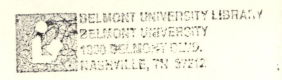

CULTURE

Control and Commitment in a High-Tech Corporation

GIDEON KUNDA

Engineering Culture

Labor and Social Change,
a series edited by Paula Rayman and Carmen Sirianni

Engineering Culture

Control and Commitment in a High-Tech Corporation

Gideon Kunda

 Temple University Press ■ Philadelphia

Temple University Press, Philadelphia   19122
Copyright © 1992 by Temple University. All rights reserved
Published 1992
Printed in the United States of America

The paper used in this publication meets the minimum requirements
of American National Standard for Information Sciences—Permanence
of Paper for Printed Library Materials, ANSI Z39.48-1984 ∞

Library of Congress Cataloging-in-Publication Data
Kunda, Gideon, 1952–
    Engineering culture: control and commitment in a high-tech
corporation / Gideon Kunda.
        p.   cm.—(Labor and social change)
    Includes bibliographical references and index.
    ISBN 0-87722-845-0 (cloth: alk. paper) ISBN 1-56639-075-3 (pbk.:
    alk. paper)
    1. Corporate culture—Case studies.   2. Organizational
effectiveness—Case studies.   3. Control (Psychology)—Case studies.
4. Employee motivation—Case studies.   5. Quality of work life—Case
studies.   6. High technology industries—Management—Case studies.
I. Title.   II. Series.
HD58.7.K86 1992
658.4—dc20   91-8652

contents

acknowledgments

The support and assistance of many people helped make writing this book both possible and worthwhile.

My teachers at the Massachusetts Institute of Technology—John Van Maanen, Ed Schein, and Don Schon—created an intellectual environment for which I will always be grateful. Each in his own way offered guidance and criticism as well as encouragement to explore my differences with them. John introduced me to the art (disguised as a science) of ethnography, pointed me toward much inspiring work (including his own), and, line by line, helped me learn the craft of ethnographic writing. Ed taught me the value of curiosity, provided a clinical perspective on fieldwork, and was a constant source of ideas and interpretations. To his always insightful readings Don added a continuing challenge to engage in both personal and intellectual introspection. Together, they helped me find my own voice.

Friends and colleagues offered their ideas, an occasional sanity check, a few laughs, and continuing support. Debbie Kolb was an invaluable and patient reader and critic over the years. Steve Barley provided the comforts and challenges of a fellow traveler. Deborah Dougherty was everything one could expect of an office comrade and more. Michael Rosen offered his thoughts, his library, and his hospitality. Mitch Abolafia, Sam Bacharach, Lotte Bailyn, Eyal Ben Ari, Nurit Bird-David, Chaim Chazan, Paul DiMaggio, Tami El-Or, Bob Gephart, Yossi Grodzinski, Eva Illouz, Ziva Kunda, Barton Kunstler, Brian Mundell, Mike Piore, Yehouda Shenhav, Moshe Shokeid, Carmen Sirianni, Boaz Tamir, Paul Thagard, Bob Thomas, and Ely Weitz made many helpful suggestions. At Temple University Press, Mike Ames, Jane Barry, and Joan Vidal provided skillful editorial support. And Lesley Rubin, in many ways a party to this work, gave not only many insightful comments and a much needed outside perspective, but a home, and all it stands for. This book is dedicated to her.

Engineering Culture

chapter 1

Culture and Organization

> "Just do a few little things for us, and—"
> "What sort of things?" Yossarian interrupted with belligerent mis-
> giving. "Oh, tiny, insignificant things. Really, this is a very generous
> deal we're making with you. . . . all you have to do in return is . . ."
> "What? What must I do?" Colonel Korn laughed curtly. "Like us."
> Yossarian blinked. "Like you?" "Like us." "Like you?" "That's
> right," said Colonel Korn, nodding, gratified immeasurably by Yos-
> sarian's guileless surprise and bewilderment. "Like us. Join us. Be our
> pal. Say nice things about us here and back in the States. Become one
> of the boys. Now, that isn't asking too much, is it?"
>
> —Joseph Heller
> *Catch-22*

"Welcome to Technology Region—Working on America's Future," pro-
claim the signs along Route 61, the region's main artery. It is early, but the
nervous, impatient energy of high-tech is already pulsating through the spectacular countryside. Porsches, souped-up Chevies, Saabs, indeterminate old
family station wagons, motorcycles, company vans, lots of Toyotas—the
transportational variety is endless—edge their way toward the exit ramps
and the clusters of "corporate parks," engineering facilities, conference centers, and hotels that are the place of daily congregation for the region's residents. As their cars jerk along, some drivers appear engrossed in thought,
a few may be observed speaking into tape recorders or reading documents
from the corner of their eyes. In "the region" the future is now; time is
precious; and for many of the drivers work has already begun.

The parking lot in front of High Technologies' Lyndsville engineering
facility is rapidly filling. High Technologies Corporation—"Tech" to most
of its employees—is one of the larger, more successful, and better known of
the Region's corporate residents, and reputed to be on the "leading edge" of
the high-tech industry. The Lyndsville facility is home to a number of Tech's

more prominent and promising engineering groups. It is a low, sprawling, ugly building squatting behind the spacious parking lot carved out of the countryside a few miles off the highway. Between eight and nine o'clock, most of the day residents emerge from their cars to take over from the night shift—a few engineers pulling "all-nighters," the cleaners, and the security guards.

Jim Davis, a uniformed guard working for a contractor who provides Tech with security services, watches the morning inflow. He is hoping— like many in his position—one day to secure permanent employment at Tech, but in the meanwhile must settle for a temporary job at the company's boundary. As the first group of day people walk briskly through the front door toward the security desk where he has spent the night, he whispers in mock terror: "They're baaaack!" Passing the desk, the objects of his feigned concern perfunctorily flash small plastic Tech identity cards at him. He nods, not bothering to look closely at the proffered signs of full membership, and as he prepares to relinquish his post he explains: "Couldn't recognize 'em anyway. They all look the same." On his way out he adds: "Same thing every day. Bust their balls and think they're great. I dunno— this place is something else."

A casual outside observer might concur. The many hundreds of people employed at Lyndsville whose day begins as the night shift ends are, on the face of it, a fairly homogeneous group. The age is predominantly late twenties to mid-thirties. Almost all are white and—except for secretaries— most are male. Many would characterize their social status as "upscale." Almost all have college degrees, mainly in fields of the technical sort, with a majority in electrical engineering and computer science. The range of compensation is wide, but the average, by most standards, is well above the comfort zone. The dress code is loose, if rather drab. Business attire seems almost theatrically out of place and suggests association with the outside world, usually with "business types." The general demeanor combines a studied informality, a seemingly self-assured sense of importance, and a clearly conveyed impression of hard, involving, and strangely enjoyable, even addictive, work. Many routinely refer to their work as "state of the art"—of considerable quality, innovativeness, and profitability, and thus intrinsically, unquestionably, and self-evidently worthwhile.

Over the course of the workday, the Lyndsville facility appears to assume the character of its inhabitants: a combination of effort and informality, freedom and discipline, work and play. After early coffees or breakfast in the open cafeteria, the labyrinth of cubicles that occupies much of the internal space becomes the stage for a seemingly chaotic variety of individual activities and complex networks of interaction that take place against a background of subdued but persistent squeaks and whirs from terminals, keyboards, and printers. At first glance, one would be hard pressed to identify differences in rank, status, or power. In many identical and modest-looking cubicles, people are tapping away at computer terminals. Meeting rooms on the periphery are occupied by small groups in apparently intense, occasionally volatile, and sometimes playful discussion. In the central lab space, people are wandering between tangled cables connecting rather unimpressive-looking pieces of equipment to each other and to the ceiling. The cafeteria is occupied throughout the day. Although it often appears that people come and go as they please, it is fairly well established that long hours are the norm. Those not present are assumed to be working elsewhere. Many will continue working through the evening, some on their company-provided home terminals. Others will do so in their minds and—a few would report—even their dreams.

The observer, comparing the glimpsed scenes of life at Lyndsville with traditional or commonsensical images of work life in profit-seeking corporations, might wonder what is going on here. Are things as chaotic and uncontrolled as they seem? How and by whom are the collective interests maintained? Why do people work so hard and claim to enjoy it? Is it the work itself that is intrinsically satisfying? Or is it something about the social context in which it takes place? More broadly: what is it like to work here? Is this the organization of the future? Or is it perhaps a futuristic revival of the past?

To insiders, the scene at Lyndsville is "typical Tech"—a way of life taken for granted, with nothing to puzzle over. If asked to address some of the observer's concerns, many would retort rather matter-of-factly that what one has observed are nothing more than manifestations of Tech's "strong culture." If this at first seems somewhat tautological, it soon becomes apparent that "the culture" is a popular explanatory concept, frequently used as a description of the company, a rationale for people's behavior, a guideline for action, a cause for praise and condemnation, pride and despair, a quality that is said to distinguish Tech from other industries and even from other high-tech companies. "It is," many would say, "what makes us what we are."

What do they mean? One answer is to be found among those who consider the "strong culture" their domain.

Tech Culture: A Managerial Perspective

On this randomly selected workday, the Lyndsville engineering facility is the stage upon which practical managerial concerns with "the culture" are acted out. A few miles away, in a fairly spacious but still modest office at Tech's corporate headquarters, Dave Carpenter is preparing a presentation to be given at Lyndsville later in the day. He is one of the more senior managers in the Engineering Division, and has been with the company a long time. Like many Tech managers, Dave Carpenter works extremely hard. He has recently gone on a strictly enforced seven-to-seven schedule that includes working breakfasts and dinners, but it is still difficult to get onto his calendar. He has just finished a series of long-scheduled "one-on-ones." The last one was with a Harvard professor wearing a fancy business suit and a prominently displayed visitor's badge, who has just been ushered out after exactly half an hour. ("Some kind of case study interview—culture and productivity; everybody wants to know what we're up to.") Dave has a few minutes to get his presentation together. The group at Lyndsville has recently been made part of his organization—"his world"—in one of the frequent reorganizations that are a way of life for Tech managers, or, as he would say, "a part of the culture."

For Dave, as for many managers, cultural matters are an explicit concern. Dave considers himself an expert. One wall of his office is covered with a large bookcase holding many managerial texts. Japanese management, in particular, intrigues him, and books on the subject take up a whole shelf. ("They know something about putting people to work—and we better find out what it is.") Dave has a clear view of what the culture is all about and considers it his job not only to understand, but to influence and shape it for those whose performance he believes to be his responsibility.

A key aspect of Tech culture, Dave often points out, is that formal structure tells you nothing. Lyndsville is a case in point. "It's typical Tech. The guys up there are independent and ambitious. They are working on state-of-the-art stuff—really neat things. Everyone, including the president, has a finger in the pot. The group is potentially a revenue generator. That they are committed there is no doubt. But they are unmanageable." How then, he wonders, can he make them see the light? Work in the *company's* interest? Cooperate? Stop (or at least channel) the pissing contests? And not make him look bad? Dave knows that whether he controls it or not, he "owns" it— another aspect of the culture. And as he reads the company, his own future can be influenced by the degree to which he is credited with the group's success. And he is being watched, just as he watches others. His strategy is clear. "Power plays don't work. You can't *make 'em* do *any*thing. They have to *want* to. So you have to work through the culture. The idea is to educate people without them knowing it. Have the religion and not know how they ever got it!"

And there are ways to do this. Today Dave will make his first appearance at Lyndsville. He will give a presentation about the role of Lyndsville's various technical projects in Tech's long-term business strategy. "Presentations are important in this culture," he says. "You have to get around, give them the religion, get the message out. It's a mechanism for transmitting the culture." Sending and interpreting "messages" are a key to working the culture. Dave is clear about what he wants to accomplish: generate some enthusiasm, let them work off some steam, celebrate some of the successes, show them that they are not out on their own, make his presence felt. And maybe give them an example of the right "mindset." In "the trenches" (a favorite expression), he is sure, there must be considerable confusion caused by "the revolving door"—the frequent changes of management. Lyndsville reputedly has quite a few good and committed people. It is a creative group. But it is also considered a tough, competitive environment. Some say it reminds them of the early days of Tech, when commitment and burnout went hand in hand. Perhaps. The company has been changing. But some things stay the same. Dave remembers life in the trenches. He was "there" years ago, he has paid his dues—including a divorce—and he still feels an affinity for the residents of the trenches, some of whom he will meet today. And, as always, he is prepared. He reaches for the tools of the culture trade— the "road show" color slides used at yesterday's strategy presentation to the executive committee—and selects the ones for today.

Concern with the culture is not just the domain of senior managers; it has also spawned a small internal industry that translates global concerns, ideas, and messages into daily activities. Near the front lobby of the Lyndsville building, a large conference room is being prepared for more routine "cultural shaping." Alone in the room, Ellen Cohen is getting ready to run her

"Culture Module" for the "Introduction to Tech" workshop for new hires, also known as "bootcamp." It will take two hours, and if everything runs smoothly, she will stay for Dave Carpenter's presentation. ("It's a must for Tech-watchers. You can learn a lot from attending.") She is an engineer who is now "totally into culture." Over the last few years she has become the resident "culture expert." "I got burnt out on coding. You can only do so much. And I knew my limits. So I took a management job and I'm funded to do culture now. Some people didn't believe it had any value-added. But I went off and made it happen, and now my workshops are all oversubscribed! I'm a living example of the culture! Now I do a lot of work at home. Isn't this company super?"

She is preparing her material now, waiting for the participants to arrive. On one table she is sorting the handout packages. Each includes copies of her paper "A Culture Operating Manual—Version II"; some official company materials; a copy of the latest edition of *Tech Talk*, with an interview with the president and extensive quotations from his "We Are One" speech; a review of academic work on "corporate cultures" that includes a key to the various disguised accounts of Tech; a glossary of Tech terms; and a xeroxed paper with some "culture exercises" she has collected for her files over the years. "It covers it all. What is a Techie. Getting Ahead. Networking. Being a Self-Starter. Taking Charge. How to Identify Burnout. The Subcultures. Presentations. Managing Your Career. Managing Your Boss. Women. Over the years I've gathered dynamite material—some of it too sensitive to show anyone. One day I'll write a thesis on all of this. In the meanwhile I'm funded to document and preserve the culture of Engineering. It's what made this company great. 'Culture' is really a 'people issue'—a Personnel or OD [Organization Development] type of thing, but they have no credibility in Engineering, and I'd rather stay here, close to the action. It's a fascinating company. I could watch it forever. Today I'm doing culture with the new hires. I tell them about how to succeed here. You can't just do the old nine-to-five thing. You have to have the right mindset. It's a gut thing. You have to get the religion. You can push at the system, you drive yourself. But I also warn them: 'Win big and lose big. You can really get hurt here. This place can be dangerous. Burnout City.' And I tell them the first rule: 'Do What's Right.' It's the company slogan, almost a cliche, but it captures the whole idea. 'Do What's Right.' If they internalize that, I've done my job. My job?

They come in in love with the technology; that's dangerous. My job is to marry them to the company."

What does "Tech's strong culture" mean to Dave Carpenter and Ellen Cohen? First, and most broadly speaking, it is the context of their work life, a set of rules that guides the relationship between the company and "it's people." At one level, the culture offers a description of the social charac-teristics of the company that also embodies a specification of required work behavior: "informality," "initiative," "lack of structure," "inherent ambi-guity," "hard work," "consensus seeking," "bottom-up decision making," "networking," "pushing against the system," "going off, taking risks, and making things happen." But, as the frequently heard metaphors of "family," "marriage," and "religion" suggest, the rules run deeper. The culture also includes articulated rules for thoughts and feelings, "mindsets" and "gut reactions": an obsession with technical accomplishment, a sense of owner-ship, a strong commitment to the company, identification with company goals, and, not least, "fun." Thus, "the culture" is a gloss for an extensive definition of membership in the corporate community that includes rules for behavior, thought, and feeling, all adding up to what appears to be a well-defined and widely shared "member role." [1]

But there is more. For Dave Carpenter and Ellen Cohen, as well as many others, the culture has a dual nature: it is not just the context but also the object of their work lives. The culture means not only the implicit and ex-plicit rules that guide and shape their own behavior and experience of work; it is also the vehicle through which they consciously try to influence the be-havior and experience of others. The "culture," in this sense, is something to be engineered—researched, designed, developed, and maintained—in order to facilitate the accomplishment of company goals. Although the product—a member role consisting of behavior, thoughts, and feelings— is not concrete, there are specified ways of engineering it: making presen-tations, sending "messages," running "bootcamp," writing papers, giving speeches, formulating and publishing the "rules," even offering an "operat-ing manual." All are work techniques designed to induce others to accept— indeed, to become—what the company would like them to be.

This duality reflects a central underlying theme in the way culture is con-strued by many Tech managers: the "culture" is a mechanism of control. Its essence is captured in Dave Carpenter's words: "You can't make 'em do anything; they have to want to." In this view, the ability to elicit, channel, and direct the creative energies and activities of employees in profitable directions—to make them want to contribute—is based on designing a member role that employees are expected to incorporate as an integral part of their sense of self. It is this desire and the policies that flow from it, many insiders feel, that makes Tech "something else."

The use of culture in the service of control in a modern corporation might seem at first strange, even unique, to those for whom culture is a concept more meaningfully applied to Bornean headhunters or to the urban literati. Tech managers, however, are not alone. A practical concern with culture and its consequences is widely shared among those for whom the corporate jungle is of more than passing interest.

Culture and Control

In recent years, the concept of "corporate culture" has captured the imagination of both students and practitioners of management. In a large and growing body of theory and research, scholars have attempted to define, refine, and apply a cultural perspective to the description and analysis of organizational phenomena. Despite the diversity, most would agree with Ward Goodenough (1970) that, most broadly speaking, culture is "in the minds and hearts of men"—a learned body of tradition that governs what one needs to know, think, and feel in order to meet the standards of membership. Others, like Clifford Geertz (1973), would locate culture in the vehicles for public expression of these meanings—signs and symbols.[2] When applied to organizational settings, culture is generally viewed as the shared rules governing cognitive and affective aspects of membership in an organization, and the means whereby they are shaped and expressed.[3] Of particular concern have been the shared meanings, assumptions, norms, and values that govern work-related behavior; the symbolic, textual, and narrative structures in which they are encoded; and—in the functionalist tradition—the structural causes and consequences of cultural forms and their relationship to various measures of organizational effectiveness.[4] Thus, culture and its family of concepts offer students of organizations a relatively new and increasingly popular vocabulary of description as well as a set of new theoretical variables with which to "build" (or recast) theory.[5]

Where we find description, however, prescription is never far away. Built into the descriptive vocabulary and the theoretical relationships is the potential for practical use. It is made explicit by the many scholars who also have an applied interest and who address their work to practitioners and consultants interested in "diagnosing" and "changing" cultures in the service of organizational effectiveness.[6] Moreover, a large and profitable body of popular managerial literature has capitalized on these ideas, proclaiming a relationship between culture and the "bottom line." Terrence Deal and Allen Kennedy (1982: 15), for example, claim that with a strong culture, a "company can gain as much as one or two hours of productive work per employee per day." The business press has granted the cultural perspective significant attention,[7] and it has made its way into the daily discourse of practicing managers and other members of business organizations as a routine aspect of organizational and corporate language. Thus, organizational culture is not only a powerful and popular etic concept; it also has a significant emic dimension.[8]

The prescriptive view focuses on the explicit and active design and management of "organizational culture." What is in the "hearts and minds" of employees, it is suggested, can and should be managed in the organizational interest. Academic observers typically point to (and often implicitly recommend) the combination of freedom, commitment, and emotional involvement that this kind of work environment supposedly generates. For example, Edgar Schein (1985) views culture as based on deeply held—often unconscious—beliefs shared by employees. In Schein's view there is an observable and potentially manageable relationship between the behavior of senior managers and cultural outcomes. In a disguised description of Tech, he suggests that the central beliefs include the equation of the company with a family where members take care of each other, and the view of members as both strongly motivated and capable of governing themselves. Others make their positive evaluation of strong cultures more explicit. In a typical statement, Rosabeth Kanter (1983: 203) describes a disguised version of Tech and claims that work in such companies offers "a high" that "may be the closest to an experience of 'community' or total commitment for many workers, a dramatic, exciting, and almost communal process brought to the corporation." [9]

The popular managerial press is even less restrained. For example, in their best-selling *In Search of Excellence*, Thomas Peters and Robert Waterman (1982) convey their ideas with almost evangelical fervor.[10] Management, they claim, is the art of creating strong corporate cultures by "shaping norms," "instilling beliefs," "inculcating values," "generating emotions." "Strong cultures" are based on intense emotional attachment and the internalization of "clearly enunciated company values" that often replace formal structures. Moreover, individualism is preserved; for employees, the companies "provide the opportunity to stick out, yet combine it with a philosophy and system of beliefs . . . that provide the transcending meaning—a wonderful combination" (p. 81). The ideal employees are those who have internalized the organization's goals and values—its culture—into their cognitive and affective make-up, and therefore no longer require strict and rigid external control. Instead, productive work is the result of a combination of self-direction, initiative, and emotional attachment, and ultimately combines the organizational interest in productivity with the employees' personal interest in growth and maturity.

Thus, in the view of proponents of strong cultures, work in such companies is not merely an economic transaction; rather, it is imbued with a deeper personal significance that causes people to behave in ways that the company finds rewarding, and that require less use of traditional controls. The company, in this view, harnesses the efforts and initiative of its employees in the service of high-quality collective performance and at the same time provides them with "the good life": a benign and supportive work environment that offers the opportunity for individual self-actualization. Broader implications are often drawn from this depiction of corporate life. The prescriptive literature goes so far as to propose that such corporate cultures are a solution to the problems created by an allegedly overbureaucratized and underperforming organizational society.[11] To accomplish this, managers are offered (often for a price) a variety of methods and techniques: participative decision making, overt uses of rituals and ceremony, the management of symbols and meanings, explicit formulation of a "corporate philosophy," and so forth.[12] All supposedly produce the kind of employee whose orientation to work, Deal and Kennedy (1982: 9) approvingly suggest, is captured in the following quotation: "I feel like putting a lot of time in. There is a real kind of loyalty here. We are all working this together—working a process together. I'm not a workaholic—it's just the place. I love the place."

The concern with culture detected at Lyndsville and the convergence of practical and theoretical notions of culture and its management in the academic and managerial literature reflect a widespread and growing managerial interest in finding innovative solutions to the foremost problem of management: the conflict of interest that lies at the heart of the relations between organizations and their members. Purposeful collective action, whatever its circumstances, requires the coordination of activities of a diverse and heterogeneous membership. There is, however, an inherent conflict between the demands organizations place on the time and efforts of their members and the desires and needs of members when left to their own devices. Thus the age-old managerial dilemma: how to cause members to behave in ways compatible with organizational goals. Bureaucratic work organizations, Amitai Etzioni (1961) suggests, have traditionally relied mainly on utilitarian forms of control: the use of economic power to elicit compliance with rules and regulations from a work force concerned mainly with maximizing material rewards.[13] The rhetoric of culture, however, indicates a shift in managerial sensibilities to a different form, one that Etzioni refers to as *normative control*.

Normative control is the attempt to elicit and direct the required efforts of members by controlling the underlying experiences, thoughts, and feelings that guide their actions. Under normative control, members act in the best interest of the company not because they are physically coerced, nor purely from an instrumental concern with economic rewards and sanctions. It is not just their behaviors and activities that are specified, evaluated, and rewarded or punished. Rather, they are driven by internal commitment, strong identification with company goals, intrinsic satisfaction from work. These are elicited by a variety of managerial appeals, exhortations, and actions. Thus, under normative control, membership is founded not only on the behavioral or economic transaction traditionally associated with work organizations, but, more crucially, on an experiential transaction, one in which symbolic rewards are exchanged for a moral orientation to the organization. In this transaction a member role is fashioned and imposed that includes not only behavioral rules but articulated guidelines for experience. In short, under normative control it is the employee's *self*—that ineffable source of subjective experience—that is claimed in the name of the corporate interest.[14]

Attempts to implement normative control in industrial settings might be considered "something else," but the ideas on which it is founded are not new. In his classic *Work and Authority in Industry*, Reinhard Bendix (1956) identified an inexorable trend in the evolution of managerial ideology from the early days of Frederick Taylor's "Scientific Management" to the formulation of the theory and practice of "Human Relations" by Elton Mayo and the numerous scholars and practitioners who followed him.[15] For Bendix, the essence of the trend was a growing managerial interest in the psychological absorption of workers by organizations. This represented, in his view, a systematic encroachment on previously private or unregulated domains of work life—irrational sentiments and attitudes—a sort of creeping annexation of the workers' selves, an attempt to capture the norms of the workplace and embed control "inside" members.

Practice has, in a fashion, followed theory. Many observers have noted the historical evolution of managerial practices designed to facilitate the incorporation of the worker into an industrial community. These include graded careers, increased job security, long-term employment, the rise of internal labor markets, the emergence of training and education functions, the professionalization of management, the growth of personnel and human resource management as managerial disciplines, decentralization and participatory decision making, job redesign, benefits, and stock ownership plans.[16]

How is one to account for this trend? Most generally, managerial interest in normative control has been seen as a consequence of the massive bureaucratization of the workplace in the twentieth century and the emergence of the business corporation as the dominant form of industrial organization.[17] Yet the explanations vary. For sociologists of bureaucracy, the need for and the mechanisms of normative control are built into the very structure of bureaucracy.[18] As Bendix (1956: 251) suggests, a shortage of control is inherent in bureaucracy: "beyond what commands can effect and supervision can control, beyond what incentives can induce and penalties prevent, there exists an exercise of discretion . . . which managers of economic enterprises seek to enlist for the achievement of managerial ends." Consequently, as Robert Merton (1957: 198) has pointed out, effective control requires that "ideal patterns of action are buttressed by strong sentiments which entail devotion to one's duties." In this view, the relationship of discretion and control is particularly pronounced in the case of the rapidly expanding white-collar labor force and for the types of work, technologies, and labor processes characteristic of what Daniel Bell (1973) refers to as the "post-industrial society." [19]

Management theorists present a similar argument but cast it as the solution to a practical managerial problem. This perspective was formulated most clearly by Chester Barnard (1950), one of the most influential of the early management theorists. In his classic *The Functions of the Executive*, Barnard says that in order to elicit the willing and predictable contributions of effort required by a large-scale organization, traditional economic inducements must be supplemented by an effort to change the "states of mind" that govern the willingness to contribute. This includes the "inculcation of motives," which means shaping not only work behaviors and activities but also the self-definitions of members as social actors, their world views, and, most crucially, their emotional responses to their condition. In Barnard's view, this required "a process of deliberate education of the young, and propaganda for the adults" (p. 152).[20]

Marxist scholars add a critical twist to the same argument. Richard Edwards (1979), for example, suggests that bureaucracy leads to the need for and the use of increasingly sophisticated forms of control. This, he explains, is due to the inevitable conflict of interest between workers and management that arises in capitalist systems as a result of managerial attempts to control the labor process. Control based on ownership, he argues, inevitably leads to worker alienation, and consequently to overt conflict and decreased efficiency, and to a managerial search for more and better control. Thus, the development of forms of control is a dynamic process. In its most recent form, bureaucratic control, the impersonal rule of company law and policy is coupled with a growing tendency to enforce not only obedience to the rules but also an internalization of the rules and an identification with the company.[21]

In sum, the recent popularity of the idea of strong corporate culture may be seen as the culmination of a pronounced historical trend in managerial ideology and practice toward forms of normative control. In the most general terms, shaping the employees' selves in the corporate image is thought to be necessary in order to facilitate the management and increase the efficiency of large-scale bureaucratic enterprises faced with what the managerial literature refers to as "turbulent environments": rapid technological change, intense competition, and a demanding and unpredictable labor force.[22]

However one views its causes, the evolution of organizational forms based on a managerial ideology of normative control leads to heavy claims against the self—the thoughts, feelings, and experiences of members of work organizations. More than ever, domains of the self once considered private come under corporate scrutiny and regulation. What one does, thinks, or feels— indeed, who one is—is not just a matter of private concern but the legitimate

domain of bureaucratic control structures armed with increasingly sophisticated techniques of influence. The significance of this development goes
beyond the boundaries of organizational life. The power of organizations
to shape individuals raises the more general problem of the relationship of
self and society, a problem that has long tantalized social theorists: how to
balance individual freedom with collective action, private and public life,
civilization and its discontents.[23] The bureaucracies that govern work life are
one arena—and not the least of them—where these questions are played out
in the course of daily interaction.

Thus, understanding the practical consequences of the ideology of normative control in bureaucratic settings becomes a matter of acute importance.
How effective, we must ask, are the corporate attempts to influence employees? What is the experience of the people against whom such heavy claims
are made? What kind of people are produced in this process? In short, if
the member role represents normative demands, what are the normative
responses and how are we to evaluate them?

The Consequences of Control

Recognition of the trend toward normative control has brought with it two
distinct views of its consequences. For supporters and proponents, it is the
wave of the future, a solution not only to the economic and organizational
problems that plague a declining West but to its deeper existential dilemmas
as well. In this view, there need not be a conflict between organization and
individual: organizational forms based on normative control are potentially
liberating; and personal development and growth are possible in the service
of corporate goals. Elton Mayo (1933), the architect of Human Relations,
troubled by the dehumanizing potential of industrialization and its political
ramifications, felt that finding meaning and satisfaction through work asso-
ciations was both necessary and possible. Numerous others have taken up
this theme.[24] In this view, the inherent conflict between the individual and the
collective may be transformed into cooperation that is in the interest of both
company and employee. Normative control is conceptualized as an appeal
to the potential existing in people. To the extent that they are shaped, that
shaping is framed as a process of education, personal development, growth,
and maturity—in fact, a development of a better, healthier self, saved from
the threat of anomie and alienation and the pathology of conflict.

If supporters of normative control in industry promise a self regained, critics warn of a soul lost. This imagery seems to have haunted the post-war sensibilities of observers of the corporate world. C. Wright Mills in his classic *White Collar* (1956: xvii) claims that large bureaucratic organizations "usurp both freedom and rationality from the little individual men caught in them." In *The Organization Man*, William Whyte (1956: 397) warns, somewhat more colorfully, of the insidious influence of organizations on the personal and emotional life of members, where a manager is tempted into a "practice of a tyranny more subtle and more pervasive than that which he means to supplant." "No one wants to see the old authoritarian return," Whyte states, "but at least it could be said of him that what he wanted primarily from you was your sweat. The new man wants your soul." In this view, then, normative control is a sophisticated and manipulative form of tyranny in the workplace, a threat to both freedom and dignity, an unwarranted invasion of privacy. Forced to explain the lack of overt coercion and the seeming cooperation of the victims, Whyte portrays the individual experience of this tyranny in a different light: "It is not the evils of organizational life that puzzle him but its very beneficence. He is imprisoned in brotherhood" (p. 12). This imagery has persisted. More recently Edwards (1979: 148) conjures it up to warn that under normative control the "workers owe not only a hard day's work to the corporation but also their demeanor and affections." Here, "control tends to be a much more totalitarian system—totalitarian in the sense of involving the total behavior of the worker. Hard work and deference are no longer enough; now the 'soulful' corporation demands the worker's soul, or at least the worker's identity."

The criticism does not stop here. Not only is normative control, in the view of its critics, the moral equivalent of tyranny; it is also dysfunctional. Some, like Edwards (1979), claim it cannot last: management, he argues, must necessarily betray the loyalty and commitment it evokes because the cost is too high. Others, like Whyte (1956) and Merton (1957), suggest it undermines organizational performance. The dire consequences of successful normative control are, in their view, embodied in the "organization man" or the "bureaucratic personality," for whom identification with the organization overrides all else and leads to the inversion of means and ends, a preference for conformity, a predilection for groupthink, a fear of creativity and initiative, and a dearth of ethics. Still others suspect that normative control is largely rhetoric, a disguise for more traditional practices, and in any case not practical.[25] Although not entirely consistent with each other, all agree that there is cause to worry about the kind of society, the kind of organizations, and the kind of citizens such forms of control produce.

Thus, the recognition of the rise of normative control generated conflicting and often contradictory images of its consequences and led to a continuing debate: is normative control a form of tyranny or a movement of liberation? Is it a failure, or does it work only too well? What the various debates concerning the practice, meaning, and consequences of normative control have in common, however, is a notable paucity of evidence coupled with a distinct preference for hyperbole, abstraction, and metaphor. That the managerial mind was and is fascinated by the possibility of normative control of subordinates is easy to document, well established, and not very surprising. With regard to the actual practice of normative control and its consequences for those subjected to it, the evidence is neither clear nor coherent. Most evaluative attempts have rested on a rather limited empirical base, often using as a basis for their claims the rhetoric of management taken out of context and away from the point of production. Students of managerial ideology focus heavily on the rhetoric of spokespersons and its interpretation and seem to ignore the actual settings within which normative control is formulated and applied and its meaning for those for whom it is formulated.[26] There is scant contextual evidence concerning the use of ideology, its meaning in the context in which it is used, the practices associated with it, the nature of life in organizations supposedly resorting to normative control, and the consequences for individuals. Particularly lacking are detailed studies of white-collar, professional, and managerial workers, among whom the trend is supposedly most pronounced.[27]

How then are we to evaluate the widespread managerial concern with "strong cultures"? On the face of it, as we have seen, the essence of the ideology of strong cultures is a restatement and a reaffirmation of the doctrine of normative control. This formulation, moreover, attempts to preempt the well-known criticisms. In the strong corporate culture, its proponents assert, normative control offers increased freedom and autonomy rather than tyranny, individualism rather than groupthink, creativity rather than conformity; and, for those concerned with the techniques of implementation, it is claimed to be technically feasible, as illustrated in numerous anecdotes (some using Tech as a model) in the self-help managerial literature. If anything, in the gospel of strong culture, what was once seen as the breeding ground for the diseases of bureaucracy is now heralded as its antidote. Normative control—or at least the rhetoric associated with its practice—once again rides high.

Are these claims justified? Does the strong corporate culture indeed foster a form of affiliation that generates personal and collective "highs"? Or is it a new guise for tyranny in the workplace—an unwarranted invasion of privacy driven by commerical interests? Or is it just another cycle of empty managerial rhetoric that obscures the real and unchanging nature of work organizations and the people they employ? More important, what do strong cultures in the workplace have to teach us about the never-ending tensions between individualism and collective action, freedom and commitment, control and autonomy, that lie at the heart of an increasingly bureaucratized society? To the extent that work organizations are powerful actors in our society, and with the soul—or the self—at stake, addressing these questions becomes a matter of considerable urgency.

Some answers may be found at Lyndsville among those for whom "Tech culture" and its demands are an everyday reality. Are the people whom we encounter there happy automatons? Brainwashed Yuppies? Self-actualizing human beings? Do they think of their experiences at work as authentic expressions of themselves or as stylized roles? Is the Lyndsville engineering facility a prison or a playground?

On this randomly selected morning, a number of different experiences of the strong culture are being played out in the large, open office space beyond the conference rooms where those who live the culture spend their day. In one corner of the building, Tom O'Brien is hunched over his terminal, his back to the opening of his cubicle. He is wearing earplugs to close off the rest of the world. Things are going well, he would acknowledge, almost too well. His promotion just came through. He is now a "consulting engineer"—a title coveted by many Tech engineers. His contribution to a number of key projects is apparently being recognized by the faceless mass that determines reputation in the "technical community," and he is getting more and more electronic mail from all over the company. In his group he is considered the resident expert on XYZ technology. This year he earned close to 60K, and for the first time he was given stock options—the secret sign of inclusion. His current role is rather vaguely defined, and he can get involved in almost anything. In fact he is expected to, and he is aware of the pressure to "make things happen" and how it works on him. "That's the culture—designed ambiguity. It sucks people in," he says. He has been invited to join a number of task forces, and is thinking of learning some of the business issues. ("A little night reading. And time out for some of the hoopla. I'll go to Carpenter's presentation later. Once I'd have laughed, but when you start getting around you need to go.") He considers his position a good balance between remaining technical and getting into management. Recollections of his burnout episode a few years back and a brief and unsuccessful stint at a crazy start-up company have lost their painful edge. He is back with Tech. And he seems to have arrived.

Right now Tom is trying to understand the intricacies of a failing project. Rick Smith, the project manager, was finally removed, and someone has to figure out what the hell was going on: the technical problems and also some of the people issues. ("A lot of egos involved!") Tom was the natural choice. It temporarily adds a few extra hours to the working day, but it's fun, it's a challenge, it's involving. Today he came in earlier than usual, and he will probably spend most of the weekend on it. "Boy, did they ever screw up," he says as he stares at the screen. Every now and then an audible beep announces the arrival of an electronic message. He fights the temptation to flip screens. "It'll take a while today just to go through the mail and stay current. Things sure pile up when you're riding the wave. That's the culture. You have to learn to work it. And to protect yourself. People can get swept away. It's great. Like the joke. You get to choose which 20 hours to work out of the day."

Many at Tech would consider Tom a standard success story, a living affirmation of "the culture" and the claims of its proponents. On the face of it, he appears to have successfully incorporated the member role. The company and his work seem to be central to his sense of self. He works hard and seems to enjoy it. He is emotionally committed. He considers himself, and is acknowledged to be, self-directed, capable of "making things happen," and in need of little explicit supervision. He sees the freedom as a source of creativity and opportunity, beneficial both to him and to the company. Income is important, not only in material terms, but also as a symbol of recognition and inclusion. Yet, as Tom's recollection of his burnout episode suggests, there is a darker side to life at Tech, and its signs are never too far from the surface. For Tom it has perhaps receded into the past, now no more than a war story and even a source of pride. Nevertheless, he appears at times wary and watchful, even cynical or ironic about the culture, the company, and himself. An observer might read into his comments, jokes, and cultural self-consciousness signs of some distancing and considerable ambivalence.

For others, the dark side of the culture looms large. In a similar cubicle not far away, Rick Smith—recently removed from his position—is slowly cleaning out his desk. He stops every now and then to light another cigarette. Mary, his secretary, is in the outer cubicle pretending to be occupied even though the phones have stopped ringing. Like many other familiar and less familiar acquaintances of Rick's, she is behaving as if nothing has happened. He is not sure if he should be grateful for this studied "business as usual" demeanor, but he plays along with it. However, the large, half-filled cartons on the table and the blank screen on his terminal—sure indications of a standstill—belie the signs of routine. Rick would acknowledge that he has burnt out. "I should never have taken this job. Can't quite figure out when things started to go wrong. Bastards just threw me into this damn project. No feedback, no guidance, no support, no warning. 'It's Tech culture,' they say. 'Do What's Right.' Some help! I was so busy with all the details, never had time to get deep enough into the technical stuff. Had to rely on the group members. And they wouldn't communicate. With each other. Or with me. And the schedules were unrealistic in the first place. Probably because of all the politics. When we started to slip, things just fell apart. Everyone was watching. Probably whispering. I found out later that my boss was checking who was logged on at night. They do that. This company's like an aquarium. And my problems at home didn't help. Drinking more and more. What comes first—sipping or slipping? It hit the fan when I told them I was taking two weeks to dry out again—right before the last schedule slip. Luckily the guys in process engineering up in Hanover were willing to take me. The EAP [Employee Assistance Program] advisor here helped—he's a company shrink. Contracted and sworn to secrecy. A real professional. They have a lot of experience with this type of thing. Finally found something for me. Had to do a lot of looking first. Maybe I should take it easy for a while. Or even reconsider this whole damn company! If I can afford to—there should be a warning out front: High Technologies—It's Hazardous to Your Health."

Rick Smith is a casualty. For most who know the company, it is an inevitable part of work there—indeed, of engineering in general. Not everyone, it is conceded, can live in such an environment: some leave, or distance themselves in one way or another from the company's strong demands. Occasionally, like Rick, they succumb. He appears to feel used, betrayed, manipulated, even oppressed: living in an "aquarium," constantly watched, driven to drink. If one wished to make a case that the culture is a guise for a benign yet invasive tyranny, he would be a prime example. Yet even as he expresses the pain of his situation, he is concerned with finding another job at Tech, plans to stay, expresses a certain gratitude to the company for providing help and tolerating failure, and cannot refrain from making an ironic observation about the company—the hallmark of successful membership. Indeed, he has made his burnout and alcoholism quite public. His personal suffering is an indication—to himself and to others—of the lengths to which he is willing to go in his desire to succeed, to contribute to the company, to adopt the member role. Economic need may account in part for this, but here, too, an observer might find evidence of considerable ambivalence.

When insiders speak of Tech culture, it is often with reference to the everyday life of engineers and managers, to the ups and downs of life in Engineering as experienced by Tom O'Brien and Rick Smith, Dave Carpenter and Ellen Cohen. But there are many others for whom the culture is of equal concern. On the other side of the partition, no more than a few feet away, Rick's secretary Mary Carmanelli is keenly aware of his quiet despair. She has been in the group for two years. She started as a "temp," a temporary worker, who, like the security guard Jim Davis, shares the physical space with residents but enjoys only some of the benefits and obligations of full membership. Subsequently, through good luck and Rick's behind-the-scenes intervention, she became a permanent employee, although here, too, the relevance and applicability of the member role are questionable. "I may not be a manager, but I know what's happening. I saw it coming. Poor guy. Look what they did to him. Burnt him out. Drove him to drink. This place is a zoo. But you can't think too much about him. And he's probably making 50 a year. So big deal. They'll take care of him. . . . Techies. They have it great. Big babies! Wimps! Fifty a year and all the perks and they feel sorry for themselves. I gotta think of myself. That's what they say about the culture: 'Tech takes care of those who take care of themselves.' They said it at the career workshop last week. Rick promised he'd get me into management. Somebody has to fight for you with Personnel. I'm sick of this job. What's gonna happen now that he's gone? Will the new guy fight for me? I really wanna get into management. Marketing, sales, it's all talk. I can do that." She looks at the people wandering by, apparently oblivious to the turmoil inside. "Well, at least they give him space. They take care of you, whatever happens. That's the culture."

The concerns of Mary and Jim are shared by a large number of people whose affiliation and status are quite different from those of managers and engineers, and who appear to experience the contrast quite clearly. There are unwritten limits to their membership and to the applicability of the culture to their work life. Yet for them too the culture holds out both promise and threat. It offers them a role, it appeals to their underlying sense of self, and it might hold in store the same suffering. Whatever the differences, the question of who they are with regard to the culture and the member role is acute. And here too, ambivalence, albeit of a different sort, appears to characterize work experience.

These glimpses into life at Tech suggest that there is more to "the culture" than unilateral normative control. Managerial ideology and managerial action designed to impose a role on individuals are but one side of the question of control—they are normative demands. As Erving Goffman (1961a) points out, members are never passive objects of control; they are free to react: if conceptions are imposed, they are also systematically dealt with.[28] Members are active participants in the shaping of themselves and of others. They may—at various times—accept, deny, react, reshape, rethink, acquiesce, rebel, conform, and define and redefine the demands and their responses. In other words, they create themselves within the constraints imposed on them. What kinds of creations have we observed at Lyndsville?

None of the people whose privacy we temporarily invaded are easily categorized as accepting or rejecting an imposed role, as subjects of a tyranny or beneficiaries of a benign environment. What they do appear to share is a profound ambivalence about their involvement. They seem aware of the company's demands and their significance. Although they exhibit signs of acceptance, they also indicate considerable wariness and even a degree of cynicism about the company's expectations, even as they are investing their efforts, planning to get ahead, or contemplating the price of failure. They all seem just as much observers as actors. Also, like Dave Carpenter and Ellen Cohen, many are in the potentially confusing situation of being at once agents and subjects of this kind of control. And there are clearly people on the scene on whom the cultural claims are made but whose status seems considerably different—like Mary Carmanelli and Jim Davis.

Thus, the managerial search for normative control sets the stage for a definitional drama played out between the imposed and received images and experiences of appropriate membership. To understand and evaluate normative control, it is necessary to grasp the underlying experiential transaction that lies at its foundation: not only the ideas and actions of managers, but the responses of members. It is with these patterned experiences of membership and with the forces that shape them that this book is concerned.

Conclusion: Studying the Culture of Culture

Tech is heralded in the managerial and business press not only for its technological accomplishments but also for having developed the "strong culture" that makes them possible. The prevailing interpretations of "Tech culture" would seem to suggest that it is an example of the successful use of normative control. The managerial and academic rhetoric would lead us to believe that the company (and others like it) has achieved what has long been a managerial fantasy: the ability to design and impose a member role that includes the thoughts and feelings that underlie work behavior. The company is thought to have accomplished the flowering of normative control without its dysfunctions and is often used as an exemplar and a source of data for those interested in these theoretical and practical issues.

These strong claims raise a number of questions. Does normative control indeed work, and, if so, how? What are the organizational practices associated with it? And, perhaps most crucially, what are the consequences for its subjects? The claims concerning the relationship of culture and control at Tech and similar companies are based on the impressionistic and often partisan views of the companies' supporters or critics and, too often, on managerial assertions. Data on the actual practices that underlie Tech culture, or, most significantly, on the responses of employees, are sparse or nonexistent. Yet answers to these questions are crucial to understanding one of the basic dilemmas of our society: does this form of organization represent an enhancement of freedom or a new and very manipulative form of tyranny?

The brief tour through Lyndsville provides some evidence in support of both views. People appear to work hard; they seem emotionally attached to their work; they live with ambiguity; and some of them experience the excitement of creativity. On the other hand, there are hints of a darker, less explored side: there seems to be potential for considerable suffering; there is evidence of manipulation and ambivalence; and there are diverse populations affected very differently by "the culture."

Thus, to begin to evaluate strong cultures in the workplace it is necessary to go beyond free-floating rhetoric to the people who live with these cultures and to the everyday lives in the course of which ideas are formed, presented, and put into effect. Culture, in short, must be studied in context and the entire normative transaction examined: managerial conceptions of the culture, their enactment, and the responses of members.

This book is an ethnography of the Engineering Division of High Technologies Corporation. Ethnography is literally the study of culture and, on the face of it, an appropriate method. But the cultural self-consciousness that permeates Tech makes it ethnography with a twist: not just a study of culture as a distant and overarching social scientific concept, but an examination of practical, scientifically informed, self-conscious attempts to design and manage culture. It is an ethnography, as it were, of lay ethnographers, an attempt to document and interpret the culture of culture management.[29]

The strength of ethnography is its concern with detail: ethnographers focus on limited settings, routines, everyday life, and strive to understand "the native point of view"—what their subjects think they are up to. Such an approach tends to shy away from the sweeping generalization, the big statement; but it is also in its power to puncture inflated or overstated ideological points of view, to bring to the surface hidden or obscured meanings, and to offer images, interpretations, and facts that, if nothing else, will allow an informed debate.

Ethnography's strength, however, is also its shortcoming. Ethnography, as Geertz (1973) suggests, coexists uneasily with generalization. The object of ethnographic observation and interpretation, in his view, is neither a controlled experiment nor a microcosm, not "the world in a teacup or . . . the sociological equivalent of a cloud chamber" (p. 23). In short, the inherent skepticism of ethnography extends, as it were, to the power of its own product. Yet the data must be made to speak to larger issues.

This study focuses on a very narrow setting: the engineering division of one large corporation and some of its inhabitants over the course of one year. How typical Tech Engineering is—and, for that matter, what "typical" means—I leave to the reader and to those who might undertake to broaden the ethnographic, or other, perspectives on these matters. But Tech exists, and its way of life therefore offers both a promise and a threat. It is hoped that this study will contribute a grounded yet skeptical point of view to the debate between those who would have it either way.

In the following chapters I attempt to provide a comprehensive and detailed account of the design, management, and experience of "Tech culture" and its relation to control as it is manifested in the everyday life of the company and its people.

Chapter 2 provides a general overview of the company and its engineering division, its history, employee population, structure, and some of the relevant practices and policies that underlie the engineering of culture.

Chapter 3 describes the substance and form of the managerial ideology of "Tech culture" as it appears in the context of everyday life in Tech's Engineering Division. The analysis focuses on texts produced by or made available to members, and a number of questions are addressed. What images of the company and of the various kinds of members are embedded in the culture? What does Dave Carpenter mean when he speaks of the right "mindset"? What does Ellen Cohen tell the new hires about being a Techie? What does "getting the religion" consist of? In other words, what kind of member role do the culture designers have in mind, and how is it represented?

Chapter 4 describes and analyzes the actual practices through which the culture is brought to life and the ideology made meaningful. The settings and interactions where ideology and experience meet are described. The analysis focuses on the following questions: How is the managerial perspective transmitted? Who are the agents of cultural design? And who are the subjects? Where and how do they interact? How do senior managers like Dave Carpenter go about conveying their point of view? What happens at presentations aimed at creating a "mindset" or "generating enthusiasm"? What is the nature and impact of Ellen Cohen's training efforts—and the efforts of the many others whose work is to "shape culture"? In other words, how does cultural engineering occur in everyday life?

Chapter 5 documents the forms of experience that are shaped under the cultural spotlight and in the shadows of its darker side. How do people construct, maintain, experience, and display a sense of themselves and of others? What do members of various types make of the roles that confront them? What is it like to "ride the wave" or to "burn out"? How does one get "swept away"? How does one "protect oneself"? In short, what kind of people are created and create themselves in the continuing experiential transactions that underlie normative control?

Chapter 6 provides an overview of the main findings and attempts to analyze their moral implications. What have we learned about the nature of normative control in industrial settings? How are we to evaluate its impact on the lives of people subjected to it and on broader social concerns?

Finally, to balance and perhaps cast a more realistic light on the thread of objective realism that runs through the book, the Appendix offers a personal and very subjective description of the history of the research project, the methods used, and some of the concerns and potential biases—both personal and cultural—that may have influenced the way in which the argument was put together.

chapter 2

The Setting

> In a community with energies constantly flowing through it, every
> road leads to a good goal, if one does not spend too much time hesi-
> tating and thinking it over. The targets are set up at a short distance,
> but life is short too, and in this way one gets a maximum of achieve-
> ment out of it. And man needs no more for his happiness; for what one
> achieves is what moulds the spirit, whereas what one wants without
> fulfillment only warps it. So far as happiness is concerned it matters
> very little what one wants; the main thing is that one should get it. Be-
> sides, zoology makes it clear that a sum of reduced individuals may
> very well form a totality of genius.
>
> —Robert Musil
> *The Man Without Qualities*

High Technologies Corporation—commonly known as Tech—is a large
corporation that designs, develops, manufactures, sells, and services a number of popular high-tech products.[1] The company is, by any standard, a high-
tech success story. In the three decades of its existence, Tech has become a
widely recognized international company; its products are considered "state
of the art"; it is profitable; it controls a substantial part of the market; and its
success is held up as an exemplar and a model to others.

Tech's beginnings were modest in practice, if not in conception. The company was founded in the fifties by a group of engineers with academic and
military backgrounds, headed by Sam Miller, a researcher in a prestigious
academic engineering laboratory. With the help of a loan from adventurous
backers, they started a small company based on strong beliefs about the technical and managerial directions they wished to take. The technical ideas—
which they felt were revolutionary at the time—led to the development of
a number of innovative products. No less revolutionary in their eyes were
their plans for the social nature of the company. Combining then-popular
Human Relations–oriented management theories with their interpretation of

the Protestant Ethic, they hoped to create a new kind of work environment. Tech was to be a "people company" offering a caring, humane environment based on enlightened self-interest and job security. This would presumably elicit the commitment and efforts of employees and release their creative energies.[2]

The company's first products proved tremendously successful. The profits provided the financial foundation for growth and large rewards for early backers and investors. The products that followed strengthened Tech's position and its reputation as an innovative and technologically strong company. Despite increasing and intense competition, growth was rapid: during its first ten years, the number of employees rose from a handful to roughly 10,000, and its revenues reached $50 million. By the end of the second decade, Tech had approximately 25,000 employees and a yearly revenue of $300 million. Today it is an international corporation with close to 50,000 U.S. employees and 100,000 world-wide. Yearly revenues in 1985 were approximately $7 billion, and net income came close to $350 million. The total worth of the company is estimated to be around $10 billion.

Despite the clear trend, however, all has not been smooth. Over its history, Tech's fortunes have fluctuated with those of the world economy and the volatile high-tech industry. During a number of bad years in the eighties, the financial indicators gave Tech investors and managers reason for concern. A number of new products failed in the marketplace, and some never reached the market. Profit margins plunged, and so did the company's stock. The company went through a number of major reorganizations and hiring freezes, yet managed to adhere to its central principles and particularly to a "no-layoff" policy that reflected the founders' beliefs. A number of the founders left, but those who remain, still led by Sam Miller, are firmly in control. In the last few years, recovery has been more than complete. Tech is seen by industry observers as strong enough to weather the cycles of prosperity and recession that characterize the industry, and many claim that it is emerging into a position of industry leadership. The future appears to be promising.

The past, however, is not forgotten. "Corporate"—Tech headquarters—is located in "Technology Region," one of the high-tech centers that have sprung up around large urban and academic centers, close to where Tech's first engineering facilities were opened some thirty years ago. Although the bulk of engineering work takes place at newer facilities (most, like Lyndsville, located in the Region), Corporate is still the hub of corporate activity and the center of politics, power, and networking. Industry watchers agree that despite Tech's growth, its heart and soul—"Tech culture" in today's terminology—are still influenced by its technical roots and its founders' ideas.

The conventional industry view portrays Tech as an organization dominated by an engineering perspective. The business press frequently describes Tech as belonging to a class of product-driven, technologically oriented companies, and contrasts it with others that emphasize marketing and "business." Much evidence is produced in support of this classification. The products are considered by those who make such evaluations their business to be of relatively high quality. Sam Miller still sees himself as an engineer and is said to think nothing of personally redesigning products before they are shipped, or of intervening in the most nitty-gritty details of product development. More crucially, Tech's management structure is built around people with engineering backgrounds who claim to have put in their time doing product design, delivering "deliverables," and "shipping steel." Addicted to their work, living from vending machines, and often (it is said) perilously close to "burnout," they have survived what is called (with only some irony) "life in the trenches": hard work, ambiguous responsibilities and roles, a confusingly complex organizational structure, a decentralized "bottom-up" decision-making process, high levels of disagreement and confrontation, all coupled with a general sense of employment security and a belief in the intrinsic value of the products. All these add up to the affectionate yet critical perception of Tech as "an engineer's sandbox."

As one would expect, engineering skills are the time-honored key to status at Tech: "technical sophistication," "practical experience," and "knowing what it takes to get a product out the door." The day of the MBA has not fully arrived. The purveyors of modern management techniques have had to look for their just rewards elsewhere; at Tech they are still considered by many to be second-class citizens. Indeed, it is rumored that managers who have a business degree prefer to hide it or at least play it down, while ambitious managers in nonengineering functions are advised to spend their evenings and weekends working on an engineering degree in order to gain legitimacy and complement whatever technical sophistication they have already achieved by osmosis.

Nevertheless, Tech's continued success has created pressures for change.

The company's rapid growth, changing markets, a more competitive industry, a number of embarrassing product failures, and what can only be called the managerial/academic *zeitgeist* introduced by a new generation of managers have all resulted in calls for more "professional management." A "business perspective" is increasingly challenging the "technical" one. Many attempts are made to simplify and integrate the product line, rationalize and "professionalize" the management system, gain increased control of product development and funding processes, engage in more aggressive marketing, and satisfy an increasingly differentiated customer base. The claim that Tech is no longer a hungry start-up with an unlimited market of like-minded engineers is gaining popularity. For proponents of change, "the engineering sandbox" perspective is a continuing source of frustration. Although admittedly fostering commitment and creativity, it is also hard to structure and control; attempts to do so periodically produce a backlash of nostalgia and calls for a return to "old values."

Tech's management structure reflects the continuing tension between the advocates of creativity and the advocates of control. It is a complex and often shifting matrix headed by Sam Miller and approximately forty vice-presidents who manage the functions and areas: engineering, manufacturing, field service and sales, finance, human resources, international groups, product marketing groups, and so forth.[3] Most have emerged from the ranks of the Engineering Division, although more recently a number of managers from other functions (and even other companies) have gained prominence. A group of senior engineers (vice-president level) head the technical direction of the company, and a number of senior committees (an executive committee, a strategy committee, and so forth) are the main decision-making bodies, which survive the frequent reorganizations and fairly high turnover at senior levels. But, despite the winds of change, Engineering is still reputed to be the most influential group at the corporate level, and those who claim to know the company acknowledge that the Engineering Division, as chaotic as ever, is and will always be "where the action is."

Tech's Engineering Division is a large and complex social system defying simple description. This chapter presents an overview of the organization, using a number of different analytic schemas. First, the organization of work is outlined; second, a taxonomy of the various social categories within the Engineering population is developed; and, finally, the physical and social work environment is described. This will provide the foundation and the context for further analysis of "Tech culture" and its management in the following chapters.

The Organization of Work

The organization of work in Engineering is often described by insiders as vague, decentralized, chaotic, ambiguous, a controlled anarchy. Like other groups at Tech, it is marked by frequent reorganizations. "If one thing is constant, it is change" is an often-heard and apparently respected cliché uttered in a combination of weariness, pride, resignation, and probably self-consolation. Members of this group believe generally that "Tech has never encouraged stable groups" and that "it is a Tech tradition not to let any group get too large or too powerful."

Organization charts are not easy to come by. Although they exist, for working purposes, for various subgroups and may be collected through the efforts of secretaries or the painstaking piecing together of information, gossip, and organizational announcements, there is an accepted tendency to frown on simple mappings of the complex network of activities, to be vague about or fashionably dismissive of mechanistic structure. It is conventional wisdom that charts are always outdated and that current ones are at best an invitation to tampering.

This posture is realistic to a degree, for it is indeed difficult to display the structure of relations at Tech. But it is also a way of conforming to what many Tech employees (as well as outside observers) see as a key element of Tech culture—"matrix management." The matrix consists of "multiple dotted lines," dense, almost indecipherable "networks" of informal relations, and an aura of ambiguity that, depending on context, is either celebrated as a source of creativity or seen as a pain in the neck. As a result, formal and informal organization are not readily distinguishable: informal organizing is formally prescribed, and "culture" replaces "structure" as an organizing principle to explain reality and guide action.

Despite the ambiguity, however, there is enough stability to allow a structural mapping of the Engineering Division and a specification of the activities of the various groupings. The Engineering Division (in the United States) consists of approximately 4,000 engineers, 1,000 managers, and support

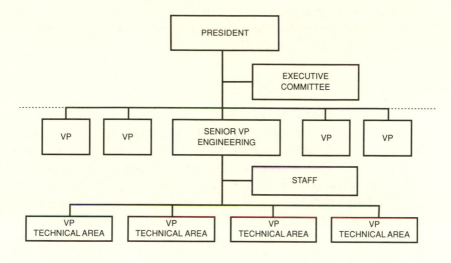

Chart 1: Top Management

staff, all of whom are charged with designing and developing Tech's products. Top management of the division (see Chart 1) is located at Corporate and consists of a senior vice-president (VP) and a divisional staff performing administrative (personnel, finance), technical (advanced research), and business (marketing, product strategy) functions. The VP of Engineering—one of Tech's first engineers—is a member of the company's executive committee. In Engineering, as at the corporate level, senior committees and task forces are key decision-making bodies. Of particular importance is the strategy and funding committee, made up of senior managers who review and approve annual plans and budgets drawn up by the various groups and then allocate the funds that support the work of the division and are the lifeblood of engineering projects.[4] The intense competition for funds and the ensuing negotiations and "politics" are a salient part of life for managers in the division.

Engineering is divided into a number of "technical areas," each responsible for designing and developing a well-defined segment of Tech's overall product set.[5] Each technical area is headed by a vice-president, who is also located at Corporate. We shall focus on one of the technical areas: Advanced Products, or AdProd.

Advanced Products Technical Area

AdProd is managed by Dave Carpenter, whom we encountered in the previous chapter. The group is responsible for developing a set of products that are seen by many in the company as part of the "new wave" and therefore critical to the company's future success. "Either we are successful or Tech is history. Also-rans. It's a bet-your-company gamble" is an often-heard though perhaps overly dramatic summary of the group's perceived importance. The group has "high visibility." Senior management pays close attention to its affairs, and its successes and failures are scrutinized and discussed frequently by those who believe that it is smart to keep a finger on the pulse of the organizational winners and losers.

AdProd (see Chart 2) is organized as a matrix and consists of a small area staff, a number of development groups, where the bulk of engineering work takes place, and matrixed program offices. AdProd staff is located at Corporate. The senior engineers in the advanced development group are responsible for the technical direction and advanced development of products, as well as research into new technologies. The strategy and marketing groups are responsible for the "business perspective"—examining market needs, evaluating profitability, and managing customer contacts and surveys, press relations, and so forth. These are Engineering's "in-house" business functions; Engineering is perceived to be a more influential organizational location for holders of this perspective. The "program offices" are matrixed groups charged with integrating the products developed by the product development groups into compatible and marketable product sets. The training and education group performs a variety of consulting, technical and managerial training, and publication functions. Ellen Cohen, the culture expert, works for the training and education group on AdProd's staff.

The product development groups in AdProd are defined as independent business units. They are located in self-contained engineering facilities in the general vicinity of Corporate. Each is managed by a senior engineering manager. One of them, the Systems and Components Development Group, is located at the Lyndsville facility.[6]

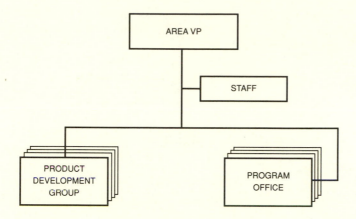

Chart 2: "AdProd" Technical Area

Systems and Components Development Group

Systems and Components—"SysCom" for short—consists of roughly six hundred employees and has a budget of about $20 million. As a business unit, SysCom has line product development groups, a staff, and a matrixed product management group (see Chart 3). SysCom's administrative staff (finance, personnel, and administration functions) report directly to SysCom's manager but also have a "dotted-line" reporting relationship to their functional managers on the AdProd staff.[7] On the staff also are engineering support groups and a product management group. Product managers are assigned to products that are being developed within the product development groups and are responsible for coordinating relations between various actors and with external groups such as marketing, sales, and field service, as well as with customers.[8] SysCom management is expected not only to manage the development process and the people, but to be responsible for the annual planning cycle, to initiate new ideas and products that are presented to the senior committees, and to meet its time and budget commitments.

SysCom's development groups are charged with developing specific products. It is in these groups that the actual engineering work takes place. A typical development group consist of engineers and managers as well as sup-

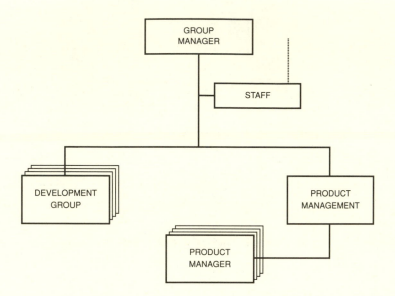

Chart 3: "SysCom" Product Development Group

port people. The organization of each group varies according to the nature of the technology and the product, as well as the preferences of the people involved. In general, however, the basic unit of organization is the project. Development group A, for example, consists of about fifty people working on six projects that are either independent products or parts of other products (see Chart 4). Reporting to the group manager are a number of project managers, who are responsible for a subset of these projects. Rick Smith was a project manager until he was replaced. In addition, some of the more highly skilled engineers are located in an advanced development group or work as "individual contributors." Tom O'Brien is an individual contributor who is part of this group, although he hopes also to manage a few development projects. He offers his expertise to others in the group when needed, works with advanced development groups at Corporate, and belongs to a number of committees that combine technical and business perspectives in the general area of his expertise.

Project managers are typically responsible for a small number of projects. In some cases the projects are part of one larger product; in other cases

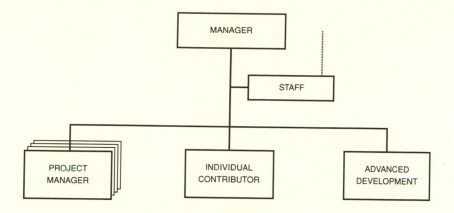

Chart 4: Development Group "A"

they are independent or even related to projects managed by other development managers in SysCom or, occasionally, elsewhere in the company (see Chart 5). The managerial responsibility for each project lies with a supervisor, the lowest managerial position and the first management assignment for many engineers. The technical responsibility is often shared with project leaders—engineers with some seniority and recognized skill. Each project has a number of engineers and technicians working on it, usually full time, as well as technical writers. Project teams stay together for the duration of the development process, ranging from a few months to a number of years. The matrixed product managers, mentioned above, are associated with projects or groups of projects and coordinate relationships as well as oversee the schedule.

To appreciate the complexities of the organizational structure, consider project ABC. The project involves an independent product that is intended to complement other products currently being developed in SysCom. The schedule is tight: the product is supposed to be ready in a year, a promise now considered unrealistic and too rashly made. The project itself is being worked on by a number of engineers, each handling a discrete part of the work. They occupy adjacent cubicles in the Lyndsville facility. Some of them frequently work at home, although all come to a variety of meetings where their work is coordinated.

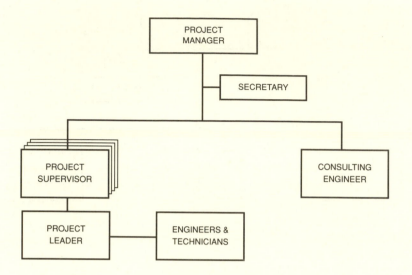

Chart 5: Project Team

The project leader considers this project "his baby" and claims to have initiated it in his spare time before selling management on the concept. He has spent much of the last two years learning the technology and interacting with others interested in it throughout the "technical community," and he hopes to become a recognized expert in this field—"the ABC space." Both he and the supervisor are under considerable pressure to deliver on time. Slips in the schedule have caused increasingly vocal concerns, and both now feel that their professional reputation is on the line. One immediate source of outside pressure is the product manager, who has made commitments to clients and to other groups in the company who have an interest in seeing the product delivered. There are considerable tensions between members of the project team, some of whom blame each other for the slips. Some have begun to look for new jobs elsewhere in the company; two have left the project. There is also increasing pressure from SysCom management.

The project's problems were reported at a SysCom staff meeting dedicated to "status reports" by the development manager of group A. The instructions were, in no uncertain terms, "Fix it!" Rick Smith, who was responsible for ABC and two other projects, was replaced soon after the meeting. Tom O'Brien was assigned to look into the problems in his spare time, and a number of engineers were brought over temporarily to help salvage the project. The personnel manager at Lyndsville is aware of the problems and is considering offering some consulting help. The manager of SysCom wants a resolution soon. He and his staff have been working on Lyndsville's annual plan for the following year. He is scheduled to announce his plans to AdProd staff in a month, prior to going before the strategy committee to present a proposal and ask for funds. ABC is a small part of his concerns, but the issue has to be resolved. Canceling the project is an option: the resources would be welcomed by other project managers, who are complaining they are "flat out"—shorthanded and overworked. Yet SysCom has made a commitment to deliver ABC and has received substantial funding; cancelation might be embarrassing, particularly since Sam Miller has been overheard to mention his interest in ABC technology. Moreover, the situation is becoming very political, since one of the AdProd program offices is expressing an interest in the project as part of its program. The SysCom manager is not yet sure what it means, but it could be a threat to "his space." And a few competing products are currently being developed outside SysCom in a group that has been making efforts to move into the ABC space. He would not like to see that happen.

As this brief description of one project suggests, an outline of the groupings, the formal reporting relations, and the work process is just a partial depiction of the organization. One reason is that projects are inherently unstable. They may disappear overnight or be recombined in different formats; they may be transferred from one product group to another as the product groups change their charters (or their managers); they may be funded, controlled, or managed by more than one group; they may be funded by external groups or subcontracted out of the organization. Similarly, staff groups and organizations may shift around, disappear, and reappear.

In addition, formal lines of authority are ambiguously defined, and there are formal and informal overlays of structure that need to be considered. Many managers and engineers are involved in temporary task forces or committees that cut across the organization. More permanent "program offices" are responsible for integrating the efforts of groups and organizations around specific issues. Consequently, working relations are loosely defined, are defined quite differently by various parties, or are not defined at all. The organization is conceived of in terms of "worlds" and "spaces"—spheres of influence that transcend the formal reporting structure. Less formal structural overlays, known as "networks," are based on communication channels between members with shared work-related or personal interests. In such an environment, the authority and responsibilities of groups and individuals ("ownership") are continuously negotiated. "Who owns what space" is often the subject of debate, conflict, and disagreement—key elements of the highly political and rapidly shifting social environment that many agree characterizes the industry, its organizations, and its people.

Social Categories

The population of Tech Engineering falls into three distinct categories that define the rights and obligations of membership. "Wage Class 4" comprises all those on monthly salaries—the engineers and the managers. They share a company-wide formal ranking system (levels one to seven) that provides a baseline for compensation, and they are entitled to flexible work hours and (should they so desire) part-time work. "Wage Class 2" consists of hourly workers. The most salient in Engineering are the secretaries and providers of support services.[9] "Wage class" status is more apparent from below. The "twos" are most aware of the distinction; from their perspective, the "fours" are privileged (and therefore envied). Employees in both wage classes are considered full-fledged members of the organization, and are entitled to all the rights and benefits of employment.[10] The third category consists of temporary workers, who are hired for specific tasks but are not considered "Tech people" even after a considerable period of full-time employment. They receive no benefits and, more crucially, may be laid off or terminated easily. Although physically present, they are exempt from the "corporate culture"; depending on one's perspective, this is either a blessing or a curse.

Engineers

"Engineer" is both a professional title and an organizationally defined employment category. In most cases, these two overlap; Tech's engineers are graduates of engineering schools. There are, however, Tech engineers (largely in computer programming) who have no formal training in engineering or computer science; instead, they are self-taught or have received company-sponsored training. To be eligible for the title, they must pass a company-arranged examination. This was easier in the past, when Tech was smaller and less formal, and when computer-related fields were less developed.[11]

Developing new products is the glamorous work. This is seen as the essence of creative engineering, what engineering is all about. It is high-pressure work: crunches, slips, and other forms of organized hysteria accompany the pressure to be creative, to produce, to be smart, and to conform to the demands and constraints of management. In development, engineers typically work on projects. Other engineering groups in the Engineering Division are involved in lower-status support activities: field service, performance evaluation, maintenance, quality. They are found in manufacturing groups, on the staff, and in support roles in development groups. Some of these engineers aspire to a job in development and occasionally make the transition; others are quite comfortable with nine-to-five jobs in a quieter atmosphere.

The prevalent image of engineers defines the nature of their identification with work and the personal characteristics that accompany it. Technology and its aesthetics are said to be the main concern of engineers, who are driven by a fascination with "neat things" or "bells and whistles"—challenging features to design, interesting problems, and sophisticated, state-of-the-art technology. "The prize for hard work," it is said, "is more hard work." If these qualities are not available in regular work and assigned projects, they can be sought in "midnight projects"—the illicit projects that dedicated engineers are said to take on in their free time for the sheer interest or pleasure of the work.[12]

"Art is what you do for yourself; work is what you do for others" is a prominently displayed slogan that captures the prevailing stereotype of the "engineering mentality." Engineers are said to prefer the former over the latter and to possess big egos, addictive personalities, little if any social skills, not to mention graces, a bent for hard, obsessive work (often at the expense of family and social life), and a penchant for "burnout," the scars of which are carried and displayed almost as one would a purple heart. An engineer's commitment, it is implied, is often primarily to the technology rather than to the company; rather than allowing business criteria to shape their work, they are motivated, it is said, by a predilection for "creeping featuritis" and the urge to move a midnight project to high noon. This image, immortalized to the satisfaction of many by Tracy Kidder (1981) in *The Soul of a New Machine* ("the only one who really understood us"), underlies the folk wisdom used by many in the organization to explain or rationalize their decisions, feelings, and attitudes. It is against this standard that many engineers measure and evaluate themselves and others; and it is this imagery that informs those whose task it is to control and channel the energies of engineers as well as keep them loyal, committed, and happy.

Despite the carefully cultivated image of rampant individualism, engineering work is not easily distinguishable from the company context. Engineers often see their work through the lens of the company interest. They own the "technical world" and see others who might interfere with their art as "overhead," "do-nothings," or, most pejoratively, "product preventers." Many are aware of the business issues. In most cases they recognize profitability not only as a precondition for the opportunity to work on more neat things but also as the ultimate measure of their success, and many therefore take an active interest in marketing decisions. Thus, organizational and professional concerns are inextricably interwoven in the practice of engineering.[13]

Within development, engineers sort themselves out by the type of work they do and their perceived skill. Engineering is a highly competitive arena in which formal statuses are supplemented by informal ratings. Informally, engineers are categorized by their skill. There are the "brilliant" and the "geniuses," their status sometimes debated ("the only way he made the list of 100 brightest scientists is if he mailed coupons from the back of cereal boxes") and sometimes acknowledged ("Peter is brilliant. There is no question about that; he is a crackerjack engineer"); and there are journeymen (and the occasional journey woman), who might be "solid citizens—no rah rah"—or just "bodies." ("They were short on the project, needed some coding [computer programming] done to meet the schedule, so they brought down a body from Lyndsville. The body's name was Bill; he's gone now.")

Formal status is organizationally recognized. The "engineering community" has a separate ranking system—the technical track. Table 1 presents the levels, ranks, numbers, average pay, and tenure of the Tech engineering population in 1985 (data are limited to the engineers defined as involved with development work).[14]

Junior engineers usually do lowly and boring work ("cranking out code" is the standard example) and engage in narrowly defined tasks. Principal engineers have proven their technical skills to their managers and typically

Table 1: Engineers

Level	Title	Population (% of total)	Average pay ($ per year)	Average Tenure (years)
7	Corporate Consulting Engineer	0.5	87,000	12
6	Senior Consulting Engineer	1.5	72,900	9
5	Consulting Engineer	5.0	59,000	8
4	Principal Engineer	26.0	48,300	6
1–3	Junior Engineer	67.0	n.d.	2–5

have senior project responsibilities, including project leadership on smaller projects. Consulting engineers may have responsibility for an entire product or system ("technical gurus") or acknowledged expertise in it. Consulting engineers are less involved in specific projects; instead, like Tom O'Brien, they engage in corporate-wide consulting, trouble-shooting, project initiation, technical task forces and committees, and so forth. At higher levels, the distinction between engineering and business is in many cases vague.

The technical track has standard stages. Almost all entry-level engineers are "college hires," recruited out of engineering schools. (Engineers with no formal training are a dying breed.) Junior engineers can progress up a rank and pay scale. At the junior level, promotions are fairly rapid. Over time, junior engineers are informally evaluated. For those who choose a technical career, promotion to principal engineer involves recognition of a status jump and occurs after a corporate committee evaluates the candidate's "technical contribution."

Approximately 10 to 15 percent of the engineers quit the technical track each year. One major reason is the lure of a managerial career.[15] Principal engineers must make a critical career decision: remain on the technical track or move into management. At this point the typical engineer has been doing project work for about four years. An abundance of folk theory explains the transition choice—burnout, ambition, boredom, a technical "Peter principle," a desire for change, an interest in "people issues." Some call it "getting the disease"; for others it is a sign of maturity. All agree that the price is involvement in "politics and all the shit that goes on."

The pros and cons of the managerial option are hotly debated. Statistics are utilized to support both sides. Some engineers believe that the managerial track promises more potential income and room for growth. Although considerable corporate efforts have gone into designing a more promising and rewarding technical track in order to keep the talented technical people doing technical work, promotion to senior technical-track positions is regarded as difficult. (Table 1 shows a distinct bottleneck at the consulting level.) One way of circumventing the perceived disadvantages of the technical track is to take a promotion into management while remaining a technical person.[16] Many would consider Rick Smith a typical example of an engineer who "just couldn't handle" management. Tom O'Brien is considered a candidate for such a transition and is therefore the recipient of much conflicting advice.

There are other reasons for quitting the track. Less successful engineers, or those not perceived to "have what it takes," may transfer to nontechnical jobs, with or without the overt signs of burnout and the stigma of being a "loser." Others might be persuaded by "headhunters" preying on engineering talent to join a start-up company, where the security of a guaranteed steady income is traded for excitement and the potential for higher monetary awards. In keeping with Tech's tradition of job security, few engineers are terminated.

For the many who stay on the track, engineering offers a distinct identity that ties working on the technology to the specific realities of the company. Beyond compensation, which is generally perceived to be comparable to what other large companies offer, the company is also thought to offer opportunities for training and professional development, relative autonomy, and interesting work for some.[17] For many, the no-layoff policy is particularly important. The company has never laid off engineers (or other employees), even during some of the more severe downturns. There are also risks, however: demands are high, burnout is a threat, and things can "get crazy." Nevertheless, most engineers consider it a "good engineering environment."

Managers

Managers are the movers, the shakers; they make it all happen. All the engineering managers have a technical background; almost all have formal engineering training and development experience (or at least Tech experience in engineering).[18] Technical sophistication is practically the sine qua non of management in Engineering; without it, one gets no respect. Tech

Table 2: Engineering Managers

Level	Title	Population (% of total)	Salary ($ per year)
7	Group Manager	9	97,000
6	Senior Engineering Manager	20	80,100
5	Engineering Manager	36	63,900
4	Supervisor	35	48,900

managers have a reputation for remaining very technical, often at the expense of developing "management skills." Conventional wisdom suggests that "amateurish management" is one of Tech's shortcomings.

The managerial track runs parallel to the technical one (see Table 2 for 1985 data). Supervisors—on the first rung of the managerial ladder—are at the same level as principal engineers. Mostly fresh out of engineering work, they typically manage small projects or parts of larger ones. For the first time they are expected to take care of "people issues," the formal and informal requirements of managing engineers and others—a skill that is not presumed to come easily to engineers. Promotion up the managerial ladder involves responsibility for larger projects and for product groups and organizations, and, of course, increased compensation.[19] At higher levels, managers become involved in budgetary questions and relations with other groups in the division, the company, and the rest of the world. Increasingly, "business" and "political" skills become important, as well as "Tech-knowledge"—a familiarity with the company, the people, and "the culture."

It is the engineering manager's job to mediate between the requirements of technology and business, the two central ideological forces in this universe. The technical world is a familiar one to all managers; it was their first love. But "business" is a pervasive force, an adult reality with its own charms. The "business perspective" is carried by senior managers (and such specialized staff groups as marketing, strategy, and product management) and driven down the managerial ranks.[20]

Business imposes two criteria for success: revenue and time. The business of business is, of course, profit. In this view, making money is not only a necessity but an ideal, the measure of all things good. Senior engineering managers are evaluated both formally and informally on their ability to "produce revenue." The business perspective is translated down the line into "time to market" requirements and "aggressive scheduling." To balance the forces of technology and profit, managers must be able to ship products on time.

Managing time is of central importance in managerial work. This is not easy. The dilemma it poses is a recognized fact of engineering life. On the one hand, managers are evaluated formally and, more important, informally on their ability to "ship on time." On the other hand, they are frequently committed to unrealistic schedules. ("Let's face it. If you want the project you have to lie! Otherwise the other guy will get it. And he's lying too. And your engineers—well, they're playing the same game.") Schedules, slips, crunches, and delays become an eternal bone of contention. "I want it yesterday" is the demand of the desperate manager. "I need more time!" is the equally desperate reply. Thus, "time to market" is the grand criterion of organizational assessment.

To meet their commitments and to generate more opportunities, managers must learn how to squeeze the most out of engineers and development groups: how to buffer them against organizational turbulence, keep them from succumbing to the temptations of headhunters or the sirens' lure of overwork and burnout, and channel their creative energies in productive directions rather than the neat things they might prefer.[21] At the same time, they must also be aware of what competing managers are up to, what senior management is thinking, and how to generate organizational support for their activities.

Thus, managerial work requires a number of skills. First, they must remain "technical" or at least conversant enough not to lose their credibility or allow themselves to be misled. Second, they must learn the language and modes of thought of the business world. Third, they must develop their "people skills." These include understanding and managing the psychology of engineers and the intricacies of social interaction. Fourth, they must learn "Tech culture"—how things get done in the company. Finally, they must hone their "political skills"—the art of doing battle in an environment perceived as very competitive and highly conflictual.

All would concur that the managers' lives are hectic. Burnout is an ever-present threat. One moves away from the dirty work of hands-on engineering, only to find other forms of "dirt." ("There is an incredible amount of crap going on as you move up. All the politics.") In addition, time pressures are great. Keeping a sane calendar is an ongoing concern for managers as well as their secretaries. Some speak privately of an early retirement or a quieter lifestyle as an alternative to the unpleasant aspects of organizational life.

Many of the managers are ambitious and upward-looking, and aspire to make it at Tech (or elsewhere in the industry, as some would privately acknowledge and others have publicly demonstrated). Mobility can be quite rapid. Managers, like engineers, carry with them a reputation, often as good as the last project they were associated with. Observers of Engineering claim that managers often attempt to bail out of failing projects or leave before the market has responded in order to preserve their reputations.[22] In this view, reputations are primarily a matter of luck or "political and presentational" skill. Thus, reputations are constantly debated, and the attribution of failure (often followed by the reality) is always a danger.

Failure may have a number of consequences. Managers reputed to be unsuccessful are often passed on to other groups with good recommendations, while those said to have burnt out might be "taken care of" by being assigned to one of a number of ill-defined jobs whose sole purpose seems to be to allow the company to live up to its public commitment to take care of its employees. More serious casualties are also discussed by managers and engineers. Stories of alcoholism, divorce, psychiatric breakdown, suicide, and even one murder are told and retold. Thus, the struggles of daily existence are highly dramatized. The extremes of winning and losing are portrayed in gory detail and in colorful language. This drama is often public and open, consistent with the image of exciting high-tech organizational life. More privately, however, one also hears that losing is not all that bad. There is a well-identified (and no doubt reassuring) class of "early retirees," also known as "deadwood." Said one manager faced with a possible loss of funding: "There is only an up side here; no down side. The worst case is to retire on the job. I know quite a few people who spend most of their time tending their investments or taking care of their yachts. . . . Life isn't so bad on 60K a year!"

Wage Class 2

The hourly workers in Wage Class 2, neither professional nor managerial, provide the services and the work that support the activities deemed central. In Engineering, they are mostly secretaries. Almost all are female. They work fixed hours—from nine to five—and make an average of eight to twelve dollars an hour. Wages are similar to those paid by other employers, but the benefits are considered excellent. Most secretaries are lifelong residents of the local towns. The younger ones frequently have degrees from local colleges, and some, like Mary Carmanelli, whom we encountered in Chapter 1, hope to move into nontechnical jobs in Wage Class 4. Others hope for a promotion within their category. Senior secretaries who have been with the company for at least ten years are entitled to a weekly salary.

Temporary Workers

Tech employs two kinds of temporary workers. Most are hired to do the dirty work (such as cleaning) or to provide security and other services. In addition, people are often hired for secretarial positions beyond those allowed by the "headcount"—the number of positions formally assigned to a group. Doing roughly the same secretarial work as employees, many of these "tags" or "temps" see their temporary assignment as an opportunity to get hired full time. For them, getting in is an achievement, a promise of more security and access to Tech's highly regarded benefits. Higher-status temporary work is performed by free-lance engineers hired for specific tasks and paid well above the corporate rate.[23]

Statistics are not available for all of Engineering, but extrapolating the percentages found in a number of subgroups suggests that temporary workers account for approximately 8 to 10 percent of the total population. Numbers change with hiring freezes and thaws and other personnel policies.[24]

The Work Environment

Tech's work environment is said to the reflect the "openness," "flexibility," and "informality" prescribed by the culture. "Open office space" is strictly enforced. In a typical engineering facility, collapsible office cubicles are clustered in the center of a spacious hall, with seminar and meeting rooms on the periphery. Close by are the labs that house computers and other technical equipment, and the libraries. Most facilities also have large, open cafeterias in central locations with good (by corporate standards) buffet food.

Offices are the primary setting for work. A typical office measures eight feet by eight feet, with five-foot-high partitions and no door. Each is equipped with a telephone and a computer terminal. Project and group members are typically located in adjacent cubicles. Engineers and managers have their own cubicles. Senior managers occupy corner offices and often have slightly more space, with room for a secretary in an adjacent office. At Corporate, senior managers might have closed offices, but all doors have glass panels. Secretaries to senior managers occupy a cubicle that is designed as the entrance to another; others occupy desks in open space. Many managers and engineers have "a space" at more than one facility. Those who do not may step into a temporarily empty cubicle and use the terminal to access their electronic mail. Thus, the setting is designed to encourage communication, enhance face-to-face exposure, and minimize status distinctions.[25]

The open office space resembles a beehive. On a typical day, engineers may be seen in their cubicles, attached to the ubiquitous terminal, often with ear plugs to keep out the unending background noise and prevent the interruptions that are inevitable in a space designed for openness and communication. Others might be observed in the labs, bent over the hardware. Managers are more mobile and less available, although their secretaries are always around.

Work-related interaction occurs in other settings as well. Meeting rooms off the central office space permit more private meetings (design meetings, status reports, staff meetings, and other configurations in which time is spent or misspent). The common space around the cafeteria is used throughout the day. During the morning and afternoon it provides the setting for informal meetings over computer output or paper and pencil designs. It is humming at lunch time as members of different statuses and levels congregate around the many tables. The lunch hour is also used for leisure activities; most noticeable are the sports crowd, the runners, and the card players. More privacy— always a concern—can be found away from the office. Much formal and informal interaction takes place in restaurants and bars close to the facilities. Local hotels provide the stage for many off-site meetings, conferences, trade shows, and product announcements. Tech also has conference centers with private meeting rooms available by reservation.

Another space within which to interact is the "technet," an electronic system that offers an instant world-wide link between Tech terminals and uncontrolled access to multinational and multicompany networks. All managers and engineers have their own mailstop directly connected to the terminal in their office. The traffic within and between facilities is heavy and smooth, and is used for both work and leisure. Thus, beyond the usual transmission of work-related documents, employees use it for everything from "underground" newsletters to the organized activities of interest and hobby groups. During the workday terminals are always on, and the arrival of mail is announced with a beep. Many engineers and all managers also keep a terminal at home that allows them to work via the telephone lines.

The flexibility of space is complemented by a flexible approach to time. Members of Wage Class 4 often use "flexitime": as long as they fulfill commitments and do not arouse attention, they are allowed to manage their own schedules and to design their workday as they see fit. Nevertheless, there are rigid and potentially enforceable standards. Time supervision is subtle, often undiscussed, and based on a negotiated relationship. If people overtly come and go as they please, they may also be covertly watched by supervisors ("If he comes late, I kinda take notice if he stays late; a private arithmetic—you never know when you have to use it.") Rick Smith's concern that the use of his home terminal was being monitored is not atypical. People in Wage Class 2, on the other hand, work regular hours.

In sum, Tech's work environment reflects the same tension between control and chaos that is central to its social worlds. On the one hand, flexibility is a key theme in the spatial and temporal organization of work. Both space and time boundaries are loosely defined and negotiable. On the other hand, subtle and implicit attempts to control—including the conscious design of the office space—are in evidence, and members experience a constant need to protect their space and time from outside demands.

Conclusion

Tech Engineering is an intense and complex environment. It couples a fluid and ambiguous structure, rapid internal mobility, and flexible spatial and time boundaries with heavy demands on the time and energy of employees, particularly those in the professional and managerial ranks. The organization consists of a complex network of relationships, with relatively few of the traditional organizing principles to comfort and guide members. Structural principles and social categories provide broad definitions with which to begin to make sense of the social environment, but many insiders consider these insufficient. There is a distinct preference for informality: Tech, as a social entity, is internally characterized as having a "culture" that provides a map to guide employees through the dramatic and routine daily events there.

The importance of the culture as an alternative organizing principle has produced a sustained managerial effort to explicate, codify, and disseminate an official version of it, with advice on how to live with it. These explicit views of the culture are considered in the following chapter.

chapter 3

Ideology: Tech Culture Codified

"Don't the people in the control towers ever raise hell?" "They all belong to the syndicate," Milo said. "And they know what's good for the
syndicate is good for the country, because that's what makes Sammy
run. The men in the control towers have a share, too, and that's why
they always have to do whatever they can to help the syndicate." "Do
I have a share?" "Everybody has a share." "Does Orr have a share?"
"Everybody has a share." "And Hungry Joe? He has a share too?"
"Everybody has a share." "Well I'll be damned," mused Yossarian,
deeply impressed with the idea of a share for the very first time.

—Joseph Heller
Catch-22

'Twas not by ideas, —by heaven! his life was put in jeopardy by
words.

—Laurence Sterne
Tristram Shandy

Tom O'Brien has been around the company for a while; like many others,
he has definite ideas about "Tech culture" and what it takes to get things
done in Engineering. But, as he is constantly reminded, so does the company. When he arrives at work each morning, he encounters evidence of the
company point of view at every turn. First are the bumperstickers adorning
many of the cars in the Lyndsville parking lot. "I LOVE TECH!" they declare,
somewhat unoriginally, the words underscored by the ubiquitous little red
heart designed into the company logo. "This shit is everywhere," he says.
"I got it on my own car."

If the bumperstickers seem trivial, almost tongue-in-cheek, the short walk
to his cubicle takes him past a plethora of more serious stylized references
to his experience as a member of the organization. Inside the building, just
beyond the security desk, a large television monitor is playing a videotape
of a recent speech by Sam Miller. As he walks by, he hears the familiar

voice discuss "our goals, our values, and the way we do things." "It's the 'We are One' speech," he notes as he walks by, "nothing new." He has read the speech in a company newsletter, and excerpts are posted everywhere. Turning a corner, he stops by a large bulletin board fixed to the wall next to the library. On one side is a permanent display including the well-known statement of the "Company Philosophy" ("It's the Bible—the Ten Commandments for the Techie: make a buck and do it right"), and a selection of personnel policies titled "Your Rights and Obligations." On the other, clippings and copies of recent references to Tech in local, national, and trade newspapers are prominently posted. He glances at the latest addition, "High Motivation in High-Tech: The New Work Force"; an anonymous hand has highlighted the company name in bright yellow. By the cafeteria, where he stops for coffee, a flipchart calls attention to Dave Carpenter's presentation ("High Technologies' Strategy for the Future—How You Fit In. The talk will be videotaped"), and to a workshop on "Career Management at Tech: How to Make the Most of Yourself." Close by, piles of brochures are stacked on a table in front of the personnel office. Tom takes one, headed, "If you are experiencing signs of stress, perhaps you should give us a call." Inside it offers some words of wisdom: "Everyone experiences stress at some time. . . . Stress isn't necessarily a bad thing. . . . You can do something about stress." He turns into the workspace labyrinth, picks up his mail, and enters his cubicle, where he plans to spend the morning.

Cultural commentary finds him also in the relative seclusion of his own space. As he sits down, he switches on his terminal in a practiced, smooth move, absentmindedly logs on, and turns to the screen. On his technet mail he notices among the many communications another announcement of the afternoon events; a memo titled, "How Others See Our Values," reviewing excerpts on Tech Culture from recent managerial bestsellers; a request to be interviewed by a consultant for a culture study; and the daily review of all references to Tech in the press. In his mail ("the hardcopy"), he finds *Tech-knowledge*, one of a large number of company newsletters. On the cover is a big picture of Sam Miller against the background of a giant slogan—"We Are One." He also finds an order form for company publications, including Ellen Cohen's "Culture Operating Manual." His bookshelf has mostly technical material, but also a copy of *In Search of Excellence*, distributed to all professional and managerial employees, and a business magazine with a cover story on Tech's corporate culture, titled "Working Hard, Having

Fun." For good measure, an "I LOVE TECH" bumpersticker is fixed to his filing cabinet. The day has hardly begun, yet Tom is already surrounded by "the culture," the ever-present signs of the company's explicit concern with its employees' state of mind (and heart).

Tom's exposure to the company perspective on "the culture" is not atypical. For Tech employees, company-sponsored references to the nature of their individual and collective work experience—their motivation, values, feelings, what they are up to and why—are taken for granted, a routine interpretive backdrop to their daily work. Although their stance toward such commentary varies considerably—for some it is "a useful guide to survival," for others "Big Brother shit," and for others yet an elaborate game or simply "the facts of life"—most insiders (as Tom would say) "speak Tech culture fluently": they easily reconstruct and often make use of its style and substance. For members, then, the company perspective on the culture is familiar, systematic, comprehensive, thought-out, well-articulated, and associated with the company's interest. It is, in other words, a pervasive "organizational ideology."

Ideology, most generally speaking, is an authoritative system of meaning.[1] As Geertz (1973: 220) suggests, all ideologies—whether political, aesthetic, moral, or economic—are "schematic images of social order" publicly offered in the name of those with a claim to authority as "maps of problematic social reality and matrices for the creation of collective conscience."[2] In corporate contexts such as Tech, ideology consists of images of organizational social reality—publicly articulated and logically integrated "reality claims" concerning the company's social nature and the nature of its members, formulated and disseminated by those who claim to speak for "the company perspective."[3]

What is the "company perspective" on Tech culture? What forms does it take? Who are its spokespersons? What kinds of authority do they claim? What versions of social reality do they offer? What kinds of member roles do they depict? What normative demands do they embody? How are the various ideological forms related? What general matrix of meaning do they combine to create? In this chapter, the meanings contained in the organizational ideology are uncovered and explicated. The focus of the analysis is on the varieties of the printed and recorded word available to Tech members— the articulated and relatively enduring inscriptions and codifications of the company point of view.[4] How ideology is interactively constructed and used, and what it means to members, is the subject of the following chapters, where ideological reality claims are analyzed in the context within which they are pronounced and made meaningful.

At Tech, inscriptions of the organizational ideology fall into three distinct categories, each of which derives its authority from a different source. First is the direct voice of managerial authority: the documented views of senior managers found in such forms as the "company philosophy," the videotape of Sam Miller's speech screened in the entrance lobby, or the transcripts in *Techknowledge*. The voice of expert authority appears in papers, reports, and memos attributed to internal experts charged with observing and commenting on the social aspects of the company: Ellen Cohen's "Culture Operating Manual" and the personnel materials on stress are examples. Finally, there is the voice of objective authority, the selective representation of materials produced by outside observers of Tech, as in the press clippings posted daily on the Lyndsville bulletin board and electronically distributed excerpts from managerial bestsellers. The form and the substance of each variant of the ideology are discussed separately, followed by a comparative analysis that specifies the main themes of the company perspective that they combine to create.

Top Management: The Voice of Leadership

Senior managers at Tech espouse a distinct and systematic view of the company and its members in written documents that formulate and codify the abstract principles underlying the managerial perspective, and in recorded speeches and interviews that offer personal interpretations of the official point of view.

Official Statements

The official company perspective is found in a variety of documents and booklets posted in public places and distributed to employees. The "Engineering Guide," widely distributed and used in Engineering, contains the closest thing to an organization chart officially distributed by the company: a listing of the groups, their managers, tasks, addresses, and locations. Most managers and many engineers keep a copy in their office. Other publications of this sort include booklets describing Tech's pay and benefits policy and education and training opportunities, a handbook on career management, and an introduction to the company for new employees.

The official statements found in these documents are brief, comprehensive, abstract, and highly prescriptive formulations of the principles management considers crucial to the definition of the company. The "Engineering Guide" reprints the broadest and best-known managerial statement —a five-page codification of the "Company Philosophy," composed by the executive committee after extensive "wordsmithing."[5] Among statements concerning technical and business matters, one finds as well a formulation of the official perspective on the social nature of the company and its employees. The following selection captures the main themes. First, the corporate goals are framed in moral terms:

High Technologies Corporation:
Our Corporate Philosophy

Honesty
We want to be not only technically honest but also to make sure that the implication of what we say and the impressions that we leave are correct. When we make a commitment to a customer, we feel the obligation to see that it happens.

Profit
We are a public corporation. Stockholders invested in our Corporation for profit. Success is measured by profit. With success comes the opportunity to grow, the ability to hire good people and the satisfaction that comes with meeting your goals. We feel that profit is in no way inconsistent with social goals.

Quality
Growth is not our primary goal. Our goal is to be a quality organization and do a quality job which means that we will be proud of the product for years to come. . . .

Customers
We must be honest and straightforward with our customers and be sure that they are not only told the facts but understand the

facts. . . . We sell our corporation and we must be sure all commitments are met.

Second, the company's social organization is said to be based on a balance of freedom and discipline:

Responsibility
Plans are proposed by individuals and teams. These plans may be rejected until they fit the corporate goals . . . but when they are accepted, they are the responsibility of those who proposed them. . . .

Management
We particularly want to be sure that management jobs are clear and well defined. . . . Meeting financial results is only one measure of a plan; other measures are satisfied customers, development of people, meeting long-range needs of the corporation, development of new products, opening new markets, and meeting the commitments made to others in the company. We believe that our commitment to planning assures freedom to act.

Third, the philosophy depicts the desired attributes of members as based on self-discipline and "the right attitude":

Personnel
We believe that individual discipline should be self-generated. . . . We promote people according to their performance; not only their technical ability but also their ability to get the job done and to take the responsibility that goes with the job. Ability is measured not only by past results but also by attitude and desire to succeed.

First Rule
When dealing with a customer, a supplier, or an employee, do what is "right" to do in each situation.

Other documents elaborate and explain these themes and add a descriptive note to its prescriptive, somewhat idealized, and very abstract requirements. For example, in the "Engineering Guide," immediately following the company philosophy, one finds an explicit formulation of the essence of the "corporate culture": the company is characterized by "informality" and "trust," its employees by "maturity" and "self-direction."

Tech Culture

High Technologies is a people-oriented company. The employees receive courteous, fair and equitable treatment. . . . Management expects hard work and a high level of achievement. . . . A great deal of trust is placed in employees to give their best efforts to a job. . . . Employees are expected to act in a mature manner at all times. . . . The matrix organization is goal-oriented and depends on trust, communications and team work. As a result, most employees function as independent consultants on every level, interacting across many areas necessary to accomplish the task.

Honesty, hard work, moral and ethical conduct, a high level of professionalism, and team work, are qualities that are an integral part of employment at High Technologies. These qualities are considered part of the Tech culture. Employees conduct themselves in an informal manner and are on a first-name basis with everyone at all levels. . . . The opportunity for self-direction and self-determination is always present.

Similarly, in a handbook titled "High Technologies and You: An Introduction to Tech for New Employees," the Company Philosophy is explained as follows:

Welcome to High Technologies. As you may have already noticed, we are a company with the spirit of informality and openness. We strive to maintain an environment where people can grow and excel. We encourage a spirit of cooperation among all employees.

The loyalty, hard work and creativity of our employees has made High Technologies a global corporation with a reputation for quality and services. . . .

To show our employees we appreciate them and to invite their commitments, we listen to them and respond to them promptly with genuine interest. Above all we maintain our commitments to them. . . .

As for your success at High Technologies, the people who prosper around here are those who care about the company, can recognize opportunities, propose solutions and accept the responsibility to get the job done.

Finally, a booklet titled "Bet on Yourself: You, Your Career and High Technologies" explains the company policy with regard to career development, emphasizing the official view of the relationship between the company and its employees. "Freedom to manage work" coupled with "individual responsibility" and "self-management" are the key:

We are fortunate that as a corporation, High Technologies places a high value on individual responsibility. While this valuing of individual employee initiative offers us varying degrees of freedom in terms of decision making, open communication and bottom-up problem solving, there can be no freedom without responsibility; and one of the most important employee responsibilities is SELF-MANAGEMENT.

Your schooling and your work experience have prepared you for responsibility but not with this apparent freedom. This freedom to manage your own work may be a shock which takes some getting used to.

In our complex and ever changing HT environment there is often the temptation to abdicate responsibility and place the blame for your lack of job clarity or results on "the organization" or on "management." But if you really value your energies and talents, you will make it your responsibility "to self" to see that you utilize them well—that means taking an active rather than passive role in managing your performance.

Thus, official company documents distill management's collective preferences into abstract principles, catch phrases, and key words openly designed to educate and influence. Three themes are apparent: Tech's depiction as an organic entity whose goals, shared by all, reflect a moral stance vis-à-vis the world; the company's "people oriented" social organization, combining paternal care and trust with an informal atmosphere, freedom of action with responsibility; and an elaboration of members' desired attributes. Required behaviors are vaguely defined: creativity, taking initiative, hard work, meeting commitments, "doing it right," are thought to reflect internalized values, beliefs, and feelings; "self-generated discipline," "attitude and desire to succeed," "caring," and "loyalty" are considered evidence of personal "growth" and "maturity."

Such documents are generally regarded as "apple pie and motherhood statements": abstract and idealized, they reflect management's desires, even wishful thinking, in formulations removed from everyday reality. They are rarely, therefore, the focus of attention. However, the principles they embody are frequently restated and interpreted in the less organized but more concrete words of senior managers attempting to explain, exemplify, substantiate, and validate the main themes of the managerial perspective.

Senior Managers Speak

The recorded thoughts, observations, and ideas of senior managers are perhaps the most frequently encountered form of ideological expression. Here, the managerial perspective is presented in the name of real people, whose experience is often used as evidence for its applicability. The focus is mostly on mundane concerns of business and technology, but explicit references to cultural matters are often present.

Newsletters are the most widespread media for disseminating the personal views of senior managers through interviews, reprints of speeches, and occasional signed editorials. Their number varies, but the average in Engineering is around two hundred; of these, most are funded by company budgets.[6] Some are limited to the ranks of management, others to occupational groups, and others still to particular organizations. They appear weekly or monthly in employee maildrops or homes; others wait around to be picked up or appear magically on the technet. All are kept in the library stacks, and clippings of key items are routinely posted.

Speeches, presentations, and interviews given by senior managers are routinely videotaped. Edited versions are found in the libraries and are used by training and public relations groups. Some tapes are used in workshops and seminars; others, like Sam Miller's "We Are One" speech, are screened in public during lunchtime sessions and shown throughout the day in strategic locations (see Chapter 4 for a description of events where videotapes are used).[7]

Senior managers address the three main themes of the managerial perspective: the company's moral purpose, the nature of its social organization, and the attributes of the member role. Sam Miller is a key figure in this rhetoric. He is widely recognized as someone with a distinct point of view, referred to by insiders as a "vision," a "philosophy," or a "religion." Regarded by many as the originator of "the culture" and a key figure in its preservation and maintenance, he is frequently interviewed, and ideas associated with him are well known and widely circulated.[8] Other senior managers repeat and interpret similar ideas.

The company's moral purpose is reflected in the frequent reference to the corporate goals, or "mission."[9] Thus, in a videotaped interview designed and used for training purposes, Sam Miller suggests that profit is not just an economic necessity but also intrinsically worthwhile:

> We wanted to make a profit, which clearly took somebody else's money—with the promise that we were going to try and get a return for that money. And so we started off from the start saying, "It's not our company," and we promised to make a return on the money we were using. That is an orientation which has stayed with us and affected us significantly. At that time *profit* was a bad word. We forget it now, you know, but we're really much more business-oriented today than we were then. After the war most of my friends in college were—not most, many of them were—honest-to-goodness communists. Openly, no problem. A few years later they're straight as could be, doing military work on the Korean War, but many of these ideas—antibusiness, antiprofit—were much stronger then than they even are today, and people would hire a scientist or an engineer and say, we're hiring you to build you up technically, to have you present papers and all that, and secretly they'd hope he'd make some profit for them. And we told them it was simple: "We've got

someone else's money, and we have to make a return on it."
And this orientation has allowed us to grow. Everybody in the
company understands we've got to make a profit, we want to
make it as consistently as possible. We plan to do something in
a quarter, we want to get it out, and we're not embarrassed to
have people work hard to get it done by the end of the quarter.

There is more to the mission, however, than profit. In this view, Tech's
goal is also to make significant "social contribution." In interviews with
company newsletters, Sam Miller emphasizes this repeatedly:

Our goal has never been just to make money or just to sell technology, but rather to do something which is unique and make an
important contribution to our customers.
    Our mission, our contribution to society, our vision, is to offer
to society our technology, which we see as being the answer to
the major problems of the world in this area.

The social contribution is construed as developing unique technologies. In
reviewing Tech's history, Miller says:

In time it became clear that hundreds of other companies would
be technically able to do the things that we were doing. It became clear that if we were to make a contribution to the industry,
we had to do something unique. So we set about to concentrate
our efforts and our resources on those things that would be important to customers and those things which other companies
would have difficulty doing.

The morality of the company's mission also extends to its internal
social organization—commonly described as "people-oriented." In a taped
speech, Miller relates that orientation to ideas derived from early Human
Relations theorists:

We almost have a moral obligation to society. We owe it to society to do it. We told them what to do; now we must show them
how! What is most important is where your heart is. When we

started Tech, the business fad was McGregor and Theory X and Y. Some tried and said: "I *knew* it wouldn't work." We made it work! And for an American company, we do it well! [10]

Miller often uses academic environments as a model for Tech's combination of openness, trust, and peer pressure. In a videotaped speech, he says:

> Now, if I asked what advantage we have, we would often say—I hope you would say—we have an environment, an atmosphere, which is conducive to creativity and encourages people to go do good work and to work hard. In fact, when we started the company there were a number of ideas we took from some of the top engineering schools. One was the atmosphere. There was at that time—and I believe still today—enormous generosity on the part of management. They didn't pay well, but enormous generosity and enormous trust, just *trust* people—not checking on them all the time. In the group I was in, there were also very clear goals so that everyone understood where they sat relative to the project they were working on. My boss there said: "We owe it to the person working for us that first of all he knows how well he's doing." It's laid out in a way that can be reviewed and he knows. Secondly, his peers know, and *there* is where the pressure is for driving hard. You see, the other thing that they had was the enormous intellectual challenge, in all ways. And that combination of generosity, trust, and emotional—I mean *intellectual*—challenge was exceedingly productive, and it was this that challenged us, challenged me, to go into business, to try to generate that atmosphere. And this is still the challenge. It produced people who were creative, enthusiastic, interesting, exciting, and worked awfully hard and enjoyed doing it.

Managers typically refer to these ideas as part of a longstanding tradition. In an interview, the vice-president of Engineering says of the "early days":

> We had a small personnel department, but had very definite ideas about how to handle people and how people should manage. We had a strong feeling for the individual and wanted to

be sure our personnel policies enabled us to provide jobs that people would be excited about and could accomplish, that had goals and measurements. Many of the same things we talk about today. . . .

Aspects of the company's "people orientation" are frequently adumbrated. In a recorded speech, the vice-president of Human Resources discusses the company's "commitment to its people":

> We have always tried to transmit the notion that people are our most important asset. In a time of crisis, our initial reaction is to protect our employees. In the past two recessions there came a time when we said we needed to stop hiring people. This is, I think, a message of how good an organization we are, perhaps much more than how much we grow or how fast we grow. During the past years our values regarding job security have been severely tested as never before. And while we do not guarantee full employment, we have lived up to our commitment to manage the business in a way that reduces the likelihood of resorting to involuntary separation of our people. High Technologies is its employees.

Much is also made of the balance of freedom and discipline that is supposed to characterize working life in the company. Freedom is reflected in enhanced autonomy for members, otherwise known as "bottom-up management." The vice-president of Engineering says in an interview:

> I believe you just can't manage a fast-growing, fast-moving organization in detail from the top. It limits the growth if you try to do it that way. So we've continuously tried to push decision making functions down inside the organizations to product lines, to engineers.

Autonomy, in this view, must be coupled with responsibility:

> One of the concepts that hasn't changed from the beginning of the company is that people are responsible for the success of the

projects they propose. "He who proposes does," and is judged on the results. That fundamental philosophy hasn't changed. I hope it never does. We have to keep working to make sure that engineers feel they can propose things and go out and do them— that they aren't powerless, that they can get decisions made.

Senior management's expectations of members (the third managerial theme) are implicit in the depiction of collective attributes: morality, hard work, excitement, commitment. Sam Miller frequently refers to the values that should or do (the distinction is not always clear) underlie members' moral orientation to their work. Some are derived from the world of religion. In a widely distributed recording of his "state of the company" speech, Miller says:

> We're told that in many religions, maybe particularly Christianity, humility, searching, the pilgrim looking, is the model of life. In Peters' book *In Search of Excellence*, his answers are sometimes too simple, but the title is interesting: the *search* for excellence. In every part of the company, every one of us, we're still just pilgrims looking.

He also calls on the values of science for inspiration:

> We need enthusiasm, the confidence, the self-assuredness to go out and win. We also need the introspection, the humility to learn, to learn from each other, to study, to go to school, to learn from our customers. There is a good tradition for this in science. You know, we're taught that the scientist is humble, he never knows the answer, he's always searching, he's looking for the construction of the atom. He's never there, he's humbly looking, experimenting, frustrated he could be so stupid two years ago, ill at ease with what he has today—there's that humility to build a science.

Tech's values are further specified by the vice-president of Human Resources in a taped speech before a senior management conference:

Values and principles and beliefs are qualities we consider inherently worthwhile and desirable. The characteristics that determine our values are found in the roots of this culture, where values are shaped by members of that culture. Values define and give meaning to societies, organizations, and people. Values pull people together by helping to preserve continuity and commonality of the group. Values do in fact actually shape behavior and determine the future and success of organizations. The core values in our personal behaviors that we encourage all of our managers and employees to share and promote are honesty, loyalty, commitment, quality, efficiency, taking responsibilities, receptiveness to both people and their ideas, simplicity and clarity in our work and how we express our views, being active and willing team members, and ultimately to follow the first rule, which at High Technologies is to do what's right, the honest thing in all situations, whether it is in our behavior inside or outside of the High Technologies environment.

Incorporation of collective values is required. The VP of Human Resources continues:

Our values grow as a practice, as a way of life. Values are not something written down and tacked up on the wall in the form of ten principles that you must follow. Values are not a list of things that you should or should not do. The values I refer to are what we represent. They are inside of us; they are qualities that rarely surface in conversation. Rather they tend to surface in actions or attitudes. Others recognize our values of high integrity by what we do and how we behave. People and their values make High Technologies different and offer us the potential for being unique. People who work at Tech . . . feel a tremendous mobility to move up and across. They feel a freedom to seize the opportunity presented to them and develop their own personal goals within the parameters of the company goals.

A certain experience of membership is thought to follow from incorporating these values. "Excitement" and "fun," in particular, are frequent glosses for the emotional outcomes of hard, autonomous work. In a typical statement, the VP of Engineering describes his view of the desired state: "We spend a lot of time trying to make it fun to work here, make it challenging and exciting, make you feel as though you can make important contributions."

The prescription for the ideal membership experience often becomes a descriptive review of history. It is a frequent and subtle shift, part of the two-pronged effort at defining reality that is characteristic of this genre. Says Sam Miller:

> Our basic strength has always been the attitude and commitment of our people. The most important thing we can do is to continue to provide challenging opportunities for personal and professional growth, while we reinforce our commitment to achieve leadership in the industry.
>
> We must keep this atmosphere which generates creativity, makes people work hard and makes them *enjoy* working hard, challenges them to learn, challenges them to do new things, challenges them to take chances, and challenges them to be careful in their approach to things so that we never gamble the whole company—and this, I think, is still the goal, still the secret of our success.

Emotional gratification should also be derived from achieving company goals. In an interview in *Techlife*, Miller emphasizes the discipline that must counteract the pure joys of technological accomplishment:

> Individual products often seem to be more exciting than total systems because they are so visible and so much fun. But we have committed to design and build the world's best systems. As we aggressively pursue our overall strategy, our opportunities are great, and we can be very successful if we're disciplined and stay with our strategy.

Discipline is the basis for accomplishing collective goals, and its emotional correlate is "pride." Thus, a vice-president comments on the company's recent financial performance: "Everyone at Tech should be proud of these figures, which result from hard work and our increased emphases on efficiency and productivity."

Such emotions are associated, more generally, with affiliation with a company like Tech. A more personal and poetic testimonial to pride is found in the recorded speech of a senior manager:

> Have you ever had the experience of going to the corner store and being asked by the proprietor, "Where do you work?" If you say Chipco or Caltech, chances are the proprietor will say, "Oh, they are good companies!" But if you say High Technologies, chances are he will say, "Oh, that's a *great* company!" and you get a little chill of pride that runs up and down your spine because you know that there is something that sets us apart from the rest. And in that difference lies greatness and the potential to be unique.

Ideally, a heavy investment in work results not only in fun and pride, but in the additional benefit of individualism: a release from oppressive collective experience, from "the horrors of modern society." A vice-president says in an interview:

> As for the future, I'd like to see a company where each individual really feels that he or she has a role to play and has the freedom to succeed or fail based on their own ingenuity.
>
> One of the horrors of modern society is "group think" or "group do," where you are never singled out as an individual. My vision of a beautiful company is one where individuals, when they go home at night, feel that they have really made an impact, that they have been able to accomplish something, and they feel proud of themselves and proud of the company they work for.

In other words, incorporation of the member role satisfies both individual goals and collective interests.

The Perspective of Top Management

In speeches, interviews, and editorials, senior managers' personalized and animated view of the ideology fleshes out and complements the abstract principles in the official documents that presumably represent all of them. Managers combine morally based prescription with a touch of commonsense description buttressed by personal testimonials. Grounding the legitimacy of the abstract prescriptive principles in their own experience and their own words, and presenting themselves as spokesmen for an undifferentiated "we," they shift between prescriptive and descriptive statements, moving easily from exhortation to anecdote, from recollections of the glorious past and the company "traditions" to predictions of a no less glorious future. Thus, ideas are related to specific and recognized sources who imbue them with the authority associated with their names and the validity their presumed experience and status confer.

Overall, the managerial perspective depicts Tech as an organic community with a history, a mission, and shared values. Not surprisingly, "technology" and "business" goals provide the ultimate sources of meaning. More crucially, the two are compatible in the service of a higher goal—"making a social contribution." It is suggested that the blend is unique to Tech. Internally, the company is presented as possessing a "people orientation," combining paternal care with an open, informal, yet achievement-oriented society lacking the trappings of status-conscious and rule-bound bureaucracies. In such an environment, organizational action is based on principles of individualism: autonomy of action, freedom, and initiative. At the same time, accountability and responsibility are enforced, not only by one's superiors but also by peers, who are the source of intellectual challenge (and, if Sam Miller's apparent slip of the tongue is meaningful, of emotional pressure as well), and ultimately by internalized standards.

Consequently, membership in this community is presumed to define one's social existence and personal experience. Membership implies not only assuming a role, but incorporating it and becoming it, making it a part of one's self. The explication of the role is largely prescriptive. Required behaviors are vaguely articulated: "creativity," "hard work," "self-generated initiative," and, of course, "doing what's right." More emphasis is laid on the articulation of underlying emotions presumed to drive behavior: working with technology means "fun" and "excitement." By implication, it is a "boy's world," an "engineer's sandbox." "Business" is not merely a constraint to be remembered even at the peaks of "fun" and "excitement"; rather, the discipline associated with business is intrinsically worthwhile and a source of "pride." These emotions add up to an emotional link to the company—a "commitment" and "loyalty" presumed to be shared by every member of this "we."

This view of the relationship between the members and the corporate community carries with it two further implications. The first is that there is no contradiction between personal and collective goals. Incorporation of the role supposedly reflects both a personal growth toward maturity, and, more significantly, participation in a moral order (similar to religious and scientific communities) that sustains the company and simultaneously provides members with an identity and releases them from the "horrors of modern society." In other words, individualism is a way to membership in the collective, and heavy self-investment in the company not only guarantees personal returns but also enhances individual freedom. As a corollary, the boundary between self and organization fades: personal meaning is derived from identification with the collective.

The second claim, made by omission, suggests that the membership is undifferentiated. Differences of class and status are discussed only in terms of performance and reward, and economic reward is underplayed as a motivating factor. Instead, unity and togetherness are emphasized. By implication, the principles of membership experience apply to all who are glossed by reference to "we."

Taken together, official statements and their interpretation by senior managers reflect a systematic point of view on the company and its employees. However, these ideas are largely framed as representing management's desired state of affairs and are directly and openly attributed to the managerial interest. Consequently, the legitimacy of their prescription and the validity of their description might be open to question. To complement and moderate the direct voice of managerial authority, the expertise of internal observers is frequently used by those who speak for the corporate interest.

Staff: The Voice of Expertise

Internal experts bring to the company perspective an aura of scientific credibility. Most are members of personnel staff groups at Corporate or in Engineering; others are temporarily hired consultants, or employees on temporary assignment. Ellen Cohen, for example, is a full-time culture expert chartered with unearthing, documenting, and preserving the "culture of Engineering." As a Tech employee, she has a "project description," submitted as part of her group's annual funding plan.[11] The culture study, one of many proposed projects, has assumed the contextual norms of engineering development—it must have "value added," measurable "deliverables," and a clear schedule.

> **Culture Project:**
>
> Goal: to uncover messages and trends in the culture which have led to successes in the past for products and people . . . and to present that information to Advanced Products and other parts of Engineering in such a way that increased productivity will result.
>
> Strategy: Publication of two culture series papers a year, mostly filled with data found out about the Tech culture. Scheduled is a "Culture Operating Manual"—Version II, with original data written by Tech people and various Tech watchers. Draft out spring 86.
>
> Herospeak II: 6 successful engineers and the beginning of an algorithm for what is success at Tech-of-the-future containing a mix of marketing, profit, technology and doing what's right (being a good manager, having vision and providing significant contributions to Tech culture).

The output of these efforts is a "native anthropology": corporate reports describing aspects of the culture and referencing academic and popular literature on Tech (complete with the unmasking of carefully disguised published material), handbooks, manuals, self-help literature, and a variety of widely distributed memos. Some of them are explicit "culture studies," while others make occasional reference to the topic or to its various aspects. Although available to anyone with an interest, such materials are usually encountered by participants in training and education workshops (see Chapter 4).

In this body of work, Tech's social environment is depicted with little reference to mission and morality; rather, managerial prescription is replaced by a quasi-scientific, seemingly dispassionate, description of the social environment with particular emphasis on the member role, coupled with advice on how to make use of this knowledge. Two documents are illustrative. The first, a report used at a conference of Tech personnel managers, describes the individual-organization relationship in ways that support managerial claims. Note, in particular, the blurring of boundaries between self and company, the emphasis on "ownership" of one's work, and the final disclaimer distinguishing this description from "motherhood statements":

> Tech seems to have achieved over its history a very strong sense of commitment and involvement with its people. This seems to be influenced by and based on management philosophy starting with the president and continuing through most of the management hierarchy. Some important parts of this philosophy which have contributed to innovation and growth are:
>
> 1. People are really considered to be important to the company, they do not take a second seat to profits. The company has followed a tradition of full employment.
> 2. Employees are involved in Tech. Most individuals do not see a sharp demarcation between themselves and the company. There is a great deal of drive and energy to keep decision making at the lowest possible levels.
> 3. People have ownership in what they do.
> 4. Successful implementation is rewarded.
> 5. There are minimal formal processes. There is little bureaucracy compared to other places. Those processes in place are considered only guidelines.
>
> While these could be seen as motherhood statements, they truly appear to be part of the operating fabric of Tech.

The second document, a study by Ellen Cohen, uses the terminology of "culture" more explicitly. Describing the "assumptions and values that support the culture" (based on a framework borrowed from external sources), the document sets out the essential qualities of the social environment and delineates the parameters of the member role: an entrepreneurial spirit and a sense of ownership.[12]

Assumptions of High Technologies' Culture:

We Are All One Family
. . . Subcultural differences are encouraged, failure among members is tolerated to some extent, . . . people are encouraged to express their feelings and to give candid feedback, . . . all doors are open, informality and working through people is encouraged.

People Are Creative, Hard Working,
Self Governing and Can Learn
People are encouraged to learn from experience . . . by the sink or swim method with some support, be a self-starter, . . . push at the system from your position (Bottom up), respect the differences of others, find a way to enjoy work, take ownership, do what's right.

Truth and Quality Come from Multiple Viewpoints,
Free Enterprise
People are working to help the company produce good products and thus make money. Individuals have different ideas about how to proceed. Some people view this as conflict. Indeed there is some conflict. The basic idea is that we are all in this business to win, that requires buy-in from key areas, selling ideas to get support, confronting ideas that are not considered good for the final outcome, taking risks and tolerating mistakes (not big ones), accepting that this is a political world. Top management feels that they are not smart enough to know every detail. Top management is able to sort out ideas.

Some High Technologies Values are:

Do What's Right
This term is a catch all at High Technologies. It means to decide what is right for the corporation, the organization you are work-

ing in and for yourself; to commit to that right thing and to do it. It is possibly the most common phrase used.

Individual Freedom

People have the freedom to be themselves and to find out the best way of getting their work done. Sometimes a person's individual freedom conflicts with another's or an organization. These are the places where negotiation takes place. Individual freedom implies individuals taking responsibility for themselves.

Entrepreneurs

This is the basic building block of the culture. The individual is an entrepreneur in a free enterprise system, High Technologies, using individual strengths for the good of the company by running a small business producing a product.

Internal experts elaborate on these ideas, focusing on the member role by describing successful members and explaining how to become one. Internalizing the organizational ideology is a primary attribute of members. For example, a paper titled "Talking Values: Heroes of Engineering Speak" attempts to breath life into abstract principles by offering members' testimonials to their own real-life experiences. Framed as "a study of Tech values," it consists of excerpts from interviews with senior Tech managers and engineers identified as "heroes"—successful manifestations of the culture. One interviewee suggests that the formal "company philosophy" is a valid description of Tech and its members:

> There is no such thing as a corporate philosophy, it is not something you write down and then somehow invest in the company. These values are inside of us and we don't tell people about our integrity and our morality—they just somehow recognize it in what we do and how we behave. We wanted to keep a sense of modest morality. Those people who know the rules of the game have it all in their heads. One way of institutionalizing some of that without writing it down is to say: "Your job is to go around and you be the book."

What would usually be a criticism of a "corporate philosophy" is here used to support its substance—a preemptive strike against would-be critics.

The resulting "mindset," incorporated by the typical successful member, is described by another interviewee:

> A lot of people we hire into this company, at least the ones that stick around, have basically the same mindset. Someone who is innovative, enthusiastic, willing to work hard, who isn't hung up on structure, and who has absolutely no concern with educational background. They demand an awful lot from themselves. The harshest critic in the system is yourself and that drives you to do some terribly difficult things. You have to be a self-starter, an individual who takes chances and risks and moves ahead. The expectation is that everyone is going to work hard, not for hard work's sake, but for the fun of it, and enjoy doing what they are doing, and show commitment no matter what it takes. A core of the environment is individual commitment, a lot of integrity, and a very high level of expectations from yourself. Hassle is the price of the organizational structure. For those who don't like it, it's very frustrating. You can wrap those three or four things together (openness, honesty, success, fairness) and you can sum it all up in one word and that is caring. Caring about your job, the people who work for you, yourself.

Once again, the abstract prescriptive principles of management are offered in colloquial terminology as a valid, experience-based description: hard work and fun, demonstrated commitment, harsh self-criticism, and, ultimately, "being a self-starter."

As befits an engineering organization, knowledge is put to practical use: cultural analysis is used as the basis for a self-help version of role learning. For example, one document written for training purposes couples cultural description with advice on how to fit into the environment. Here "technical" role advice—covering behavior, belief, and feelings—is stated clearly. Points 1 through 9 characterize Tech and give advice on appropriate behaviors and interpretations of organizational reality. Adapting to informality and flexibility is the key to success, as is being a "self-starter." Point 10 adds the required feelings, on the assumption that these too are manageable, and that they lend coherence and a rationale to the behavioral patterns.

1. Things get done by an informal face-to-face system—not by memo through the formal system.
2. The Tech world will overload you if you let it. Only you can say no. An absence of a no connotes a yes. Making aggressive commitments and meeting them is a success. Making foolishly aggressive commitments and missing is failure even if the actual result is the same as the aggressive commitment.
3. Understand the word fail. It does not mean you are a total failure as a person—you failed to accomplish something.
4. The control system appears loose as a goose. Don't ignore it or you will get caught. If you plan to deviate from a plan tell someone ahead of time.
5. You must be a self-starter and a self-director. Only you can decide what is the right thing to do. If you really believe something, do it, even if you are told no. Be prepared to get killed if you are wrong. Tell the right people what you are going to do even if they disagree and say no.
6. The Tech world is more dynamic than you probably realize. To accommodate growth and the need for flexibility there needs to be reserve in the system. To an outsider, reserve looks like lack of control. The winners are the managers who know when, where and how to put reserve into their system.
7. Listen to the message not the words. Successful Tech managers like to think out loud and are comfortable doing so. The danger in this is that words are frequently not well thought out. Listen carefully for the underlying message. Don't take words literally.
8. Get accustomed to radical changes in the organization and jobs people are doing, including your own. Be prepared for surprising and unpredictable changes every couple of years. Be flexible in your thinking about jobs people can do outside their traditional career path.

9. Tech is a trust rather than a power culture. You will get nowhere without being trusted. You gain trust by being open, talking straight (saying what is really on your mind rather than what you think people want to hear) and listening well. Trust is not just personal integrity but being well enough known that people can predict how you will act.

10. Tech hates a mercenary. Working for money as a prime reward will be abhorred. You have got to like your work and have an interest in people.

The tone of this material is pragmatic and realistic, suggesting a measure of "academic freedom" enjoyed by the authors and an appeal to the common sense of the audience. To distance their claims from others of the "motherhood" variety, the documents call attention also to the "down side" of life at Tech, to the problems, the threats. Such a stance is even more explicit in Ellen Cohen's "Culture Operating Manual—Version II." Modeled after high-tech technical publications, it opens with a lexicon of key Tech terms and their implications for role performance. In it, the author balances the ideas of "networking," "ownership," and "do-it-yourself careers"— the mainstay of the member role—with potential costs: burnout, losing, unfunding, loss of reputation. All terms are drawn from everyday usage.

> The following is a list of terms used at High Technologies. They are a clue to the nature of the way the culture works and the skills needed to operate within it.
>
> **Beat up**   A person gets beat up when they are overpowered by the person with whom they are interacting. It is not a pleasant experience.
>
> **Burnout**   A person is considered burnt out when they are unable to contribute. Working too hard, worrying too much, stress, frustration etc. cause burnout. Many times manifestations are serious to the person involved. This person may also be called one of the "walking wounded." Burnout will damage a personal reputation as people want to be sure they can rely on each other.
>
> **Do it yourself career**   Employees at High Technologies are expected to make their own career plans and to pursue them. The company is not responsible for creating your career path for

you. A service manager once said that he and Sam Miller had one thing in common, they both had gone as far in the company as they wanted to go and were happy with the job each had.

Losing   Being unsuccessful, failure.

Networking   A person creates individual support networks either in person or over the established automated networks. They are a way gossip is spread through the company. They provide personal friendship support. They provide political safety support. They are the way the culture is spread.

Ownership   You own the piece of work for which you are responsible. This applies to every job no matter how small. . . . You own your own success or failure. . . .

Sink or swim   New employees are left to their own devices often for months. . . .

Personal Reputation   . . . It opens the doors you need. . . . Some causes of bad reputation are lack of honesty, not being supportive, only being a taker, nonproduction and being negative. Some causes of good reputation are production, quality, honesty, being supportive, good people skills. . . .

Unfunding   Your resources are taken away from you. You lost.

Following the lexicon, the author offers more elaborate advice on managing one's experience within the culture. A number of "scenarios" describing typical experiences of new employees are presented. The following excerpt is called "The Valley of the Shadow of Tech":

They have just been hired into a new group or are going to try out a new task. They receive a lot of encouragement. This is called the walk-on-the-water point of entry. For a while they vacillate and finally they reach decision point B. Feedback is given. Not all is positive. The employee may even be beat up. For some the experience is not so good. . . . The employee falls into the valley. The passage of time will cause some better feelings. . . . Other employees will console the injured person. . . . Some people do not risk again, some choose to update their resume and leave the company. Most people get to point E, "full recovery," and find better ways to interact with the system, a wiser employee.

There are limits to in-house academic freedom, however. A study titled "the antiheroes" paper was proposed by the same author. The outline suggested a study of "living examples of how not to manage at Tech." It was very quickly shelved as a "sensitive document," and all copies were deleted from the terminals that had received them.

The Voice of Experts

Internal experts present what appears to be a relatively independent perspective, a "scientific" description of the company in which the ideological facade is acknowledged and made to creak a little, commonsense knowledge and everyday terminology are used, and moralistic exhortations are toned down, if not eliminated.

Much of the substance of the description is consistent with the managerial perspective: the environment is depicted as nonbureaucratic and informal, while the associated member role is based on an entrepreneurial spirit coupled with blurred boundaries between self and organization. Behavioral requirements are ambiguously defined, and required knowledge and nuances of emotion are specified: incorporation of the organizational ideology, self-control, the association of fun and hard work, adherence to rules for appropriate emotional response, and the need for self-presentation in an organizationally acceptable light as a way to full membership.

There is, however, a key difference between the managerial and the expert perspectives: for the latter, it is a more real world. The unpleasant realities of life—the "down side"—are acknowledged and described: it is a political world; there might be some "pain"; "burnout" is a threat; failure might be tolerated, but only "to some extent"; and "motherhood statements"— untrustworthy versions of ideology—abound. Similarly, the prescriptive statements are pragmatic, and the moral high ground is either assumed or ignored. By implication, successful role performance is based on the ethic of personal success and self-help.

Although a measure of independence from the managerial perspective is implied, the views of internal experts are still clearly partisan: the free spirit of inquiry is funded (and occasionally censored) by management, and its findings complement and largely substantiate the managerial point of view. Moreover, although its spokespersons attempt to demonstrate an insider's knowledge, quote "heroes," and rely on high-status outsiders, they themselves are largely lower-status members.[13] The reality claims of internal experts, therefore, are also potentially suspect.

To bolster the legitimacy and the validity of the ideology's claims, a third form of ideological expression is used: a selective and occasionally edited representation of the views of supposedly credible, nonpartisan outsiders.

Tech Watchers: The Voice of Objectivity

Tech is the target of much observation, discussion, and analysis by outside observers—"Tech watchers"—whose output is widely available to the general public. Three categories of Tech watchers are recognized: academics, consultants, and journalists.[14] Some of the main themes addressed by these observers have been summarized in Chapter 1; here the focus is on the manner in which these materials are brought to the attention of members.

Academic Research

Tech has been studied by scholars (primarily in business schools), and their findings are available to insiders in traditional academic form: unpublished manuscripts, working papers and theses, and published articles and books.[15] Typically, these materials consist of extensive descriptions of the company, disguised at the insistence of the Tech legal department, ever watchful that "proprietary information" not fall into the hands of competitors. Nevertheless, identity is rarely a secret to insiders. Copies and summaries of findings are used mainly by members of personnel groups to design training and education events and materials. Senior managers also have access to them (and to their authors, in consulting roles).[16]

One such study (Dyer, 1982) is a disguised, interview-based description of Tech culture. (It served as the basis for Ellen Cohen's depiction of Tech culture, cited earlier.) In the concluding section, the author articulates a view of the essence of that culture:

> the data gathered from this investigation primarily reflect three underlying assumptions of the company's culture: 1. We are

one family; 2. People are capable of governing themselves; and 3. Truth is discovered through conflict.[17]

The equation of Tech with the notion of "family" is central to the description. Most crucially, this imagery suggests that members have strong emotional ties to Tech to the point that they are "inextricably connected" to the company.

> The term "family" suggests that they are inextricably connected to a social group and are oriented towards preserving and maintaining the integrity of the group. Maintenance of the group supersedes individual motives and desires, and strong affective ties bind the "family" together.

Such academic studies maintain the appearance of neutrality based on a scientific descriptive stance. Their main claim is that member behavior is driven by an orientation to the company based on an identification with the collective that, in turn, is achieved through incorporation of "the culture." The boundaries between self and company are blurred, and attachment has an emotional component. The focus is on the professional and managerial employees as natural representatives of the collective.

The Popular Managerial Press

Books and articles written by consultants belong to a distinct genre oriented to a broad managerial audience.[18] Copies are found in the small management sections of Tech's various technical libraries and in the bookshelves of many Tech managers and engineers. Internally generated summaries of this type of literature, typically prepared by members of staff groups, are easily available. Excerpts are occasionally distributed to members.

This genre combines a conceptual overview of "corporate culture" with practical advice for managers. The following excerpt comes from a widely distributed paper titled "Overview of Corporate Cultures," written by an internal consultant.

Overview of Corporate Cultures

Introduction

This is an overview of the concepts of corporate cultures. It is the introduction to a series of papers giving a picture of the cultures of some of the corporations in the computer industry. The research was in the area of successful management practices, successful corporate practices, and corporate cultural personalities as seen by business analysts, sociologists and anthropologists.

Definition of Corporate Cultures

"In looking at the underlying values and beliefs of an organization one can begin to understand the activities of the employees. . . .

"These common understandings or general acting company philosophies provide the standard of response to problems. . . . They account for the company image. They affect the individual self image of the employees."

". . . If integrated into the workings of the corporate staff, the development of organizational cultures can, in part, replace the workings of outdated cumbersome bureaucratic methods. Research has shown that corporations with rich nurturing cultures which are appropriate for the individuals hired by the company will have a better shot at not only becoming successful, but also staying that way through the generational changes of economic cycles and the aging of human beings." (Peters and Waterman, 1982)

Corporate culture is the essence of the personality of the corporation. Without facing this fact and managing it many important assets to the corporation are lost. There is much research in this area currently that supports this.

Culture is established by the founder and maintained by the executives of the corporation. Culture must be managed. Excellent corporations already know this and have taken steps to manage and control their culture.

To illustrate these ideas, more specific descriptions of Tech and similar companies are offered. For example, an inventory of "Tech values" gleaned from the managerial literature is used in training and education. In the following excerpt, note the characteristic use of terms such as "fetish" and "zeal" to describe members:

The Importance of Tech Values:

1. Quality
At High Technologies the chaos is so rampant that one executive noted, "Damn few people know who they work for." Yet High Technologies' fetish for reliability is more rigidly adhered to than any outsider could imagine. . . . High Technologies pursues quality with quixotic zeal. The corporate philosophy states that "growth is not our principal goal."

Managerial techniques for accomplishing what this genre claims is possible are widely publicized. The following memo was prepared by the manager of one of the education groups. It was sent over the technet to a number of senior managers, who forwarded it automatically to others. Hard copies were also distributed, resulting in a chain communication.

High Technologies

to: John Brown and staff   from: Bob Rogers

cc: Jim Smith   Corporate Quality
     Bill Nixon
     Mike Sutherland

WAYS TO PUT EVERYONE IN TOUCH WITH CUSTOMERS
from Peters and Austin
A Passion for Excellence
The twin themes of the book are:
1. Take exceptional care of your customers
2. Constantly innovate
    Several lists or devices for doing the former caught my eye. You'll enjoy reading the book, and these brief quotes are no substitute. But as we continue to work towards making High

Technologies #1 in customer satisfaction I thought it might be handy to have some of these ideas briefly summarized for reference. In particular, we can give or send this excerpt to participants in workshops. It might help those who aren't sure exactly what concrete steps to take.

Awareness

Apple prides itself on having gotten its entire executive staff (the senior officers) to volunteer for a regular stint of listening-in on the 800 call-in number.

Three mornings a week, all executives of Castle find a 5" × 7" yellow sheet of paper on their desks. The title: "Daily dose of reality." Below is the name and phone number of a customer. . . .

People Express has an internal TV network, a daily news show . . . a highly visible bulletin board in each facility . . . where almost everyone must pass by. Good news customer letters are flaunted on the left side; the right side displays bad news letters. . . .

LucasFilm (Star Wars, etc.) . . . has few rules, but one is this: on any LucasFilm softball team, there shall be no more than one person from any one department.

Reward System

Domino's Pizza . . . measure service systematically—and weekly. . . . The survey not only covers quantitative technical issues e.g. response time—but also qualitative ones: did anything we do bug you? Monthly evaluation and compensation for all hands (up through the president!) are predicated on the results, which are instantly summarized and made available to everyone; in fact they are publicly and prominently displayed in all facilities. . . .

The tone of the popular managerial literature is one of pragmatic common sense, based primarily on anecdotal evidence but occasionally bolstered by quotes from academic studies. The emphasis on membership as total involvement is similar to scholarly claims, but the language is more colorful

and exaggerated: the metaphor of "family" is replaced by the more compelling imagery of a cult characterized by binding emotions such as "zeal."
This genre, however, goes beyond scholarly assertions to make the additional claims that cultures may be designed by managers who have at their
disposal techniques for "inculcating" beliefs and feelings, and that the result
is, without question, enhanced performance and economic success.

Journalism

Business sections of the national press, journals such as *Business Week* and
Fortune, local papers, and the high-tech trade press cover business, technological, and managerial aspects of Tech and its competitors. This is the most
widely visible medium whereby the point of view of outsiders enters Tech.
In many cases, the focus is on everyday affairs, with cultural commentary
an aside consisting of a few platitudes. Occasionally, more extensive articles
offer a systematic perspective on particular topics.

The Tech environment is saturated with press reports. Major features
in the larger and more influential organs are widely read and discussed,
particularly by managers. The information is monitored both formally and
informally and finds its way onto the walls and into the communication networks. Clippings of stories with Tech relevance, often highlighted in glowing yellow, are posted all over and are hard to miss. They are also used to
decorate cubicles. The libraries monitor the press as a matter of routine, and
collect and file all materials. Technet bulletins offer summaries. On a typical
day at Lyndsville, up to twenty articles and press clippings are available, all
published in the preceding two weeks.[19]

In routine news reports, technical and business information is interspersed
with thumbnail descriptions of the company that follow a standard formula.
The following review of a major Tech trade show appeared in the business section of a large metropolitan paper. Conventional wisdom framed
as journalistic insight relates company history to current developments and
emphasizes the organic view of Tech and the recurring images of "anarchy"
and "pain" that describe everyday organizational life.

> Back then solid engineering and product execution coupled with
> price and performance were enough for success. This "pumping
> iron" strategy was shared by competitors. There was less need

for broad brush–stroke marketing. Nearly all products were directed to engineers. But that has all changed. Tech's brassy show this week signals the company's completion of its painful reorganization. Instead of the hurly-burly of product groups competing for corporate resources and incurring forecasting problems, Tech claims a new, sleek, streamlined image. It now appears that this fallen archangel of excellence, condemned for everything from superannuated technology to bloated management, has landed squarely on its feet. Indeed the industry may soon have to contend with an expansionist Tech capable of defending its traditional turf, but now also a threat to competitors' territory.

Similar snap analyses have a critical tone, yet employ the same imagery.

Tech slowed in part before because of its complex matrix organization that meant managers on the ground reported to too many different bosses at once back at Corporate. A VP is pictured in the company newspaper juggling at a barbecue to illustrate the point. "They make a big play of their reorganization," says a consultant, "but it is still a kind of controlled anarchy."

When the focus is on internal Tech events, Sam Miller is frequently the topic. He is characterized in the press as a dominating figure, and his picture graces many of the reports. Aspects of the culture are attributed to him. He is Tech personified.

Tech's founder and president has been a lightning rod for Tech critics. The company has been described as too loosely organized and too tightly organized. He has been criticized for exerting too much control over a company that has outgrown him. Tech is doing well despite some major weaknesses. Although his product sense has looked good lately, no one would ever call him the greatest manager. . . . Unlike many rivals, Tech has observed a no-layoff policy throughout the slump. "That costs them," Johnson says, "but it is a big qualitative plus." "In theory my word is an order," says Miller, reputedly a strong-willed manager, but in fact he now watches initiatives flow to his desk instead of pumping them away from it.

Members' loyalty is a repeated theme. A report on Tech's international business starts with a typical cultural comment: "Of course Tech people world-wide still work to agreed corporate targets and remain fiercely loyal to the company ideals, but their style is effortlessly suited to local custom and local customer needs." Articles that explicitly elaborate on the meaning of "loyalty to the company" implicitly suggest which groups are seen as representative of Tech employees. Ways to achieve loyalty and commitment are described. The following sketch of "high-tech people" from *Business Week* was posted for days in front of the Lyndsville library. Here, the sources of description overlap: a weekly business magazine cites a Harvard professor using the favored terminology of the consulting world to describe employees' "missionary zeal." Although the statements refer to "workers," the focus is on professional employees: engineers and managers. When Tech people are discussed, these are clearly the representative group.

> "Fulfillment oriented people are looking to achieve, to learn more, to grow," says Stephen B. Smith, group senior vice-president at Yankelovitch. "They want to do the next thing in their jobs not because it means a promotion but because they get a high from moving ahead. . . . The issue for management is not money, but rather how do you reward these people so they will be more productive and more committed." "At the heart of most high-tech companies' efforts to find and keep their innovative workers is a sense of inclusion in a unique undertaking and a sense of missionary zeal," says Calvin H. Pava, an assistant professor of organizational behavior at Harvard University. To motivate people, most high-tech companies make sure that each worker understands the role that his or her creative effort plays in making a product successful. "The most important thing you can do is infuse people with the importance of what they are doing by giving them a feel for market impact," declares Richard L. Crandall.

A more extended report on Tech's personnel management techniques (in the business section of a large metropolitan newspaper) emphasizes self-motivation and the use of the "whole person":

> Tech is trying to increase productivity with fewer people while at the same time emphasizing individual involvement in the process and personal pride in the product. As Norwood says, the company is trying to achieve a balance between the social part of one's life and the work part of one's life. . . . "We're trying to balance work and family," Babbitt says.
>
> Babbitt says the goal is to have an atmosphere that is informal, relaxed and trusting, where people are self-motivated, creative, open and flexible. "We don't want a lot of clones here," he says. "We want a lot of individuals. Everybody here knows everything I do. We're not paying you for a job here; we're trying to use the total person. Primarily this is an investment in our most valuable asset and that is people."
>
> "Everybody is a teacher here and everybody is a learner," Babbitt says. "People are responsible for themselves; that is the trick."

More critical analyses are rarely seen at Tech. Exposé journalism is not in vogue in the business press, and the few examples that exist are not publicly displayed. A clipping on a drug bust at a competitor's facility might be posted on private initiative, and an article critical of Tech might be circulated surreptitiously, but these are few and far between. An article in a regional monthly magazine reviewed the impact of Tech on the towns in its environment. The training manager who showed it to me considered it "yellow journalism" and wrote a letter of protest to the editor. Copies of the article were circulated informally, but not posted or referred to on the technet. Its characterization of Tech culture is largely borrowed from the popular literature.

> The company also has projected a full-blown culture of ideas, a gospel . . . : thrift, paternalism, self-reliance, and the belief that a hard-working elite can expect to get rich through its devotion. . . . Tech philosophy is fully in step with the romanticized

individualism of the high-tech industry as a whole. Like most high-tech firms, Tech culture aims at reconciling individual creativity with the demands of large organizations by shattering bureaucratic and social norms.

What Tech has brought to the towns' social life, the author suggests, is marital instability, alcoholism, overachieving children, crumbling institutions.

The press is the most frequently observed and referred to of all outside observers, the main channel through which outside perspectives are imported to Tech. Press reports are the genre least subject to internal control, but the more critical examples are not publicly displayed or circulated. The descriptions tend to focus on Tech as an organic, acting entity. The internal references focus primarily on the person of Sam Miller and secondarily on the professionals and managers as representatives of the work force. The imagery uses stock phrases, some of which overlap with internal terminology, while others are borrowed from consulting jargon. The most general image is that of loyalty and high involvement related to the nature of the work.

Internal Representations of Outside Perspectives

The differences between the three external genres are largely stylistic and characteristic of the forms of knowledge they claim to embody: science, practical common sense, journalistic observation. The available scholarly work, claiming the authority of science, focuses on a general description of the culture, emphasizing similarities between members. Although these texts are in the public domain, they are not widely distributed. The existing ones are used as inspiration by translators, interpreters, managers, and professional ideologists, for whom they serve as a foundation for their reality claims. Popularizers quote scholarly sources, but base their authority on a pragmatic, no-nonsense attitude, familiarity with managerial jargon, and a variety of illustrative anecdotes. To general description they add techniques for managing culture and the promise of financial rewards. Journalism offers a more dense, repetitive, and continuous perspective—the ongoing chatter that fills the gaps between distinct ideological events. Drawing on the claimed (and generally granted) authority of the press as a disinterested observer/critic, their reports are the most frequently seen by members, yet the least consciously attended to. Mostly concerned with global and company-wide issues, they gloss or slip in specific reality claims concerning the culture as assumed truths. The rare critical perspective is edited by internal hands. Overall, the observations of Tech watchers are not intended solely for a Tech audience, and they may therefore be seen as disinterested; it is this "objective third party" status that insiders wish to emphasize when making use of the material to support and legitimize the managerial point of view.

Despite their stylistic differences, however, external views appear to be variations on one theme: membership in Tech implies heavy involvement and a strong emotional bonding of the individual to the company, characterized in such terms as "missionary zeal," "fierce loyalty," and "family affiliation," and leading to the collapse of boundaries between the self and the organization. This type of involvement—presented as the key to economic success—is accomplished by designing an environment based on individual autonomy, informality, minimal status distinctions, and seeming disorganization.

Conclusion: Culture Decoded

The texts produced and disseminated in the name of top management, internal staff experts, and outside observers bring to the members' attention a distinct organizational ideology. The depictions of social reality offered by these spokespersons are formed around key words and strong images, and they appear to feed on themselves in the course of their own reproduction as the different genres make use of each other's formulations, clichés, and metaphors. These images provide a backdrop to everyday life in the organization, forming a dense matrix of meaning that is constantly, if peripherally, in a member's view. Relentless repetition is the rule. The material is circulated on the technet, posted in public places, distributed in the mail, encountered in workshops, and used as decoration. Consequently, ideological formulations—ready-made words of wisdom, platitudes posing as insight—become a constant background noise.

Both differences and similarities are to be found in comparing these texts. The divergence is largely a matter of emphasis, style, and claimed basis of authority. Senior managers focus primarily on the attributes of the collective—particularly its goals and history—as a way of lending membership a moral significance and defining its broad parameters. Their rhetoric combines prescription and description (although the boundary between the two is not always clear). Official company statements offer abstract principles as the collective managerial view—the "party line." Recorded interviews and speeches add volume and flesh to these skeletal principles. People are quoted, their memories and experience used to bring principles to life; management is personified and made intimate. Senior managers are openly partisan, making their views suspect, yet they also possess the insider's claim to a strong, empirical grounding in personal experience.

Internal staff experts tend to focus mainly on the attributes and requirements of the member role, while ignoring its larger moral significance. Also speaking as insiders, they present themselves as more independent, scientific, pragmatic, and descriptive; their documents suggest a semblance of academic freedom, and their prescriptions appear as detailed, instrumental, "real world" advice.

Tech-watchers claim a nonpartisan and supposedly objective perspective, and add running commentary, a comparative view of other companies, a hint of criticism, and a set of techniques for managers. Their focus is primarily on the internal workings of the organization, and secondarily on the experience of membership, and their views are disseminated in support of internally produced reality claims.

Despite the variation in form and focus, the underlying meanings conveyed to members are consistent. The essence of the organizational ideology may be found in the convergence of content: where the genres overlap— in the articulation of the member role—there are no contradictions, and a coherent interpretive framework emerges. In addition, each variant adds certain dimensions to the ideology that remain unchallenged by others. Overall, the organizational ideology consists of two main themes: an elaborate depiction of the social attributes of the company, and a specification of the member role.

The metaphors used to characterize Tech as a social entity are based on the imagery of "family" or analogies with morally sound institutions: religion and science.[20] Externally, the imagery is suggestive of clear, legitimate, and unquestioned purpose, and this is frequently articulated and specified by senior managers. Tech is presented as having a mission; in its dealings with the world, its unique blend of business and technological principles provides not only a challenge, but a moral purpose; and its economic success and unique social contribution are consistent with the ideological principles of the larger environment—profit, progress, and individualism.

Internally, Tech's distinct principles of organization are captured in the notion of "culture" as opposed to "structure." Traditional forms of control associated with bureaucracy are relegated to a supporting role. Instead, control is thought of as the internalization of discipline reflected in the attitudes, orientations, and emotions of committed members. The company is presented as informal and flexible, and its management as demanding yet trusting. The community is characterized as "bottom-up," loose, free, a "people company." In this view, members are not constrained by enforced or traditional structures and the explicit behavioral rules associated with them. On the contrary, they are expected to engage in a form of creative chaos where decisions emerge through a political process of negotiation between innovative members. Discipline is not based on explicit supervision and reward, but rather on peer pressure and, more crucially, internalized standards for performance. There is little mention of the economic structure, and the importance of economic rewards is underplayed, even frowned upon. It is a fact of life, but not one to be emphasized; instead, rewards are seen as arising from the experience of communion, of belonging, of participation in the community as organizationally defined.[21]

Describing a "culture" in this fashion does away with the sharp differences between categories of people that were once the hallmark of organization and focuses instead on the similarities. Thus, the functional and hierarchical distinctions between categories of members are underplayed and vague. The image is of a collection of undifferentiated individuals fulfilling the general requirements of appropriate membership. Unity and similarity are emphasized, authority and power deemphasized or legitimated: the distinction between management and employees is conveyed in the unquestioned imagery of parental or religious authority, while marginal people and groups are only peripherally mentioned. The condition of membership is a particular orientation to the community, one that is said to be achievable by any employee through incorporation of the member role—organizationally defined norms for behavior, beliefs, and feeling.

The central image for the member role is that of the self-starter, the entrepreneur. Behavioral rules are vague: be creative, take initiative, take risks, "push at the system," and, ultimately, "do what's right." Much more attention is paid to developing what Mills (1940) calls a "vocabulary of motives"—a specification of the emotional dimensions of membership that supposedly explains behavior: loyalty and commitment, caring, identification, fun, excitement, enthusiasm, the joy of hard work, a "high" from achievement, "rigidly adhered to" fetishes, a feeling of ownership, pride in organizational affiliation.[22] Moreover, one is well advised to make these aspects of oneself public and—the final touch—to appear to be authentic in so doing. The "down side"—Tech's negative and problematic attributes—is presented by those committed to demonstrating a balanced approach (journalists and, using a constructive tone, some internal experts) as a dysfunction that is at least potentially correctable by the individuals involved and not inherent in the system.[23]

Central to this view of the member role is the blurring of boundaries between self and organization. The member role is "incorporated," based on "strong identification," an inextricable connection to the company, with little "demarcation." It involves "the whole person" and is based on powerful emotional ties expressed in "zeal" or at least "enthusiasm." The role is linked to the collective in the imagery of "growth" and "maturity," and beyond that a moral and ethical existence associated with appropriate role performance. The ideal state is one of "self-control" and "self-discipline." When that is achieved, the organizational interest and self-interest are one.

Thus, Tech's organizational ideology clearly articulates a system of normative control. Extensive involvement is specified: encouraged by organizational forms and a variety of promised outcomes, members are expected to invest heavily not only their time and effort, but also their thoughts, feelings, and conceptions of themselves. The consequent removal of a clear demarcation between self and organization is presented as the basis for effective organizational action.

What is the impact of this pervasive rhetoric? Ideology is but one side of a normative transaction. The content and presentational form of the organizational ideology help at least to shape the language with which these matters are thought and spoken of, and contribute to the stock of "received wisdom," conventional knowledge, and notions of reality that is the foundation of everyday life. Yet these reality claims are open to a variety of interpretations, and their meaning emerges in the course of social interaction. To understand the realities that are shaped in this environment, let us examine the social contexts within which such claims are made and enforced. The symbolic action through which ideology is brought to life is the topic of the next chapter.

chapter 4

Presentational Rituals:
Talking Ideology

> They rebel in their heart against a subordination to which they have
> subjected themselves and from which they derive actual profit. They
> consent to serve and they blush to obey.
>
> —Alexis de Tocqueville
> *Democracy in America*

"It's not just work—it's a celebration!" is a company slogan one often hears
from members attempting to describe life at Tech. Less formally, many refer
to Tech as "a song and dance company." And, more privately, some agree
that "you have to do a lot of bullshitting in groups." Like much of the
self-descriptive conventional wisdom that permeates the company, these observations—whether offered straightforwardly or cynically—contain a valid
observation: everyday life at Tech is replete with ritual.

Ritual, most generally speaking, is "a rule-governed activity of a symbolic character which draws the attention of participants to objects of thought
and feeling which they hold to be of special significance."[1] At Tech, as
insiders well know, members regularly participate in a variety of such structured face-to-face gatherings: speeches, presentations, meetings, lectures,
parties, training workshops, and so forth. Dave Carpenter's planned appearance at Lyndsville and Ellen Cohen's culture seminar are examples,
along with more routinely occurring events such as Tom O'Brien's weekly
team meeting with the members of the ABC project. Whatever else they
are intended to accomplish, these events are also occasions where participants, speaking as agents for the corporate interest, use familiar symbols—
presentational devices, stylized forms of expression, company slogans and
artifacts—to articulate, illustrate, and exemplify what members in good
standing are to think, feel, and do. In short, these gatherings, which I will

refer to as presentational rituals, are where the organizational ideology—the managerial version of Tech culture and the member role it prescribes—is dramatized and brought to life. How this occurs, and what it means to members, is the topic of this chapter.

The meaning and consequences of ritual have long been an object of sociological and anthropological inquiry. Despite the emergence of conflicting schools of thought, most students of ritual see it as a crucial link between ideologies that provide the framework for collective life and the associated forms of individual experience.[2] In this view, rituals—ranging from the mass spectacles of modern politics to the seemingly inconsequential routines of everyday social interaction—are collectively produced, structured, and dramatic occasions that create a "frame," a shared definition of the situation within which participants are expected to express and confirm sanctioned ways of experiencing social reality.[3] Such displays have the power to affect participants profoundly. As Steven Lukes (1975) suggests, ritual may determine the manner in which social reality is perceived, interpreted, and understood. Moreover, Victor Turner (1974: 56) points out, when ritual "works," the reality it portrays assumes emotional significance for participants, resulting in an experience that he calls a "symbiotic interpenetration of individual and society."[4]

From this perspective, then, ritual may be seen as a mechanism of normative control. As David Kertzer (1988) illustrates, ritual has been used throughout history to symbolize authority, to gain legitimacy for rulers, to reinforce adherence to particular ideologies, and to generate and intensify solidarity with and loyalty to collective ties.[5] Similarly, in organizational settings, ritual "offers its managers a mode of exercising (or, at least, seeking to exercise) power along the cognitive and affective planes" (Van Maanen and Kunda, 1989: 49). In this sense, rituals are "mechanisms through which certain organizational members influence how other members are to think and feel—what they want, what they fear, what they should regard as proper and possible, and, ultimately, perhaps, who they are."

It is precisely this quality of ritual that appeals to Tech managers. At Tech, concern with the shaping of members' thoughts and feelings is high. Conventional managerial wisdom has it that extensive and recurring participation in ritual gatherings where the organizational ideology is enacted causes members to "internalize" the culture and infuses them with the right "mindset" and the appropriate "gut reactions." In short, those with an interest in engineering culture consider presentational rituals a mechanism for transforming the abstract formulations of Tech's organizational ideology into the lived experience of members. "They are," in the words of one manager, "where Techies are made."[6]

The experiential outcomes of ritual performances, however, are a more complex and ambiguous matter than those who stage them might claim (or hope). For one, rituals may not always "work." As Jack Goody (1977) argues, ritual often loses its transforming power and conveys little, if any, meaning;[7] and when they do work, as Turner (1969) points out, rituals typically have multiple, complex, ambiguous, and changing layers of meaning that are only partially articulated, understood, or acknowledged by participants.[8] Thus, neither prior theoretical assumptions nor native accounts—informed and sophisticated as they may be—are sufficient to determine what participants actually make of ritual performances and how they experience them. Rather, the meaning of ritual is context-dependent; it is always an interpretive empirical question.[9]

What, then, do presentational rituals at Tech actually accomplish? Depending on the observer's perspective, their significance could be interpreted quite differently. Some, perhaps partial to managerial designs, might indeed find in these gatherings evidence of a "symbiotic interpenetration" of member and company; others, more suspicious of the machinations of authority, might detect little more than meaningless lip service in response to invasive demands for compliance; those attuned to the stereotypes propagated by pop sociology might discover only opportunistic and self-serving adherence to managerial rhetoric fueled by hopes for pecuniary gain. To determine what thoughts and feelings are actually engendered in members, a detailed and contextualized analysis of the form and substance of the performance of presentational rituals is required.

In this chapter, I offer examples of several types of rituals commonly performed at Tech. The analysis focuses on the processes that underlie the construction of the ritual frame in each type of event.[10] What is (and is not) said and done? By whom? How is it understood by those present? What rules govern the unfolding of these interactions? How are they enforced? To what extent do the different kinds of events have different consequences for the experience of participation? And, taken together, what do they reveal about member-organization relations at Tech?[11]

The analysis begins with those ritual occasions on which senior managers—the primary representatives of the company—convey their message to members of considerably less seniority.[12]

Talking Down: Top Management Presentations

Senior managers meet with members on a variety of occasions. Such events usually consist of presentations in the course of which the speaker articulates the managerial perspective on Tech, its business, organization, and culture. The presentations are usually scheduled well in advance; the audience in most cases is large and consists of members of Wage Class 4; the atmosphere is often festive; and the proceedings are typically recorded and made available to those not present.

Dave Carpenter's presentation at Lyndsville is an example of perhaps the most common encounter between a senior manager and a large group of members. As in most such presentations, the speaker focuses on technical and business issues but uses the occasion to make ideological points as well.

In the Trenches

"Tech's Strategy for the Nineties," Dave Carpenter's presentation, is scheduled for three in the afternoon, but at two thirty the Einstein Room—Lyndsville's largest conference room—is already full. The VP's appearance—well advertised in advance and open to all employees at the facility—promises to be a distinct happening. Lyndsville has only recently become part of Dave's organization, and this is his first presentation here. Most managers, many engineers, and a number of members of the support staff are present. The comfortable swivel seats are all taken; people line the walls, while others gather at the door or sit outside within hearing distance. The business decor seems to underscore the significance of what is about to transpire: a speaker's podium beneath an etching of the room's namesake; a large screen; high-tech projection equipment; a teleconference hook-up; a video camera waiting to record the event for posterity. The work routine at Lyndsville has temporarily broken down, and a simmering excitement, anticipation, and curiosity seem to permeate the waiting audience.

The pre-meeting is a transitional stage during which the participants gather and jointly shift from routine to ritual. As they wait, members engage in a variety of interactions. Some take the opportunity to make small talk; others indulge in company gossip (the significance of the recent reorganization and the reputation of the speaker are favorite topics). Many interactions have the quality of light, improvisational bantering that allows members to comment on the experience of work. For example, as members of one project group stand around the coffee table outside the room, engaged in animated discussion, John, their project manager, wanders over. Noticing his approach, someone says in a stage whisper: "Quiet, don't talk, John is coming!" John responds: "Careful, you'll burn me out!" Everyone laughs. He adds ominously: "And the next one might not be as good as me."

At a few minutes before three, Dave Carpenter enters the packed conference room, accompanied by Jack, the manager of SysCom, who reports directly to him. Dave's appearance marks the end of the pre-meeting and the transition into the ritual frame—the main event. Other discussions lose their animation and cease as he walks slowly to the podium, smiling at acquaintances in the crowd. All attention focuses on him as the noise gradually subsides and Jack, after a few light taps on the microphone, begins his introduction: "We finally have Dave here. Our seminar series often features outside speakers, but it is hard to get upper management here. So block him if he heads for the door." Some smiles and laughter acknowledge the seemingly lighthearted references to backstage realities that usually precede such sessions. Lyndsville is known for its independent spirit, and it is no secret that Jack and Dave have had their differences since the recent reorganization. Jack allows a few seconds for the whispers to subside and then, in a more ceremonious tone, adds:

> "Like many of us in Engineering, Dave came up the hard way, through the ranks. He knows what it takes to make products and what it takes to get them up and out the door. He is one of us."

Dave appears to concur with this view. He adjusts the microphone, nods almost imperceptibly at the video operator, and says:

> "It's a pleasure being here. It justifies the work we do, and gives meaning to being in Tech. The further you get away from people the more you miss the past! You are doing a good and important job. I know you're having fun; and you're doing good work, really neat things. You're the perfect example of what we mean by 'bottom-up.' And that is not a Tech stroke; it's a *real* stroke!

> Now let me tell you about the challenges we are facing and the role of your group in what lies ahead."

As he prepares his slides he adds: "I gave this presentation yesterday to the Jackson group; I pulled the slides out from my road show. I hope they're in order." The allusion to "Tech strokes," the sharing of some backstage information, and the self-mocking dig at the requirements of the business world are a sign that he feels at home in a crowd of "technical folks." The lights are turned out. The room is momentarily plunged into darkness, and then the large screen behind Dave is lit up with the first of his professionally designed multicolored slides. "High Technologies Corporation: Business Strategy," the first one announces. "Here we go," whispers my neighbor, the veteran of many such affairs; "we're on the air." The transition is complete.

The mildly ironic tone ending the transitional stage disappears, and Dave is all business as, half-turned to the screen, he leaps into his presentation. The presentation follows a standard format used by presenters at all levels. It is built around ready-made slides that are flashed on a screen behind the presenter. On each slide a number of "bullets" are listed: several words succinctly summarizing a point. Each "bullet" is exposed as the point is made, and then a few minutes of elaboration or anecdotes follow.

> "Today we'll talk about what it takes to win and win big. The technologies you're working on—the XYZ series—are a key to our strategy; the potential revenues are enormous. At the executive committee meeting in Atlanta, Sam repeated our commitment to the "We Are One" strategy, and you guys have a key role to play. The challenges are great, but we're ahead of the competition, we can kill them in the marketplace. [First slide.] There are three main pieces to the strategy. First, we want to be the quality vendor *and* the vendor of choice. Not only be, but be *perceived* to be [smile] by the *customer*. [Smile. Heads nod.] This stuff came out of the Atlanta meeting and the new long-range plan that came out of the meeting. So now people can go off and. . . .

Dave continues in this vein, the rapidly changing slides summarizing and illustrating his claims about "customer satisfaction," "market share," "revenue streams," and the kinds of products that are needed to "win and win big."

Much of the discussion is highly technical: Dave reviews the technological intricacies of projects and products and discusses the business issues involved. The hushed crowd seems absorbed, taken by the speaker's enthusiasm. Laughter answers his disparaging references to the competition, and vigorous nods and knowing smiles follow his comments sometimes serious, occasionally humorous—about Tech and its management, organization, and style of doing business. Quite a few people are taking notes. A distinct sense of togetherness, common purpose, and shared excitement appears to permeate the now comfortable, almost intimate, semidarkness typical of such presentations. Temporarily, at least, the reality Dave conjures up seems all-encompassing; he is speaking for an undifferentiated "we," and there appears to be no distinction between the words and the collective experience of the participants.

All, however, are not of one mind. Some people have wandered off (I'll wait for the video"), while others—mostly support staff but also some engineers and managers—continue to work in their cubicles, seemingly unperturbed and oblivious. For the former it is "another Wage Class 4 party" and of no particular concern. The latter consider it at best a waste of time. "I don't need all that happy horseshit," one engineer tells me. "It's the old song and dance, and you hear about it anyway."

Reservations of this sort are not limited to those who stay away. In the room, there is also evidence of some distancing from the proceedings. As the presentation continues, Jack and a number of the senior managers move out into the corridor, away from the crowded doorways, and engage in animated whispering. There is not much new in the presentation for them. "This is more of a pep talk, keep the troops involved type of thing. There is more important work to be done; you know—people issues, politics," one tells me.

The side events, however, go largely unnoticed. The distancing that does occur is usually reserved for private moments and trusted confidants, or cloaked in protective humor. Within the publicly drawn boundaries of the ritual frame, the presentation unfolds in the manner typical of such events. Dave continues for about an hour and forty minutes. He concludes with an exhortation to work hard, meet schedules, and have fun, and then adds:

> "We're growing 50 percent on the gross margin. The profits are high and growing! We're the only group in all of Engineering, the only really profitable business. We should be making gobs and gobs and gobs of money! Our products are better. Yesterday we increased the prices by 10 percent [pause] to get gobs and gobs . . . [Laughter.]

Dave sits down, and the audience responds with a round of applause.

The presentation is followed by a question and answer period. This is a structured opportunity for members of the audience to participate more actively in the proceedings. Most ask routine questions that indicate an acceptance of the speaker's point of view and an affirmation of the ritual frame, and the speaker uses them as an opportunity to repeat, elaborate, and reemphasize his claims.

The first question comes from the front row, where the head-nodding through the speech was most noticeable. Flushed, half-turned to face both presenter and audience, and emphasizing the pronouns, a manager from a locally based marketing group says:

> "Dave, given what *you've* said about finances, from where *we* are sitting, what single thing could *we* do to help *you* fulfill *your* needs?"

In the back, an engineer, seemingly offended by the overenthusiastic tone, whispers to those around: "Gimme a break!" Dave smiles, thinks briefly, and responds:

> "Each of us needs this undying quest for excellence. We set tough goals and seldom meet them but feel good if we are close. That is good, but in tough times we might be tempted to back off, accept only partial fulfillment. My real goal is to pull *together* in *tough* times and go off and *do* things!"

He lists a few projects where this would be in order and takes more questions.

The question and answer period is also the occasion for a member of the audience to challenge the speaker's point of view. Ron, an engineer considered one of the "walking wounded" since the well-publicized demise of Jupiter, a project he worked on, raises his hand, stands, and says:

> "How is the new management team going to work together? It looks like some of the groups are still pulling in different directions. We might have Jupiter all over again. I think. . . ."

The open reference to "politics" on Dave's staff causes Dave to change his tone. He interrupts the question and says:

> "We are not yet a team, and we have to go through some tough times and pain together. [Turning to Ron with a smile.] Ron, you know a little bit about that, don't you?" [Turning away again.]

Ron sits down. Members of the audience exchange knowing looks; some whisper to each other; others turn and stare at Ron. Ron leans back in his chair, then makes some notes to himself. The speaker continues:

> "We have a few off-site meetings scheduled to work on our process. But let me say this about working together: we need the right mindset. I had a library full of books on Japanese management. But they have a rigid managerial system. Once a decision gets made by consensus, there is no questioning it. We need to use a combination of their and our culture. What we really need is some new heroes in Engineering. I took that word from Deal's culture book, and I'm trying to identify the Engineering heroes. People who are strong enough to come forward and then go off and make things happen. Since '79 our theme has been discipline. Jim Morrison from Advanced Technologies is an example of the new kind of hero. I've been pushing it on the executive staff, trying to get the message across without hitting them over the head with it. I learned this in the school of hard knocks. That's enough politics. Any more questions?"

As usual in Engineering crowds, the questions become increasingly technical. The atmosphere is one of friendly combativeness, and Dave is openly challenged by a number of engineers on "the company's technical direction"; a highly technical and quite emotional debate between different versions of "doing what's right" seems to satisfy the participants. But as five o'clock draws near, others grow restless. At five sharp the meeting breaks up.

The final stage of the event is the post-meeting—a transition from ritual to routine, a return, perhaps, from the sacred to the secular. Participants begin to draw their own meaning from the event. It is an opportunity to savor and interpret their experience, perhaps get a few final words in. Other realities, temporarily submerged, reappear. In the post-meeting interactions, these realities blend. Some participants leave; others stay, talking in small groups, or wander around, lingering, moving between groups. A few approach Dave, who briefly answers questions and then, indicating that he has a late afternoon meeting scheduled, leaves with a few of his managers in tow. One of them says to Dave as they depart: "That was super. You put some important messages in the system and you got their juices flowing." Dave nods and adds: "We have good people—but we need to get their heads in the right place."

Senior managers meet with members in different configurations. In the following example, a vice-president presents a group of engineers and managers drawn from across Engineering with an explicit, comprehensive, and somewhat abstract view of the organizational ideology. The event's essential structure, however, is the same.

Culture in the Cafeteria

The vice-president has been invited to speak to a luncheon meeting of graduates of an internal educational program. The organizers of the lunch— members of a staff group responsible for the program—are lobbying for continued support. Designing such "song and dance" events is one tactic for gaining visibility—some laughingly refer to this as the "hidden agenda." For the participants—managers and engineers from across the Engineering Division with few or no current work connections—lunch is a chance to network, to gain visibility, to learn, and perhaps to take a break. The VP considers it one more opportunity to "spread the word." He has agreed to discuss his view of how to succeed at Tech, and his talk is titled "My Career and What I Learned on the Way."

The pre-meeting stage occurs around an extended and fairly elaborate catered lunch, served in a large meeting room behind the corporate cafeteria. Roughly fifty people are present: some old-timers who know each others from past battles; a number of senior engineers and managers; some new hires; a manager, chain smoking, who is known by all to be "on the way out"; and all the members of the staff group. All are wearing name tags prepared by the organizers as an aid to (and a symbol of) networking.

Lunch is an opportunity to interact, meet new people and old acquaintances, introduce oneself, gossip, badmouth, observe others, pick up and pass on information ("Isn't that the notorious Bill Jones? He looks burnt out. They say he's drinking again!"), and attempt to make sense of it all. When it draws to an end, and the vice-president indicates readiness, the crowd is transformed from a loose, complex, energetic network into a hushed, focused group ready for the next stage—the main act. The rapid moving from table to table, the huddles, the jokes, the watchfulness, draw to a close. The VP stands up, arranges the viewgraph, and taps the microphone. In the background, unnoticed, moving in a different space, the contracted workers clean up under the eye of a discreet supervisor. All eyes are on the speaker. The transition into the ritual frame is complete, and the presentation begins.

First, the VP describes Tech. He states a cultural principle and elaborates it with supporting maxims and anecdotal evidence. The top of the first transparency reads: "Tech is a bottom-up company." Below this maxim, exposed one by one as he talks, is a list of "bullets" summarizing Tech wisdom in this regard:

- "If ideas came from me we would be in trouble."
- "He who proposes does."
- "Earn your reputation."
- "Your boss can't make you fail—*you* can!"
- "You get what you inspect."
- "You're second-class if you think you are."
- "If you see a problem fix it."
- "Committees live forever, task forces get to conclusions."

The VP accompanies each bullet with anecdotes from high up ("Sam told me . . .") or from the distant past ("Back when Engineering was still . . ."). When he completes the list he offers a graphic summary. "This is the Excellence Triangle," he says, turning to the board and drawing a large triangle.

Along each side he writes one word: "quality" on the left, "discipline" on the right, and "commitment" on the bottom. "That is the foundation!" he says, turning around again. A number of people jot it down. "It is what 'bottom-up' is all about." Each pronouncement is greeted with nods and smiles of acknowledgment from the audience.

The VP then offers advice on how one is "to be" and what one is to feel in a bottom-up company. Success will follow, if one is to judge from the speaker's experience. He reveals the first bullet, "RESPECT":

> "Treat others with respect and the consideration you expect, the way they want to be treated. I get *very* upset when I hear someone say 'that turkey.' It says you don't value people. Build on what others have done. Avoid the NIH [not invented here] syndrome. Nothing is more fun than making; but if others have done it, for God's sake use it!"

Nods increase in vigor as the speaker's gaze moves across the audience. He reveals another bullet: "TRUST."

> "Cooperate with other groups. Hell, its not Middletown and Lyndsville [sites of two engineering groups embroiled in a well-known finger-pointing duel] that are enemies. It's Chiptech! It's Silicon!" [More vigorous nodding; another bullet: "HONESTY."] Say what you intend. Make it public at Tech. Avoid situations where you can't be honest."

The presentation lasts for about an hour and is followed by a lengthy round of applause.

The question and answer period follows. After a number of routine questions, an extended challenge to the speaker develops. A member of the audience—an engineer known as an outspoken veteran—stands up and says with the air of a celebrity:

> "I'm Rick Danko. You said this was a bottom-up organization. That's the way it was and that's what made us so good. Are you aware that the new technet network security regulations get in the way?"

The theme of this question is familiar to all: engineers versus managers, freedom versus control. Members of the audience exchange glances, smile, raise eyebrows; they have seen and heard this before. But the tone is sharp and all seem interested as the tension rises. The vice-president reviews the policy briefly and adds:

> "We need both: security *and* communication. The new trend in the culture is security! We need to give our new engineers the full picture. We are open but we need security. Next question?"

Most questioners would have given up here. But Rick, standing again and obviously fired up, persists:

> "I disagree! People are cutting back in the name of security! Some things don't get around internally any more! I send stuff over the net all the time and I'd get upset if management said stop, or if they made it difficult! Networking is one of the ways this company works! Tech was an engineering bottom-up company, but not all Tech managers behave this way these days. Some managers actually think they run this place! I don't know what *you* think, but you've got managers who work for you, and there aren't mechanisms to get rid of them or educate them!"

The tension peaks. Rick has gone beyond the customary exchanges of the question and answer period to challenge the fundamental assumption that all present—and particularly the presenter, share the principles of the ideology. A brief silence follows, and then the vice-president smiles. Everyone in the room laughs, releasing the tension that has been building up. Rick sits down looking satisfied. Someone says to him: "I'm on your distribution list and your information is wonderful. It keeps us all up to date." Someone else says: "Loose lips sink ships. We have new hires from other companies who still have friends there." The presenter waits for all this to subside, makes a note to himself, and says:

> "Security of info is your personal responsibility! We tracked down a competitor's phone tied into a node on the net. It was plain dumb! Next question?"

The challenge is over. The VP's smile was a subtle reframing of the situation, eagerly and loudly joined by the audience and—willingly or not—accepted by the challenger. An event that came close to an open attack on the ritual frame has been reinterpreted as a playful, humorous incident, an affirmation—albeit an overeager or even eccentric one—rather than a rejection of the presenter's point of view. The roles of manager and engineer have been dramatically pitted against each other, but both can claim to share the member role. Bottom-up communication and the legitimate conflicts it requires have been enacted, and their limits subtly enforced. The rest of the questions seem mild and good-natured in comparison, and the session is declared closed.

The post-meeting is an occasion for more interpretive interactions. Ellen Cohen, the resident culture expert, still scribbling at her table, exchanges impressions with the editor of *High Performance*, the in-house publication.

> "I got some *super* quotes for my next paper!"
> "I liked the 'Excellence Triangle'; maybe we should do a piece on it."
> "Did you notice how many times he said the word 'system'? It's the new buzzword."
> "Yeah. The message from the culture is *systems*!"

Two engineers talk on the way out:

> "These speeches are interminable, like the Kremlin."
> "I was falling asleep but it was worth coming. I've never seen this guy before."

Some petitioners approach the speaker. A few ask for copies of his transparencies. A group of young engineers address Rick Danko. One says excitedly, seemingly awaiting his approval:

> "We had this jerk for a supervisor; she thought she could run the project alone, but we went to her manager and got rid of her. . . ."

Rick, however, is clearly not interested; he nods perfunctorily and wanders off in the general direction of the VP, who is still at his table. The intimacy of the spokesman role was reserved for an earlier setting. It is a sentiment that exists only in the ritual frame. The rejection is a lesson in ritual life for the new hires: ideological articulation has its place and time; now status and tenure begin to reassert themselves. As the younger engineers move to leave, the VP walks out with Rick and two of his staff members. The few stragglers are quickly gone, leaving the room to the cleaners, who have been patiently waiting at the door.

Discussion: Talking Down

As these two top management presentations illustrate, such events follow clear rules for the construction of the ritual frame. The main act, the presentation itself, is characterized by expressions of what Goffman (1961b: 106) calls "role embracement": participants publicly embrace the ideologically defined member role as an authentic expression of their experience as members. The speakers, whose words are recorded, videotaped, highlighted, amplified, and decorated with graphic devices, use vivid images that draw on an inscribed version of the organizational ideology to describe the company and its members. In particular they emphasize the company's communal nature; they attempt to speak for the collective interest; they imply a certain intimacy with the crowd; and they present themselves, their experiences, and their presumed accomplishments as an example of the successful enactment of the member role and its just rewards.

Members of the audience, although a more passive and undifferentiated group, are also expected actively to affirm the ritual frame. For the most part this consists of collective nonverbal responses—laughter, applause, nodding, note taking; questions and comments confirm the speakers' claims and demonstrate a sharing in the required emotional tone. Occasional debates on specific technical points are typically conducted in the spirit of "doing what's right" and dramatize the legitimacy of conflict in the context of commitment to collective goals. Thus, the ritual frame consists of articulations and enactments of role-prescribed beliefs ("the centrality of profit," "the importance of technological accomplishment") and feelings ("loyalty," "commitment," "excitement," "fun," "togetherness").

The main act and the collective expression of role embracement it occasions are bracketed by transitional stages: relatively unstructured periods prior to and following the presentation where participants are present and interacting either informally or around staged events such as meals. These phases seem to be governed by different rules for appropriate participation; here members typically engage in what Goffman (1961b: 108) refers to as "role distancing": "effectively expressed pointed separateness between the individual and his putative role." In these rituals, role distancing takes a specific form: participants improvise playful, yet critical, renditions of life at Tech, make joking references to known facts that are not about to be discussed, self-consciously qualify their own ideological statements, or engage in interpretive discussions. Members of the audience assume a "wise" or "cynical" stance that focuses on creatively exposing hidden meanings, debunking explicit intents, parodying conventions, and conveying an instrumental interpretation of events and an awareness of their theatrical nature. The speaker remains more reserved but may subtly convey an awareness of these undercurrents; such knowing hints are generally appreciated and applauded. Thus, role distancing, for the most part, is subtly, playfully, or humorously expressed within recognized and mostly self-imposed boundaries that protect the ritual frame and the expressions of role embracement from overt challenges or open contradiction. If anything, such episodes are considered manifestations of the company's openness and informality and, when properly performed, become a recognized feature of the event and part of the prescribed ritual form.

In short, the construction of the ritual frame appears as a sequence of stylized stages in which participants collectively and voluntarily follow the rules for appropriate role performance, shifting from playful role distancing to serious role embracement as the situation requires. Occasionally, however, the rules are broken and the underlying and often disguised workings of power in the construction of a shared reality are exposed. Thus, Rick's persistent questioning of management's commitment to the principle of "bottom-up decision making," and Ron's frame-breaking reference to politics are "out of order," raise tension, and require the speaker to draw on his authority to enforce his views. Since the gap in formal status between presenter and audience is large, and there is little to be gained—and often something to be lost—from such challenges, the speaker's smile, a raised eyebrow, a dramatic pause, a well-placed word, along with the more raucous assistance of an audience adept at reading such nuances and typically impatient with disruptions or eager for scapegoats, are enough to restrain the challenger and maintain the dominance of the ritual frame and the manifest allegiance of the participants to what it requires of them.

In sum, talking down is a ritual in which a member of senior management uses his authority and status to frame and elicit support for the official version of the organizational ideology. Yet, although senior managers are well placed to speak for the collective interests, their authority also potentially belies their own message: it is easy to interpret participant support as obsequious, opportunistic, or contrived; and the speakers' use of their status to enforce a particular view potentially contradicts their own depictions of Tech as an open, nonauthoritarian community.

The following section illustrates presentational rituals in which the organizational ideology is conveyed by formally designated spokespersons much lower in the hierarchy.

Talking Across: Training Workshops

Training and education workshops are carefully choreographed to convey to members, in a nonauthoritarian "learning environment," aspects of the organizational ideology and the knowledge and skills that members are thought to require.[13] Trainers or invited speakers on a temporary assignment are usually lower-level managers or engineers. Higher-status presenters make occasional videotaped appearances but are not the main focus. Participation typically involves lower-status members: Wage Class 4 employees up to level 4 (principal engineer or supervisor), and some Wage Class 2 employees. Higher levels are presumed not to need "training," or receive it more privately under the label "development" or "consultation."[14]

Two training workshops are described here. The first is an off-site introductory workshop for new hires, limited to pre-enrolled Wage Class 4 employees, where new members are first exposed to a systematic and comprehensive view of the organizational ideology.

Bootcamp: Learning the Culture

The Orientation Workshop, titled "Intro to Tech" but often referred to as "bootcamp," is a two-day training event offered several times a year. Designed for engineers with a few months experience in the company, it is fairly popular and draws attendees from beyond the target population.

Since the workshop is thought to transmit valuable knowledge about the company, participants occasionally sign up for more than one session. More experienced managers from Engineering and other functions occasionally participate too, believing that understanding the company and its engineers provides an edge over the less knowledgeable.

Like other in-house training events, the intro workshop must be marketed and sold in order to survive the internal entrepreneurial process. "Bootcamp" has made it in the marketplace. It is a flagship event and an important vehicle for "getting the word down" and "getting the message out." Each session is advertised across the technet, and enrollment averages about twenty.

The workshop has a carefully planned and well-defined structure. The history, business interests, products, and culture of Tech are covered in sequence. Each topic is treated in a discrete module: a two-hour session based on a presentation by a trainer or an invited guest speaker. Participants sit around a large table. Each is given a name tag and a package of materials: paper, pencils, markers, the "Engineering Guide," an employee handbook, copies of Tech newsletters, a booklet describing the history of Tech, a number of internally published research papers on Tech culture, and a mimeographed copy of "The Sayings of Chairman Sam"—a compilation of anecdotes about Tech attributed to its founder and president. The schedule is heavy, running from early morning coffee through lunchtime yawns to five o'clock fidgets on two consecutive days. There are short coffee breaks between presentations, and a one-hour lunch break.

The module on Tech culture comes first. Ellen Cohen is the invited speaker. Introductions are made. The twenty-five participants give brief descriptions of their organizational location and technology. Most are "new hires" three to six months out of school; some have transferred from other companies. One or two have vaguely defined jobs in Corporate, there is an older engineer from Manufacturing, a fairly senior finance manager from Engineering, and a technician from Field Service.

"Culture" is not a notion that engineers take to easily, and newcomers are often unfamiliar with the appropriate behavior in Tech training seminars; consequently, the module—designed as a series of interactive exercises— requires some goading. After passing out handouts summarizing the talk, Ellen writes the word "culture" on a large flipchart and says:

"The topic today is culture. We have a spectrum of people here from all over the company. Feel free to chime in. 'Culture' has become something of a fad. First, what is 'culture'? What do you think?"

A young engineer slouching in the corner answers: "Fungus. I had a culture for my senior science project. But my dog ate it." Some laugh. Ellen smiles too, but continues undaunted. "We're looking at behavior, at people. What is the characteristic of people at Tech?" She waits, marker in hand, with a warm, inviting-looking smile, nodding in anticipation, perhaps indicating the signs of affirmation she is looking for. Her question hangs. No answers. Some coffee sipping. "You feel like you've all been chosen, right?" she says, nodding her head more vigorously and still smiling. Still no replies. The stony silence highlights the incongruity of her demeanor, but she persists. "What else? What are people like at Tech?" Some volunteers speak up, drawn in by discomfort, if nothing else: "Friendly." "Amicable." She writes it all on the flipchart. The tempo picks up: "Individual- and team-work." "I'm expected to be a good corporate citizen." "Strong customer orientation." "People tend to like Tech no matter how confused," she says, and adds: "How do you feel?"

Some of the participants raise their hands. She calls on each in turn.

"I like it here. I hope for profit. I respect Sam Miller a lot. Where I worked before you'd hope they fail! Here the executives aren't as ruthless as in other companies; they are more humane. I haven't met anyone here I don't respect."
"I flash off on the technet and get to people without them wondering why; they are open and willing to share information."
"People understand. There is tolerance for new people."
"There's a supportive atmosphere."

As they speak, Ellen makes encouraging sounds and lists key phrases on the chart: "profit; not ruthless; humane; respect; open; share info; tolerance; supportive."

When the sheet is full, she pulls it off the flipchart, pastes it to the wall, and says: "This is what makes Tech a different kind of place. People are relaxed and informal. What else?" Someone says: "There is little difference between engineers and managers; it's hard to tell them apart." "Authority Not a Big Deal," she writes in bold letters on the flipchart. Then she adds: "In other places you're incompetent till proved otherwise; here it's the other way around, right?" Not waiting for an answer, she writes "Confidence in Competence," and says: "They know what they are doing, or believe it." "A little too much," the guy sitting next to me whispers to his neighbor.

Disagreement soon surfaces. Jim, a technician who has been around the company for a number of years, raises his hand. In the interchange with the instructor that ensues, she uses his objections to make additional cultural points:

> Jim: "You may be right. But I've noticed subcultures. It depends on where you work. Technical writers are considered lower than the dust on the floor. They are there to serve the engineers. In Field Service we are considered above them but not equal to engineers."
>
> Ellen: "Tech is a technical company founded by engineers. Engineers hold a special place in some people's eyes. There are status differences based on what you know. But if we don't work together—we don't sell."
>
> Jim: "Another thing I've noticed: Tech is in continuous meetings. Decisions are made by committee. It stifles creativity—"
>
> Ellen [interrupts]: "You find ways to break loose yourself. It is a company of continuums. There are pockets. There is no such thing as 'no'; it depends on how far you wanna push. You'll get uncooperative people, status-conscious people. But I've threatened people with talking to Sam Miller. It works!"

Ellen turns to the flipchart, writes, "We Are A Family," and says:

> "This is the most important one. We have a no-layoff policy. It's the ultimate backup plan. It would break some people's hearts if we had to do it. We face it as a family: cutting costs, hiring freezes. Every member is asked to contribute."

A young woman from Corporate who has been silent so far bursts out in a concerned, almost angry tone:

"I work in Corporate. A lot of the stuff is only a myth there. I see the very high up people fighting to the death. There is no clear person with the last word. They bounce responsibility around."

She starts to give an example from a well-known failed project, but Ellen interrupts her rather brusquely:

"Tech isn't wonderful or glowing. It's not. It's human. But it's the best I've seen! I was a nomad before I came here. I'm sorry you haven't seen the rest of the companies so you can appreciate Tech. [Pause.] That is another thing about Tech. People are quick to point out faults, as if they didn't have any. Where I worked before there was rampant empire building. Tech is much better. We are a state-of-the-art pioneer. There is great love and great criticism of the company."

The challenger has been reprimanded and temporarily silenced, and her challenge reinterpreted to support rather than undermine the ritual frame.

For some participants the culture module appears to make sense, and they join the discussion as supporters, challengers, questioners, or learners. Others seem more skeptical. They smile to themselves, or to a neighbor, or pull out computer printout, clearly indicating their lack of interest. They prefer the "hard data" and the facts. They see explicit cultural analysis as "fluff," the engineer's term for discourse identified with the social sciences or with "people-oriented" managers.

The emotional intensity of the module's conclusion, however, seems to captivate all the participants. Ellen flips off the viewgraph, puts down the marker, and gives a short talk that sounds off-the-record, very personal, almost motherly:

"There is a down side to all of this! There can be a lot of pain in the system! Be careful; keep a balance; don't overdo it, don't live off vending machines for a year. [Laughter.] You'll burn out. I've been there; I lived underground for a year, doing code. Balance your life. Don't say: 'I'll work like crazy for four years, then I'll get married.' I heard this from a kid. But who will he marry? Don't let the company suck you dry; after nine or ten hours your work isn't worth much anyway."

The sudden switch to a subversive-sounding message creates an air of rapt attention. All eyes are on her as she walks slowly from the flipchart to the center of the room. After a brief pause, she adds the finishing touch: "What kind of company do you think allows me to be saying these things to you?" Nobody stirs for a few moments, and then a break is called.

The next event is a videotaped interview with Sam Miller. His "philosophy" is presented in his own words. As the equipment is being prepared, an instructor frames the event with a transitional reference to backstage realities.

> "It was shot over three days. It is a selection from the material. He is really good in this one. It's not like the times we handed him a script to read."

The lights are turned out, the large screen flickers to life, and the tape begins. After the fancy graphics and titles fade away, the familiar figure of Sam Miller appears. He is sitting in a room very much like the one we are in, speaking to a group of people in business attire. They ask earnest questions that serve as cues for lengthy monologues. After a question is asked, a full frontal image of Miller's head and shoulders fills the screen. His eyes are unwavering as he talks rapidly, punctuating points with a quick smile.

Confident, charismatic, and very personal, the image of Tech's founder seems to capture the attention of everyone in the darkened room. First, he uses the history of the company to illustrate the "philosophy" that guides him.

> "In the university nobody cared. I wanted people who wanted to be artists. So we started Tech. In the beginning we cleaned the johns ourselves. I put linoleum up alone! When pigeons came in through the windows, we chased them till they fell. We said we were manufacturers, not scientists. And we wanted to make a *profit*. [A quick, punctuating smile.] Everyone here *knew:*

we are out to make a profit. And we weren't embarrassed to
make people work hard. [Smile; a brief shot of nodding heads.]
We made a profit, and we were very proud. People still didn't
believe we would make it. 'Nobody succeeds this soon and
survives,' they said." [Smile; laughter.]

Questions from the filmed audience elicit his rendition of the ever-ready
abstract principles.

"Sam, do you have any tips on how to better understand the
culture in order to succeed?"
"The company is big now. Work at it. Get to know everybody.
Volunteer for jobs. There aren't rules for how to succeed. But do
a good job. The job counts. We tolerate all sorts of schedules. I
just worry when it hides incompetence. Some people look odd
to hide incompetence! Learn. Stay in an area long enough to
learn from mistakes."
"Sam, what is unique about Tech that you want to preserve?"
"Keep the openness, trust. We hired consultants to examine
things. They came back and said: 'We found trust, openness,
and cooperativeness, little selfishness.' Those were the words I
wanted to hear. [Smile.] They knew how to flatter me. But it *is*
important. Growth is not that important."

It is dark. Workshop participants are barely identifiable silhouettes. All attention is on the screen. As he talks, the company's history and philosophy
are personified. A larger-than-life image takes over and seems to control the
room. He is far above, but the first name, the image, and the dark all suggest
intimacy and closeness, if only temporarily.

The tape lasts for half an hour, but it seems to have a lingering effect on
the bootcamp audience. When the lights finally go on, the participants stay
seated, clearly impressed. The session generates a lot of discussion.

"I keep noticing his eyes. It's the second time I've seen him, but
I've never seen him in real life."

"He is really impressive."
"He actually spoke to me a few times, but only in groups."

The participants hang around for a while talking about Sam Miller, a legend in his time. The instructor is happy to talk to all of them. She seems to consider the awed reaction of the crowd a personal success.

Another module focuses on technology. This is the real thing; this is for engineers. It has everybody's attention. An instructor introduces the guest speaker:

> "John is a consulting engineer and was project leader for Poseidon. Good stuff! Without it, the company would have been history! Even though it was a little late [smile]. Perhaps he can tell us about that too."

John takes over the floor. He is a tall, blond, bearded man, clad in jeans, sneakers, and a shapeless striped shirt, well-built, with a slight paunch and a tremor in his hands that is revealed as he arranges the transparencies on the viewgraph. Poseidon has just been completed, and he is between projects, giving talks, making himself known.

He does not acknowledge the introduction, as if the trainer has not earned the right to make it. Turning on the viewgraph, he launches into a soft-spoken description of the project he was leading. A set of ready-made transparencies ("my road show") presents his view of what can be learned from the project. Bullets capture specific points:

- "Your work can be killed by a large number of other people."
- "You can ruin the work of many others."
- "Cooperate."
- "Discuss."

For each rule he has an anecdote fitted into the time it takes to change transparencies. It is practical advice: how to communicate with others, where to find information, how to avoid "finger pointing," fights, and "pissing contests." "It can save you six months! Six whole months!" he says, and, dropping his voice, adds ominously: "and a lot of pain!" The latter refers to the generally recognized experiential price of fast-track engineering.

Finally, technology has its say, as the talk reaches a crescendo. The participants are alert. They ask technical questions and the discussion comes alive, capturing the attention of those who have so far been passive. The nontechnical people look helpless, yet they are swept along. John passes out a prototype of the product his team has designed, and explains its attributes. It is passed almost religiously from hand to hand, each person turning, looking, feeling, with more, less, or no authority. The finance manager, holding it, hears John matter-of-factly describe its revolutionary qualities. "My God! My God!" he says out loud. "This is awesome! Think of the business implications! It will cannibalize the whole product line! It will eat the competition alive!" He passes it on to the young engineer from Advanced Development, who is enjoying the reaction of the older, more senior, yet nontechnical person next to him. "Neat, huh? What does cannibalize mean?" asks the engineer. But he doesn't wait for an answer. The air of rapt attention persists. Here technology, not business, reigns supreme. Question follows question, and the speaker is kept on well over the scheduled time.

The session finally dissolves under pressure from the lunch schedule and the temporary workers waiting impatiently at the door with the lunch trays. While lunch is served, a few of the engineers capture the speaker in a corner and continue with questions as he lights a cigarette. He takes some of their names for consideration for future projects and invites them to communicate with him on the technet. The finance manager and the engineer from Advanced Development remain in their places. The younger man is engaged in a monologue, and the older man is listening in fascination and with almost paternal pride. Others continue to talk over the buffet lunch. The instructors are pleased. The module seemed to work. "John gave a *super* talk. He got them all excited. They learned a lot. We'll invite him again."

The next module focuses on business issues—an attempt to put the involvement with technology into a business perspective. The module is thought by those in charge of framing reality to deliver an important "message": the realities of business are something engineers need to learn early on; the joys of technology are inextricably tied to the company and its financial concerns.

The speaker is the manager of a staff group reporting to a vice-president. He starts by collecting and listing the reasons people are at Tech. Participants are now adept at this and respond easily: "State-of-the-art work." "Corporate philosophy." "I didn't want to sell soap." Then he gives the engineers a business view of their work.

> "We're no longer in the business of boxing other people's stuff. Other companies can manufacture us out of existence. You're the only ones who can get us to quality products. You came to work on neat things. What makes 'em neat? They are close to the state of the art. Others are forced to develop garbage and be compatible with shitty products. We're state-of-the-art for people who are turned on by technical things."

Discussing the company profits, he paints a rather bleak picture: "Our current rate of return is below the bond market! Without Poseidon we'd be history!" Using the flipchart, he illustrates the declining profits as an engineering problem. At the center of his causal map is the goal in big red letters: "MAKE MONEY." Little blue arrows point into the statement, and participants are asked to label them. ("It's a little technique I learned in Japan. A neat engineering tool.") He takes suggestions: "Quality." "Neat Design." "Low Cost." The suggestions flow in, and he places them in appropriate places. Soon the chart is complex, colorful, almost indecipherable.

Learning occurs on many levels. The speaker calls on a participant who has raised her hand. When she begins: "I'm not an engineer, but . . . ," he cuts her off with a quick: "So get out!" in an exaggerated high voice, apparently meant to indicate an attempt to parody accepted practices and points of view. The participants, mostly newcomers, are not ready for this, and there is a moment of embarrassed silence. He laughs and asks her to continue. The incident illustrates for the newcomers conventional wisdom concerning status at Tech, but they also learn something about the correct ritualistic behaviors—in this case the joking style of dramatizing cultural awareness used in many presentations.

Timeouts offer a release from the intensity and emotional grip of the main events. In the course of timeouts, participants often discover a different reality lurking in the background, usually expressed in the form of humorous interchanges. For example, when five participants enter the toilet together in the break following the business module, still talking about Poseidon, profits, and neat things, they encounter three older engineers from the local facility who are getting ready for a basketball game. They are talking about life in Tech.

> "To make it here you have to have made a lot of friends here."
> "No. It's more important not to make enemies."
> "You're both wrong. You have to not make waves."

On the way out of the toilet a participant observes: "Maybe we should move the workshop in there."

For some newcomers, the timeouts are an opportunity to express confusion and attempt to make sense of the multiple realities they encounter. During one break an engineer says, over coffee, to others at his table:

> "After the first day I was high; I thought: 'What a great place.' I went and put all these glowing messages in the system. But this business stuff really depressed me. I was shocked to find out that we were just saved by Poseidon. But my boss wouldn't cooperate with them. He told me not to answer any questions that Poseidon people would ask!"

The last session of the workshop captures and enacts the multiple and confusing realities and demonstrates one way of living with them. It is a study in the management of ambiguity. Mike, the guest speaker, works in Sales and is an expert on every product the company has to offer. He has agreed to review the company product lines. He has been to the workshop before and is liked by the organizers, who consider him a "good show." For a salesman, he is very knowledgeable about the technology. "The engineers like that," says an instructor.

Mike rushes in a few minutes late. The organizers breathe a sigh of relief. Mike doesn't waste a minute. He takes off his jacket, loosens his tie, unbuttons his vest, and pulls slides from his brief case. His transitional opening comments are rather extended. First, he comments on his three-piece suit: "You can tell I'm from Sales, right? I'm dressed to the image," and then jumps to the side, pretends to be an engineer looking at Mike the salesman, and pulls a face suggesting laid-back disdain mingled with feigned horror. "Jerk!" he says to the audience. He laughs quickly, and leaps back into his earlier position. As he is readying his slides he talks rapidly, offering a general characterization of the company:

> "In the beginning, *we* were Tech, *you* were the customer; we were the best, and if you had a problem, that's tough. We made a huge revenue. We make it in rupees, yens, pesos. Read *Tech-world* if you want to see where the money goes. But then the shift came. Last year we had a hiring freeze. Still, we hired you."

He leans back, rubbing his hands, and imitating a Fagin-like dirty old man, he says: "We wanted your ripe young minds."

Mike's high energy and stylized performance wake up the late afternoon group. Some laugh. Others look at each other as if ready to comment, but they are preempted by his self-mockery and exaggerated takeoff on them. He straightens up and continues:

> "But seriously—there are people here not working. Our clear commitment is not to let people go. It hurts but we're still paying them. This seeming lack of any organization forces on you the need to communicate, to network. It'll be nerve-racking but it'll be fun. The big problem here is info: too much! Forty percent of the technet is used by the car clubs, the freaks, the photographers. Walk around, bump into others. Find out. No one has charts. As soon as they're published, it changes, so why bother? Go and do one yourself; I'm not facetious. It's the most disturbing thing for newcomers: no structure. Especially for people out of school. Assume there is constant change. It keeps you on your toes and your desk clean. So communicate. Get on the phone, get on the technet. Reinvent the wheel. If you don't like the job, wait a minute—it will change. Move around. Your project might just disappear. Do more than one thing; you could find yourself anywhere: in Manufacturing, in management, in a dark corner growing mushrooms. And a final thought: never give up. There are a thousand places. Go next door; ask for more challenge—you'll get it. And remember: you'll own your mistakes forever."

The last statement is ambiguous. It is seemingly in contrast to the earlier, straighter presentations and draws a correction from one of the instructors, an ever-alert master of ceremonies who suspects that the speaker has gone too far in his playful deviance:

> "It's hard to get fired. You'll have to club your manager over the head. If you don't draw blood, you still won't get fired."

"You might get promoted," Mike adds with a knowing smile, drawing another round of laughter from the participants. He adds:

> "Now that you've heard the song and dance, let's get down to the real thing: T-e-c-h-n-o-l-o-g-y. What else is there in life— right? Right!"

Mike shifts into his main act, a review of the company's entire product set. Using high-quality color slides, he displays one product at a time, and discusses each. He seems genuinely excited and impressed with technological achievement and conveys an insider's view of engineering life. He asks participants to name the projects they are working on and comments on the technological aspects of the projects they mention. Identifying the technical shortcomings in a particular product, he says:

> "Yeah! That is what we need. If you wanna be a hero, figure it out. Do it in your spare time! Someone will be interested."

Everyone in the room seems interested. The review lasts almost two hours. When it is over, Mike hands out evaluation forms and says:

> "Tech is considered an engineering company. In the field we are proud of it! The commitment to engineering pleases us! The products are great! I sold for other companies, but here I feel good. Wonderful products. There it was real selling—pure skill, selling shit. You should move to Sales. It's good work! Give me a call or flash me a note. Come down and see what we're selling. We have a party there."

He jumps aside, imitating a distressed engineer: "What?! And compromise my soul? Lie?? Never!!!! I'd rather die!" and then answers:

> "Yeah! No big deal. I come from Engineering myself. Sales is a good career if you're looking to be a vice-president. Sales reps can be rowdy. We're into hype, into pep rallies [salute]. We're very competitive; it doesn't have to be over anything, so long as we can drink and sing songs [hand on heart]. We don't have these Techie decorations. [Points at the large etching of Von Neumann on the wall.] We have these big flash cards on the walls: Success. Enthusiasm."

He turns around and faces the imaginary cards, arms spread. Then he turns around again and says in a lower voice:

> "All this altruism. The bottom line is: if I win megabucks tomorrow—hey! Am I coming to work? [Shakes his head slowly.] Damn right! The bottom line: it's the check! Every Thursday! M-o-n-e-y!"

An instructor laughs, another subtle attempt to frame all this. As the participants fill out the questionnaires, Mike sits on one of the tables and imitates the call of the sirens in a barely audible singsong: "Come work for us. Where do you wanna go? Paris? London? We can arrange it for you—you won't be sorr-eeeee."

Bootcamp ends quietly. A trainer thanks everyone and makes a final pitch asking them to send others, to come again. Some file out slowly, some remain talking to new friends. They each get a printed certificate with their name on it, proclaiming them graduates of the "High Technologies Orientation Program." It might be used as an office decoration. Some are friendly, saying it was a useful program, commenting on its various parts. Others pick up their certificates politely, even shaking the trainer's hand in recognition of the attempt at a parting ceremony. A tall young engineer with the fixed smile and awkward posture of the overly bright (the one whose dog ate the culture) refuses the certificate. The instructor, holding it out, insists. He declines. She pushes it toward him. He relents, takes it from her, and, still smiling, tears it up and deposits it in the wastebasket under the table with all the Tech material. He is the last to leave. The trainers collect their materials and then meet to review the event and perhaps finetune the design for the next time. Bootcamp, they agree, appears to have earned its reputation once again.

Such comprehensive views of the company are offered only to newcomers. Most training workshops are designed for experienced members, and they focus on specific topics, as the following example illustrates.

The Career Seminar: Working the Culture

The Career Seminar is a packaged workshop offered by one of the training groups to interested groups in Engineering. It is intended to teach personal skills and an understanding of Tech culture, making participants better able to "design their own career." The seminar was contracted by the manager of the Lyndsville facility, who wants to emphasize "people issues" in his group. It is offered to the entire group on a voluntary basis and was advertised well in advance. Repeated reminders were sent over the technet, announcing "a three-part series on career management—three two-hour sessions over three weeks." Notices are on the library board and, on the day of the seminar, on a flipchart next to the cafeteria, highlighted with yellow marker. It is scheduled in the time-slot of the regular bi-weekly technical seminars at Lyndsville.

Toward three o'clock the seminar room starts filling up. Alan, the trainer, paces the corridor nervously. He is worried about his own career now that training budgets are being cut. "Overhead" people are always nervous around this time of the year. "My wife told me this morning to start applying some of this stuff to myself," he tells me.

At three, about fifty people are sitting in rows in the seminar room. Almost all the members of a development team that is in serious scheduling trouble are here. They have just come out of a reorganization meeting with their new manager, who has "read them the riot act." Their presence is the public version of getting one's resume ready, being in a career-evaluation mode. Also present are two or three principal engineers and a few supervisors from other groups. They are the most senior people around. Most others are junior engineers. Five or six secretaries are grouped together in a corner. Two are temps with a strong interest in becoming permanent. There are quite a few outsiders from other facilities who have somehow heard of the event, as well as people from Sales and support groups affiliated with

SysCom. One of the group personnel managers sits against the wall. Her aloof manner makes it clear that she is there as an organizer, not for herself.

The transitional phase of the session is quick and perfunctory. The manager of the sponsoring organization enters. He often refers to himself as a "people person" and takes great pains to display this orientation. This seminar is another opportunity. He puts the microphone around his neck and gives a brief introduction:

> "I just want to say two things. This is in response to requests. It is a kickoff in SysCom for activities planned for the last nine months but delayed because of changes in the personnel organization. You asked for topics beyond the technical stuff usual in our seminar series. You wanted more exposure to management issues, information, opportunity. We will get involved in the process of career management and development. We will put formal procedures in place. This is a beginning."

He moves to the business of the day with an oft-repeated "message":

> "*You* own the responsibility for the management of *your* life and career. Not your boss, your spouse, your organization, your company, but *you*! We want to *help* you take responsibility for your career and life because [smile] I don't want you to blame it on me. [Laughter.] This will start a process for you to help you understand if you are realistic or not, if you need to finetune your plans. That is it."

He turns and leaves. The personnel manager joins him. Alan takes over. He seems comfortable, exuding an air of practiced public speaking.

> "I wanna wholeheartedly support Jack's perspective: *Your career is your own responsibility!* Your career, your life, is in your own hands. I found at Tech that there is an expectation that management takes care of you. Tech expresses that in the form of lifetime employment. It is an expression of commitment to you. If the company goes down the tubes, you will find out

soon enough. But if it doesn't, take an urgent look at career management just the same. We will take a look at the why, what, and how of career management."

As he shifts to the main act—his prepared script—he tries to establish a bond of similarity with the participants. Fumbling with the transparencies on the viewgraph, he gives personal testimony, evoking the image of a chaotic Tech and its long-suffering employees:

"I have been fired once, unfunded twice, reorganized twice. I was moved like a piece of old meat, and when I finally found something—"

"They canceled it!" someone in the audience completes his hanging sentence, as others laugh in recognition. He ends the introduction with an Arlo Guthrie imitation:

"I *wanted* to work at Tech. I've been reorganized, disorganized, relocated, dislocated. But despite all the frustrations—it is exciting."

The transparencies are ready. He hands out photocopies. The session begins. The first one, titled "Why Career Planning—The Use of Time," moves the discussion to the realm of the personal. Alan walks a thin line between humor and seriousness as he elaborates:

"We are all on a train. Moving toward the inevitable: Death. [Pause. Silence, then a few nervous laughs.] You all know it. We only have a certain time on this planet. And death is inevitable. We all have aspirations, what we want to do, to be. [Pause.] Basketball was mine."

He straightens up, attempting to add a few inches to his rather short frame. More laughter, and quiet glances between engineers, public questioning of hype, of style. But he has the attention of the crowd as he adds: "Think of your epitaph. If you assume you will perish, you get control of your life."

In the course of the presentation, Alan keeps up a constant stream of chatter through which the central ideas are repeatedly conveyed: self-reliance and individualism serve everyone; employees are expected to take initiative; there is no contradiction between loyalty to the company and to oneself; to serve the company one must take action in one's own interest. The message is framed in a number of modes. It is supported by anecdote:

> "I was down in Everett; a lot of reassignment. I worked with them, had conversations. People there felt like their devotion to the corporation and product was enough. No need to take time for career management. 'But you're being redeployed,' I said. 'Would you have spent your time differently?' 'You're advocating disloyalty to the company!' they said. 'No! I'm advocating loyalty to yourself. If there is something you don't like, change it. What's your 'to-do' list? If part of your job stinks, change it! Talk!' 'But I have considerations, children.' 'This is not some primitive agrarian society—we're talking moving in the company. And they *pay* for it!' "

To reinforce the idea, he involves the participants in dialogue, calling on people who raise their hands:

> "What actions have you taken?"
> "I spoke to another group to find an opportunity."
> "*Good* for *you*!"
> "I spoke with my manager."
> "Yeah! *Good* for *you*!"
> "I came to this seminar."
> "*Great*! [Pause.] But it's not enough!"

Cultural analysis serves to convey the same idea. Familiar scenarios and experiences are sketched. But instead of the critical tone with which they are often accompanied, the tone here is upbeat: you can, indeed you should, do something. The next transparency is titled "Do you know any of these people?" Alan reveals the bullets one by one, reading them out loud and commenting:

"Here is one you all know: 'My project has just been canceled.'
[Laughter.] How many times have you heard it? It's got to be
up there with 'Do what's right'! Look at this one: 'I'm burnt
out. My manager is a turkey and my work is unrewarding and
confusing.' [More laughter.] Here's one who needs help! What
is the phrase you use? What is the tape in your head that keeps
you from doing something?"

Social science is cast in a supporting role. The next transparency reads: "Responsibility in the Process. Employee Self-Understanding." Alan explains:

"There are a lot of snake charmers: books, everything you
always wanted to know in fifty pages. It's fun, it's astrology.
But not many good ones. A famous psychologist, Rogers, says:
'The ego does two things. It seeks information that confirms
itself and throws out things that it doesn't like.' So seek feedback; find what you really need, what suits you, and do it! I'll
give you the literature [holds up two books], without the redun-
dancies. There is a lot of garbage out there. But these two books
are the best: *The Three Boxes of Life* and *What Color Is Your
Parachute?* Good stuff!" [15]

The session flows smoothly, having struck an acceptable balance between
seriousness and humor. But soon an open challenge temporarily disrupts the
collective mood. Jill, a gray-haired woman in her late forties who has been
taking an active, assertive role in the proceedings, raises her hand. She is a
temp who has been working as a secretary for one of the development groups
for about a year. Like other temps, she makes it well known that she wants
to become permanent. Alan calls on her.

Jill: "You're assuming we are lifetime employees, always here
in Tech."
Alan: "No I didn't. Find something, dabble. Wanna be a song-
writer? Tech doesn't employ songwriters? Are you sure? Maybe
there's a newsletter? *Tech-sing?* [Turns to the audience.] Maybe
Sing Sing if we keep shipping to the USSR."

Jill [loudly]: "Maybe I should look somewhere else?"
Alan [turning back to her]: "*Good* for *you*! I wanna open a shop in Vermont someday myself! Alan's Antiques. Any more comments? You, in the back.

The challenger is from the lowest rung of the hierarchy, and even though she persists, she is easily silenced. She tries to respond, but someone else is talking, and the session continues. The incident appears to have caused some discomfort, but it is soon buried under Alan's cheerful chatter and other questions from the audience.

The transitional post-meeting stage, a shift from ritual to routine, provides participants with an opportunity for sense-making, for interpretation. Alan concludes his presentation with an attempt to sell the next session. His headcount is important.

"Come next week; I'll give some tools. We have this joke among trainers. The guy is too stressed to take a stress workshop, doesn't have time for a time-management seminar. Think about it."

People begin to leave. On the way out a temp says:

"I wonder why the company is doing this; maybe they believe that turnover prevents burnout? It sounds good, but I still want to know if they practice what they preach. Will they really offer me a job? Or else why encourage us? I've started networking. I go over the job book every day and call up these marketing people."

Two engineers talk on the way out:

"It was a lot of common sense turned into observations with gobbledygook thrown in. He fit thirty minutes into ninety. But some of it was useful."
"Maybe; but a lot of the stuff was written for the real world, not this company!"

Others come forward, some to browse through the stacks of self-help books. A secretary pulls Alan aside and asks in a low voice: "How should I tell them in the job interview that the reason I want to move is to be closer to home?" She appears not to want others to hear her concern. He thinks for a while, furrowing his brow, and finally pronounces loudly: "Honesty is the best policy. Always tell the truth in job interviews!" An older technician says: "You should teach this stuff in high school. Used to be that it was start at the bottom, finish in the middle, gold watch, and out. Now it's getting real fancy."

The next two sessions follow the same format. The topics become more specific: a review of the career-management resources at Tech (job posting, counseling, and so forth) and an introduction to a technique for personal career planning. Between the lines, the characterization of the company and its members remains the same. Some attendees have dropped out, but most are back for more, and the room appears full, much to Alan's relief; informal ratings are of central importance to him.

Discussion: Talking Across

The dramatic structure of talking across is similar in many respects to that of talking down. In both cases formally designated company spokespersons use similar techniques and formats to frame the same ideological "messages" for a specially gathered audience. However, important differences in the presenter-audience relationship stem from the "educational" nature of the event. First, the status gap is small: most presenters are professional trainers, considered low-status by engineers, and are often roughly equal to participants (and occasionally lower) in formal rank, income, seniority, and tenure. Ideological expression is their work, and they depend on participant approval and support for their livelihood. Guest speakers are also close in status to participants. Second, the groups are usually small, and active participation is encouraged: speakers frequently call on all participants to make statements, ask questions, articulate their opinions, and express their feelings. Third, participation is not perceived to have organizational ramifications beyond the event itself and whatever individual changes might occur. Participants are there to learn, to take a break, to have fun, to network; in most cases, their groups have paid a fee and expect a service in return.

These qualities of the presenter-audience relationship have two consequences for the construction of the ritual frame. First, compared with top management presentations, the rules for participant behavior are less rigid and prescribed. The speakers, with little or no formal authority and no assurance of audience support, use more elaborate techniques for eliciting expressions of affirmation and controlling dissent: they present facts, offer insider knowledge, argue, cajole, debate; they engage in catchy monologues and improvised comedy to identify themselves with the experience of members; and they use public ridicule, open interruption, and sharp responses to silence challenges. This results, on the one hand, in more heated debate: role distancing and open challenges to the ritual frame occur frequently and quite openly. On the other hand, expressions of role embracement are less suspect: when they occur—the sign of a good workshop—there are fewer reasons to doubt sincerity, to question stances, to search for hidden agendas. Thus, displays of role embracement are experienced as more authentic and spontaneous, and may therefore be more compelling.

Second, the appropriate performance of the speakers' role is more complex. Although the speakers are temporarily acting as agents of the company and its ideology, they are less identified with it than senior managers. They do not have the mystique of perceived power to fall back on, to protect, or to justify, and it is more apparent that they are not only agents of the ideology but, like the audience, its subjects as well. Consequently, they are in a bind: they need both to establish some authority for their claims as agents and, as subjects, to justify their recourse to ideological formulation beyond the routine (and therefore less trustworthy) doing of a job. Thus, whereas senior managers subtly indicate their awareness of alternative realities, trainers engage in an elaborate and careful presentation of a self- and culture-conscious stance based on frequent and skillful shifts between expressions of role embracement and expressions of role distancing.

In sum, training workshops, like top management presentations, are company-sponsored attempts to generate commitment to the organizational ideology. Here, however, debate is more open, audience responses are experienced as less contrived, and the speakers' claims are more ambiguous. At the same time, participants seem to have less stake in the proceedings and consequently may treat the event as possessing little or no significance.

The messages of spokespersons, whatever their status, are qualified by their formal and open association with the managerial perspective, and are limited to events that, from the point of view of individual participants, occur relatively infrequently and at some remove from "real life." [16] In the following section, the focus shifts to the third type of presentational ritual: those gatherings where the members themselves talk ideology in the course of their routine work life.

Talking Around: Work Group Meetings

Work group meetings are planned face-to-face gatherings of members of formally defined work groups. Although they are explicitly intended to accomplish specific organizational purposes, all are occasions for members to engage in structured forms of ideological discourse. Tech's complex organizational structure has spawned many different meeting configurations, reflecting different types of association and reasons for meeting. Most meetings, however, fall into one of three main categories. Team meetings are periodic work-related meetings of a manager and his or her immediate subordinates (also known as "direct reports"). The team is usually the members' primary formal affiliation in the organization.[17] Intergroup meetings involve members of different groups with formally defined work-related interests in common. Members from many levels may be present, but there is no single reporting relationship.[18] Timeout meetings are periodic meetings of members of work groups where the explicit goal is not work-related. Rather, the meeting is intended to provide some collective respite from the intensity of work requirements.[19] In this section, examples are offered from each of these three basic meeting types.[20]

Team Meetings

Team meetings occur at all levels of the organization. The meetings—referred to as *staff meetings* by managers and *project meetings* by engineers—are where information sharing, communication, and joint decision making are thought to occur. They are typically closed, but guests are occasionally invited. Most meetings occur on a regular basis (usually weekly) in one of the meeting rooms close to the main working space. Senior staff meetings with heavy agendas might take place off-site in one of the Tech conference centers. The following descriptions are taken from team meetings at several hierarchical levels of the organization: VP staff, product development group staff, and a staff organization (see Chapter 2 for organizational charts).

The transitional pre-meeting stage of team meetings is often quite elaborate: since members work together, they have much to discuss. A staff meeting of the management of a large engineering group begins early as members arrive and congregate around the coffee pot. Some of their conversation is personal, but most is company-related. The content is informational: company events ("I heard about your talk at the state-of-the-company meetings. I heard it was great." "Yes, they're making a video out of it. But they're taking out some of Sam's stuff; they really have to edit him these days . . ."), company policy and strategy ("We have a window of opportunity before . . ."), technical ("They found a bug in the new X-101 . . ."), political ("I hear Smith's program is in hot water these days . . ."). These interactions are an opportunity to collect, disseminate, and exchange information and draw conclusions for oneself.

Bob, the group's manager, is late, and as they await his arrival, the staff members gravitate toward the table and take their places. In the group discussion that develops, members self-consciously balance their organizational roles with seemingly light-hearted references to alternative realities.

> "Who owns the T-675? You?"
> "No! Ken Smith does, but he reports to Cranston, so now he has that monkey on his back—or some other animal."
> "I hear he is hanging out the window by the shoelaces."
> "He could slip any minute!" [Laughter.]
> "He must be getting midnight phone calls. [Pause, then a loud feigned sigh.] It's such a nice day outside."
> "Let's start without him."
> "No. Let's break up."
> "Let's take a vote. It's a perfect day for golf."
> "Why do we have to be here?"
> "I just want to be a beach bum. But I'm trying for the big bucks now."
> "We all had the same reason to come."

One manager seated at the table notices the late arrival of a peer with whom he has been involved in a well-known and protracted finger-pointing duel—a public conflict concerning the allocation of blame for the failure of a particular project. He calls him over. Others at the table, recognizing a "political situation," watch with interest. The following interchange ensues:

> "Jack, I'd like a one-on-one with you soon; we have some stuff we need to do. Off-line."
> "I don't have my calendar here."
> "Oh. The old 'I forgot my calendar' routine, huh?"

Everybody laughs. The rejection is real, but the script has been named, its meaning noted and filed. Jack joins the group, and the bantering discussion continues until Bob arrives. "We were discussing why we have to be here," one of the more outspoken members informs him. "Because you are a member of the staff," he replies in a clipped tone as he seats himself at the head of the table. He pulls a sheaf of papers from his brief case and, glancing over the day's agenda, says in a more conversational tone: "Any big ones? Any bombshells? Anything off the street? Any names?"

The request for company information and gossip indicates a shift into a more structured mode, typically dedicated to the sharing of information by the group manager, who has access to more senior forums and more privileged information. The discussion that follows seems to mobilize the role-appropriate energies and emotions held at bay or very self-consciously displayed during the pre-meeting phase.

> "I heard that Geerson is leaving."
> "And Spencer is in a career-reevaluation mode."
> "Guess who's getting promoted: Jim Abbot!"

Then, in an enthusiastic tone, Bob relays some information:

> "The state-of-the-company meeting was *superb*! I spent three evenings with marketing people. We had serious discussions; none of the rah-rah stuff. And thanks to Jim, who gave a *super* presentation. It was by far the best Tech talk I've heard! They walked away with powerful messages. It was *fantastic*!"

Heads are nodding. Some of those who were present at the event give their own interpretive comments:

"Sam is moving to another level now. He got people to be successful, and now he is challenging them."

"Yeah, and he took Jackson to task."

Others ask questions, and Bob answers:

"Is Jackson going to change directions?"

[Pause.] "The statement I would like to make at this point is this: Sam asked me what were the three major issues over the next four years. I said: One, get Engineering thinking business. [A round of vigorous nods.] As an old Tech watcher, let me tell you—and this is only an hypothesis—that the matrix will shift again and Engineering will take up more of the Marketing space. And Marketing will have clearer deliverables. Let me also tell you the mood on the executive staff. There is a general swing in the company to get out of the happy horseshit of 'go off and do your own thing.' And I am one of the proponents of that swing. We are going to take a harsh look at projects."

The discussion continues in this vein. The tone is excited and animated. The focus is the company and its success and, in particular, on the role of the present group (and its enemies) in the great achievements. Members appear fully engaged in the proceedings. After a few minutes Bob says:

"OK. That's enough. Now let's get down to business. No more intergalactic stuff. I don't want another 'where the rubber meets the sky' meeting today. What's the first agenda item?"

The transition into the ritual frame is complete.

The main act—the working part of the team meeting—consists of the discussion of prearranged "agenda items," business or technical subjects usually presented by one or more of the regular participants, or by a specially invited outsider. The time spent on each agenda item is often limited. Some items are designed to convey information to participants or solicit their input. In other cases a decision is expected. Many agenda items consist of a formal presentation followed by a group discussion.

The presentations focus on substantive discussion of the issue at hand, yet they are frequently the occasion for explicit references to aspects of the organizational ideology. These references are often initiated by the group manager, but other participants also make ideological comments as a feature of their own presentations or as part of the discussion. For the most part, such discussion occurs within the context of apparent consensus and commitment to the group goals, validated by the ideological correctness of this stance. A typical example occurs at the staff meeting of a large development group. On the agenda is a review of the group's projects by the product manager. Using a viewgraph, he runs through all the projects, emphasizing schedule slips and resource shortages. He concludes with one of the more problematic projects, now a few months behind schedule:

> "The main issue here is that X-121 is in trouble. So we'll have a group review every week to meet and review the process. We *own* it, and we have to *work* the issue."

As the presenter returns to his seat, the group manager looks around the table. The air is one of solemn concern. The implications of "ownership"— a central ideological principle—seem clear to all. He emphasizes and elaborates the point:

> "I agree! When you own it, you *better* work it! Before you comment, I want to say something. I feel damn good about the business. I'm only upset about X-121. Very upset and frustrated. We have to get control. We *own* it. If we have to, 80 percent of our efforts will be focused on this. We'll manage it. And we're going to play it by the culture—bottom-up. We'll get our proposal ready. We'll take it to the VP staff for their buy-in. Then we'll take it to the strategy committee and say: 'This is what we can do for you and this is what we need.' And from there we go to the executive committee, and if that isn't enough to Sam, and say: 'Use your individual prerogative money, use your skunk money, anything.' We'll be polite, but we'll play real hardball."

A round of comments from the participants follows. A project manager who is responsible for X-121 says:

"Jim and his people have been giving an arm and a leg and a brain to make this happen. Some of them are flat out."

Others nod. Another staff member adds a suggestion:

"We need to give a rah-rah speech to the development managers so they understand the implications of a slippage. My people on the X series saw it in all its seriousness, but everyone should know."

After the comments, the group manager concludes:

"They all know it's in trouble, but they must understand the magnitude of it. I'll give a state-of-the-group talk and say some macho words. We'll invite everybody out even if we have to fill the cafeteria twice. It's important to get everyone. My belief about teamness is that we must also get the secretaries, the techs, the writers, the manufacturing people. I want teamness."

Next, some "actions" are assigned to various participants—Tech terminology for the responsibility for getting something accomplished. A date and a list of participants for an X-121 review meeting are set, and responsibility for preparation is allocated. Then the group manager leans forward:

"Before we move on to the next item, I'll give you one of my one-minute lecturettes—I can't stifle myself. This group is getting into a leadership position. Others will follow using the same tools. I'm pleased we're in the single largest growth industry. *But*—engineers are the worst strategic planners. We teach them, we beat it into them: micro thinking. Control, specify, and understand all the variables. An engineer can't see the large scheme, can't work with loose concepts, with unspecified stuff. It's right for engineers—that is the way they should be doing things. Or else they should be doing something else—like being managers. [Laughter.] But seriously: we have to help our engineers. We have to have a small number of strategic goals. Three,

> maybe four. Macro ones that can last for five years. Some-
> thing like: 'Reach a billion in sales in '88.' Something they can
> understand and don't have to micro it to death. Or maybe: 'Use
> standards to competitive advantage.' So if someone comes to a
> meeting we can ask them: 'How does that help us, or is there a
> new goal?' I wanna see buttons, posters, repeated over and over
> again: 'Use standards.' 'Make a billion.' So even secretaries
> understand and know the strategy. We'll become well-organized
> and aggressive. But we'll still get quality products out the door.
> That's always the number one priority. It's always being tops.
> Maybe there is only one thing above it: being honest. Boy, I
> didn't know I would be getting philosophical [laughs]. This is
> the end of my presentation; I'm not good at this."

His words are accompanied by distinct signs of affirmation from those
present. He calls for the next agenda item.

Not all interchanges are consensual. Conflicts of interest between the
participants frequently surface, and in the interactions that result, central
tenets of the ideology or their interpretation in specific contexts might be
challenged or debated. This may occur in conflictual interchanges between
peers. Here, for example, the no-layoff policy occasions a heated exchange
between senior staff members. A manager presents a forecast for future
hiring needs to the group. John, one of his peers, introjects a suggestion that
the company "get rid of some of the deadwood in Manufacturing" so that
more engineers can be hired. The presenter responds hotly:

> "Sam's position on the corporate culture is clear: no layoffs! But
> the business types are anxious, and they say that the solution is
> obvious—change the policy. Well, let's get it straight. I don't
> care about the profitability! Nothing gets my loyalty to this com-
> pany more than the current policy! These are people out there,
> real people and real bills. I was laid off once and I know what
> it's like."

His emotional rendition of commitment to a central ideological principle
silences the group momentarily, but John retorts with a well-known company
joke: "And I thought they were interchangeable work units." They stare at

each other as the tension rises. But the agenda is heavy, and a third party offers a compromise drawing on an equally central principle—profitability:

> "Tech's run on emotion too much! We need facts, not religion! The numbers can get us out of all this emotional stuff, all this 'do it my way'! The only thing that is real is making money!"

On this all seem to agree. The tension visibly subsides, and the issue is temporarily suspended. The ritual frame is restored, and the meeting moves on.

Overt challenges to the ritual frame are handled more directly. For example, Jim, a development group manager, is specifying to a VP staff meeting the resources his organization requires. The presentation goes smoothly until he mentions that he wants to hire people who have left Tech and now want to return. He is under severe scheduling pressure, and he wants people, good people. The group's personnel manager says that the corporate policy is clearly against rehiring. Others are concerned that Jim's increased headcount will come at their expense. The tension rises as participants offer different interpretations of the corporate policy. Finally, the vice-president intervenes to explain the ideological underpinnings of the policy, until Jim interrupts:

> "In the past people left and returned. Now you need a VP approval to rehire someone. Some people left and returned with higher salaries. Sam was mad. He claimed there was no loyalty. That is why the policy is there. We can't hire back anyone who left 'for significant financial advantage,' or who 'competes against Tech,' or who has 'burnt bridges.' "
> [Loudly] "Do you want this product? Right now we are flat out! Either we cut back expectations or we OK outside hires. And forget this loyalty crap!" [Silence.]
> "Jim, I'll take that with you off-line."

The suggestion to take it "off-line" is a mild rebuke. Jim is a group member of relatively high status with whom a continuing working relationship is necessary. The vice-president, aware of his dependence on Jim, knows he must be careful and at the same time preserve his authority. Likewise, Jim knows he has gone too far and takes the opportunity to withdraw. He continues his presentation, and the subject of rehiring does not resurface. During a break they schedule some time for a one-on-one. The issue now becomes a private one. Whatever action is taken will not get in the way of the ritual frame within which members may claim to share comfortable ideological formulations.

Occasionally, group members who challenge the ritual frame do not respond to subtle attempts to silence them. Here, more blatant techniques of control are used. For example, at a meeting of a project team, the group manager tries to close a debate by describing the "Tech disease":

> "We think that we're in terrible shape, but in fact we're in good shape. We are very self-critical and love to beat ourselves up. There is an 'ain't it awful' attitude. A lot of good people left because of it. It might be a self-fulfilling prophecy."

It is an often heard observation that many members almost automatically acknowledge as true. However, Mike, who has recently joined the group after his project was dramatically "unfunded," and who has been quietly but demonstratively leaning back in his chair, sits forward and bursts out:

> "What is all this talk of Tech? I don't see any Tech! What is this 'we'? I haven't met anything called Tech! I work with some people and get a paycheck!"

There is a brief, tense silence. The manager swivels his chair back to the flipchart and says loudly: "Moving right along . . ." as he brings up the next agenda item. Some people exchange glances, and a few under-the-breath titters are heard. Mike's presence is keenly felt. But the next time he starts talking ("I don't understand. What exactly do you *mean* by 'leadership'?"), Bill—an older manager known for his outspokenness—laughs and says: "I figured out a way to get him to stop." Turning to Mike, he takes a dollar bill from his wallet and says: "I'll buy you a beer if you stop talking." He puts it on the table. The next time Mike tries to intervene, someone throws the bill at him and somebody else pastes it on the wall next to the charts they are working on. Mike is quiet for a while and then joins in the discussion. Later someone explains to me that Mike was "burnt out" in his previous job and is now recuperating. "Bill handled him just right."

The intense, highly charged, and often conflictual interchanges that are characteristic of the working stage of the meeting are interspersed with short timeouts. During these, participants temporarily suspend their show of emotional involvement in the proceedings and assume a shared interpretive, often playful, stance. A VP staff meeting illustrates a sequence of conflictual engagements and interpretive timeouts.

A presentation proposing the funding of a new development effort—considered "an emotional issue" by those involved—turns into a shouting match between the presenter and a manager who is competing for the funding. The emotions seem real and dangerous, and the protagonists almost attack each other. The vice-president says nothing. The personnel manager, one of the few women in the group, intervenes a number of times in an attempt to calm the discussion, but to no avail. Finally, after a decision to take it "off-line," the episode is closed and a short break announced. The presenter walks out and lights a cigarette in the corridor.

The next scheduled agenda item is a guest presentation by a manager from a competing development group reporting to a different VP. Frank, the scheduled presenter, has been waiting outside. He is here to talk about a product he is developing and its connections to this group. There is potential for disagreement. Frank sticks his head in. He knows a good number of those present. "Is it safe to come in yet?" he asks, opening the door just enough for his head to pass through, holding on to an imaginary helmet and ducking to avoid flying shrapnel. The participants laugh, and someone replies: "It's OK, we're ready for you, we have you all set up." He is referring to the collusion among members of one group to cause the failure of others—a well-known scenario frequently referred to and often used. They all laugh. Frank makes his way to the front of the room, exchanging pleasantries with the VP:

> "I heard about your talk at the state-of-the-company meeting. Did they tape your session?"
> "Yeah."
> "Good! I'll catch it."

The VP formally introduces Frank. Frank slides up the blackboard covered with leftovers from previous discussions. The one revealed underneath, however, still has the day's agenda listed on it. Frank does a double take and says with mock horror: "Aha! A hidden agenda!" This causes loud and lengthy laughter. As he is arranging his slides he offers some additional cultural commentary:

> "This company is really 10,000 ten-man companies—and everybody talks! I sent out a draft of this proposal over the net to a few people and got back comments from people I've never heard of. The presentation takes an hour—*without* participation."

The last words are accompanied by a meaningful wink, indicating he knows what to expect. Frank begins his presentation. The timeout is over.

Frank is all business as he works his way through his prepared slides. Everyone in the room is clearly opposed to his ideas, and the hostile comments reflect it. Occasionally, however, the tone shifts from his serious presentation and open conflict to a brief, dramatized, humorous observation, as in the following interchange between the VP and Frank:

> "It'll never get across the executive committee!"
> "I hear you, but in spite of it we're gonna get our funding—eighty big ones."
> "Does Sam know? I would make sure through some mechanism (not yourself!) that he does."
> "You're right. Give us the 'didn't happen on my shift' option if anything goes wrong."
> "And then stand back."

Frank steps back against the wall, raises his arms, and remains for one second in the crucified pose, recognized by all as the penalty for tangling with Sam. Everybody laughs. Someone says: "Well, Frank, you know we're behind you!" Frank retorts: "That's the problem!" All share the joke and the good cheer that comes from this interchange. There appears to be comradeship—even mutual appreciation—in the lighthearted acknowledgment of enmity between groups and their representatives and in the playful naming of conflict-laden scripts: the set up, the hidden agenda, the crucifixion, the backstabbing.

Frank is followed by a lawyer from the corporate legal department, who warns the group to be careful in their documents to avoid antitrust issues and trouble with the Federal Trade Commission. He explains the law and concludes:

> "We're not the little old high-tech company from down the street any more. You can't round 11 percent market share into 20 percent. I've seen letters say: 'We have 85 percent of the market share and by God we'll get it all!' Your mail is claimable in court. Think of everything you write as being forwarded to the FTC! One case is enough. You don't know where it will hit us from—a disgruntled distributor, an irate ex-employee."

It is "we time." The group responds with solemn nods, confirming their concern with the company good. A coffee break is called. The corporate interest is not something to be openly questioned, but humorous interchanges during the break allow members to express alternative views. A group of managers stand together in the corridor discussing the presentation and its implications.

> "It's bullshit. Nothing to worry about. A lot of the documents we write are on the technet. So they're here today, gone tomorrow. I always keep my mail in order. Delete the sensitive stuff is the first thing to do."
> "You're forgetting one thing. They can go over the tapes! Everything stays on tapes!"
> "What?!"
> "Uh-oh! Someone better run through the tapes with a magnet! I'm gonna be more careful."
> "Did you hear? Alan just had a great line. The lawyer said: 'Don't get the documents in the wrong hands,' and he said: 'I know what he meant. Keep them away from the executive committee!' " [Laughter.]
> "Yeah, especially anything with funding on it!"

Team meetings usually end abruptly, particularly when the session has gone over the scheduled time. Thus, the post-meeting stage is often short. Members indicate that they are under time pressure. Many have scheduled events elsewhere or have planned meetings with one or more of the team members on specific topics. Participants leave rapidly, but the events of the meeting are often discussed between friends, acquaintances, and confidants for days, and some are reported by participants at other group meetings.

The Intergroup Meeting

The second type of work group meeting involves members of a number of different groups and teams. Tech's matrix structure (see Chapter 2) requires members from a variety of functional groups to work together on shared or interdependent projects. Program managers, for example, hold formal responsibility for projects that involve many different functional groups and organizations. Authority is vaguely defined and often the subject of dispute. Program participants meet in a variety of configurations, but less regularly than team members, so that participants are less familiar with each other.

The ABC program is a corporate program aimed at linking technologies and products from a number of independent groups into a unified package designed to appeal to customers. The program is highly visible and, like many similar matrixed programs, the subject of considerable debate: some in the company are opposed to it; others feel that they should own it; still others would rather not be involved. The program manager calls meetings when necessary. Most involve relevant small groups (for example, all the marketing managers, or all the project leaders responsible for a particular technology). Occasionally, all the members involved in the program are invited to a program review meeting. The meeting is convened by the manager responsible for the program and is designed as a mini-conference, an opportunity for representatives of all groups to interact, exchange information, views, and impressions, negotiate, learn, network, scout the opposition, and build coalitions.

The ABC program meeting takes place in a large conference room at the local Hilton. It is a fancier setting than most Tech affairs, befitting the importance of the event. Carefully choreographed ahead of time by the program manager in consultation with managers of participating groups, the meeting is organized around a series of presentations by members of the various interested groups. Over a hundred people are present. This well-publicized event has drawn participants of several statuses and functions: managers from the level of supervisor to group manager, and engineers from junior engineer to senior consulting engineer. Also present are representatives from

Marketing, Manufacturing, and other functions. Many know each other or of each other. The gathering reflects the tension between group interests. Potential conflict is in the air.

The transitional stage begins as participants slowly arrive. The milling around is cut short at nine when Jane, the program manager, opens the proceedings with a short talk. She is in her late thirties, chain smoking and apparently nervous. These events are important for forming the public opinion of the program, and of her. Many participants are of higher rank and status; it is on such occasions that reputations are made and take on a life of their own. This kind of visibility is essential both to her career and to the program. She starts with some interpretive comments and a joke.

> "Welcome to the meeting. The point is to share info, to get people together. So introduce yourself. The person next to you may be vitally important to what you are doing. We need consistent communication. We need to keep talking. To start it off I have a joke. A policeman stops a man driving a car full of penguins. He orders him to drive them to the zoo, to 'do what's right'—'do what's right' is a Tech term, you know. The next day he stops them again, this time all wearing sunglasses. He gets mad and says: 'I thought I told you to do what's right!' The man answers: 'I did. I took them to the zoo yesterday. Today I'm taking them to the beach.' "

The joke falls flat. People are still walking in and seating themselves behind the rows of tables, looking around to get a sense of who is there. A series of presentations begins. Participants listen carefully, watching for any sign, any message, any clue, to the various hidden agendas. The words of each presenter are important, and so are the reactions in the crowd. First to speak is Tony, who heads one of the larger development groups involved in the program. He starts by conveying a "message":

> "I have no jokes. I'm a warm-up show. Not much content, like at a rock concert. A group that may make it someday, but now is getting everyone to scream, jump, and clap. [Pause.] My message to you is this: ABC is a *corporate program*. It's not ours. We don't own it. But we do support it, and encourage others to.

[Pause.] I delight in heretical, paradoxical things; well, here's one. The ABC program is bad! It's to our disadvantage. It will homogenize the products and take away our edge! People with crappy products get the advantage back."

As he speaks, the audience becomes engaged in interpreting the significance of what he says. Some whispering starts. ("He wants to be a good corporate citizen and cover his own ass.") Next to me, a manager from Tony's group turns and studies the reactions of senior engineers and managers. Tension rises in the row in front of us, where the English contingent sits. They are known to be strong supporters of ABC. Others turn discreetly to eye the group that might be taking offense, now huddling with their heads together, whispering. Someone near me says: "He'll get things thrown at him." Tony, noticing the reaction, smiles and says: "Sorry to those of you who have to make it happen!"

After establishing his reservations, Tony moves to the viewgraph with transparencies listing the reasons for supporting the program. He turns it on. A typical presentation ensues: dim lights, a rather eerie setting, the presenter shaded, the messages glowing in the semidarkness. The lighting dims participants' views of each other and creates the impression of a darkened mass focusing on the issue, the person, and the message. It is against this background that the ritual frame is constructed. Tony reads his first transparency:

"Well, here is my warm-up message: 'ABC is a competitive weapon.' We're doing it not because we're good guys, not for religious reasons, or because it is best. We're doing it to use as a competitive advantage. It is suited to what we have to do as we move to the future."

The message is clear. This is business. Advantage. Pragmatism. Hardball. No "religion," no "fluff." We. We in Tech. As he uncovers each bullet, he reads it out loud, chanting rhythmically as he emphasizes each "we":

"*We* believe that Silicon Tech is our primary competition.
We believe that Silicon Tech is stuck with crap.
We believe that they cannot move into ABC technology easily.

We believe that this is our great opportunity.
We believe our other competitors will have the same problems.
We have to put our energy, our creativity, into development.
We have a strategy.
We believe it is the way to go.
We think it's a win. [Another transparency.] We would like to be the leader in ABC. People worked hard to make ABC acceptable. We normally knock ourselves for not doing this, but this time we did it well. We increased the market share in the Far East! Many believe that 60 percent of revenues will come from there in the future."

Tony is followed by a long series of presenters. Each says some personal words. It is an opportunity to get known, to work on one's reputation. A marketing manager is next. Assuming the reflective style and "wise" approach that many adopt for such occasions, he introduces himself and starts:

"We want people to think of Tech and immediately of this product. It is better than sex! And to think of Silicon and theirs as slavery!"

There is little response. Hype from marketeers is familiar, now standard and without shock value, not even worth an engineer's raised eyebrow. He continues:

"We have to enhance the Tech image, appeal to the consulting industry, cultivate them, use them as press announcers, have them become our missionaries, carry our messages. [Chanting rhythmically.]
We need to maintain high levels of quality!
We need to give customers the warm fuzzies!
We need to make management feel good all over!
[Lowered voice.] Our assumptions: Engineering will continue to produce quality on time. The competition will be tough. We need Engineering's support. We're not technical people. We need help in setting it up, getting it running. Marketing got in-

volved late in this process and is behind. We need to work as a
team, to further define and enhance this product."

As the presentations continue, the elements that make up the ritual frame
—the "messages," the jokes, the metaphors, the exhortations—become repetitive, even stale. Yet it is the seemingly endless flow of public platitudes,
the style of their delivery, and the audience acknowledgment that provide
the framework and the means for interaction. In their substance and their
rhythmic chanting, these expressions celebrate the organizational ideology:
the unity and integrity of the company, the "we," the common purpose.

Tech's organizational ideology, however, is interpreted not only within
the ritual frame and in the familiar words and phrases of the speakers, but
in the backstage activities of the participants. Quiet reactions and whispered
conversations must also be monitored, decoded, and stored for future use.
Here the focus is on the subgroup rivalries, the conflict, the politics. A number of participants have moved outside. Discussions are taking place near
the coffee, just outside the main door. Inside, flurries of whispers accompany the presenter's words. A woman sitting next to me scans the room and
explains the scene. She points to a ruddy-faced man sitting in the back row
and engaged in energetic whispering with his neighbors:

> "That is Cliff Laing! He is God! He is one of the chosen! He
> made the president's list last year! And that is Bob Howe next to
> him. There was a reporting line, but now it's dotted. They both
> are gurus. And if they are having a fit right now, they are right!
> But it isn't serious, or else Cliff would have spoken up."

She notices her boss, a few rows away, making notes, and turns her attention
to the presenter, opening her own notebook with renewed interest.

Since it is a large and open forum with many strangers, the felt tension
between public unity and private strife, between the ritual frame and the
reality, is rarely acknowledged. Nevertheless, tension between organizations and their representatives is not far from the surface. Occasionally, the
differing perspectives clash and erupt into open conflict. The first indication
of disagreement between the presenter, who has been extolling the virtues

of a project titled Jupiter, and a member of a competing group working on Apollo comes during the question and answer period:

> "What is the probability of a slip? What would you do?"
> "It's like asking me what I would do if my house burned down. That means that on the date we said we'd deliver we won't deliver. I guess that is the definition of a slip. [Laughter.] Well, in the event of a disaster I have no plan. You are actually asking what is my contingency plan. I will tell you that when it happens. Next question."

Open hostilities emerge in the course of the next presentation. Tom, who manages Apollo, stands and interrupts: "Jupiter is not known in the U.S., while Apollo is. It doesn't help the company to keep pushing it." The presenter responds sharply, and Jerry, a member of the Jupiter group in the audience, says quite loudly: "Those Apollo people, they are a closed community and are on the inside looking out." When the presenter is interrupted again, he becomes visibly more agitated, raises his voice, and says: "What you are proposing is high-risk; you don't want to argue about that now!" The debate ceases for a while, and the presentation resumes its earlier tone.

Both sides have made their points, and the show continues. The level of open aggression rose too high and was managed in a rather curt way. But it reappears when the marketing manager for Apollo makes his presentation. Jerry gets involved again, surfacing the conflict that started earlier: "Forgetting all the religion, . . ." he says of the just presented technical and business arguments, and makes his own point. It is an open challenge, but the scene is cut short again by the program manager, who stands and calls for the lunch break. "Have those conversations that you were dying to have," she says, as behind me people laugh quietly. The room empties rapidly as lunch and "those conversations" beckon. But Jerry is not done yet. Tom saunters over to his side of the room. Jerry is still lounging, paging through industry journals, waiting, pretending not to notice the approaching challenger. Others, expecting a juicy showdown, wait too. Jerry closes the journal and looks up. A heated exchange follows. Ideological formulations are a resource in such exchanges. Opponents are accused of breaking the norms, of being "countercultural," of misunderstanding or not manifesting the appropriate membership role:

> "The industries don't care about your product! The financials don't give a shit either! So I don't have to agree to the markets defined by XYZ!"
>
> "Read the popular media, see who has more references! No one mentions your stuff!"
>
> "You're raising flags and alienating people. If you don't quietly sell people on the religion, you won't get anywhere in this company."
>
> "I'm arguing that XYZ is the way to go."
>
> "That's religion! What evidence do you have? What numbers?"
>
> "Take the popular press—"
>
> [Interrupts.] "That is not my measure. Ask the companies. And you're not successfully selling people in Tech; you're alienating them. You move in with your whole contingent and you're beating 'em over the head with it."

It is getting distinctly unpleasant. Tom has a fixed smile on his face, and Jerry rises. They move away from each other, Jerry almost walking out on Tom as they make their way to the door. It is lunch time, time for a temporary suspension of hostilities.

There is a long line for a buffet lunch. Lunch is an extended timeout that allows participants some respite from the effort to navigate through the rule-bound events. Plate in hand, people move toward the dining room and sit around large tables. Discussions seem animated. Participants may relax and feel freer to associate with like-minded others, to enact realities of their choice, to inhabit a more comfortable place on the continuum between engagement and detachment. Lunch is also an occasion for interpretive discussions with people of one's choice ("Did you notice he didn't mention John Cummings and the chips folks in his org chart?"), an opportunity to mingle, to exchange information, to impress one's superiors, to have a drink, to check the box scores or the Tech stocks, to play politics, to wander off. After lunch, there is time for leisure activities. Senior managers are still in shifting huddles. Others line up at the public telephones, taking care of other business. Some of the engineers wander off alone. Three or four Englishmen make a show of walking off in search of a bar. One responds to a question with the grin of a naughty boy: "Where do you think we're going? We're English!" They spend the lunch break in the bar.

Toward one o'clock, people are again congregating at the doorway of the still-darkened conference room. The earlier showdown remains the topic of discussion. "XYZ are the new kids on the block. They have to push and shove to get recognition. That's the way it always works," a manager explains as he watches the protagonists return to their seats. "And it isn't over yet!" Such conflicts are not resolved; rather, they develop into ongoing battles that erupt whenever representatives of the warring factions cross paths. These feuds are an openly acknowledged and much discussed part of the Tech scene.

The rest of the day is dedicated to more presentations. Some people leave early, others show up late; the conference room and the adjacent corridors are constantly in use. At five o'clock the day is formally closed.

Timeout Meetings

The third type of work group meeting occurs when members gather as part of a formally designated timeout. In contrast to other work group meetings, these events are designed to introduce leisure—or at least relaxation—into work settings for the explicit purpose of "building morale" and increasing "motivation." Rules that govern work life are, at least partly, suspended, and standard configurations are broken down. Thus, timeout meetings have the almost oxymoronic goal of formalizing and authoritatively prescribing the unstructured playfulness and self-awareness that characterize informally occurring timeouts in the course of regular meetings. Consequently, the ritual is a mirror image of rituals in other settings: the playful, tongue-in-cheek component is emphasized, while the transitional stages preceding and following it contain reminders of the serious side of organizational life.

At Tech there are many occasions for timeout meetings. "It is never too late to party," members often assert, and the company is generally thought to encourage leisure activities and socializing. However, the boundary between work and play is vague: the definitions of organizational time are flexible; there are many attempts to annex and colonize members' time; and work and play are often combined. Thus, as the following examples show, what is "time out" and what is "time in" is never quite clear, and the distinction is a matter of degree. The monthly meeting of the SysCom development group is close in style and substance to regular work group meetings, whereas the playful component is dominant in the preparations for "the SysCom Olympics."

The Monthly Meeting SysCom's monthly organizational meeting is open to all employees. It takes place before lunch in the cafeteria of SysCom's new facility. The cafeteria is in the corner of the building and has large windows that open onto a spectacular view. All managers, many engineers, and some secretaries—about 150 people—appear. The manager has made it known that he would like full attendance, and this has been informally encouraged.

The pre-meeting phase is short. Members gather at tables, busy "talking shop." All work in the same facility and see each other on an ongoing basis. In front of the crowd, ready for presentation, is the "golden bull"—a monthly award. It is a garish trophy, roughly six feet high, of fake gold. At the top is a miniature bull. Underneath it are an assortment of others: a bust of Einstein, a dolphin, a golfer on a stage supported by golden columns, and a faithful reproduction of the *Manneken Pis*. Around the golden bull on a table are twelve statuettes of golden angels about eight inches tall. Some members examine the trophies up close.

The transition into the main act is quick. Jack, the group manager, stands. Quite a bit shorter than the trophy and seemingly oblivious to it, he begins with a review of the group performance, focusing on the feelings appropriate to membership in this group.

> "The new building we will be moving into is great: three floors, *windows* at the end of the corridor, plenty of lab space. The old building will be taken by someone outside Engineering. They want a cafeteria, and it will be a significant improvement for them. You look at those funny things [points at the window] and it will make you feel: I'm a professional, I'm valued. I sense the beginning of momentum, feeling good about ourselves. We've shipped some important products. Those who have been down on us can look now. We're shipping and we're even going to make a profit this year. I want to salute the Poseidon people. They nursed it and brought it back to health, and we're even making a bunch of money on it! The overall product strategy is coming together. I feel really good about it, and so should you."

He spends about fifteen minutes discussing the status of various projects. Despite the golden bull in the background, this portion of the meeting is straight and serious in its dealings with the group's success and is similar in tone and style to other types of meeting.

When he has concluded his speech, the manager smiles broadly, steps aside, and looks at the trophy. The mood in the room is transformed as the golden bull becomes the center of attention: it is now more playful, semi-serious, almost tongue-in-cheek. In an intentionally exaggerated dramatic tone, he says:

> "And now—the golden bull award, representing the spirit of the bull: put your head down and plow through the problems. [Pause.] It goes to—Ed Williams and the people who made X-101 happen." [Applause and some cheers.]

Ed, the project's development manager, walks to the front of the room, waving at the audience. The group manager gives an account of the project's difficulties and its current business success, naming major corporate clients. Then he reads the names of the project team, stumbling on the foreign-sounding ones.

> "Sorry if I slaughtered the names, but it's Ed's fault. I asked him to spell the list carefully. I was going to get money for a restaurant, but money is short these days—the squeeze is on. Maybe we can afford McDonald certificates, though. [Laughter.] Today I also have new trophies. We'll have to find a reason for each. These are genuine metal—not plastic. They come in male and female versions, so if you get the wrong sex, let me know."

Everyone seems amused. When the laughter subsides, it is back to business. Jack introduces a new manager, then asks if there are questions. No answer. "No problems?" he repeats. Someone near me snorts audibly. The meeting is adjourned. The golden bull is transported to Ed's office by an engineer who carries it horizontally in one hand, highlighting its nature as a prop. For a month it will protrude into the open space above Ed's cubicle, visible from anywhere in the building. The crowd disperses rapidly.

The SysCom Olympics Every summer SysCom management sponsors the "SysCom Olympics," organized sports competitions that occur during the lunch break or in the late afternoons. Art, the manager of one of SysCom's main development groups, is responsible for organizing the event. Invitations have been out for weeks. All nodes on the technet were informed by Art's secretary. For the marginal, the unconnected, or the disconnected, notices were posted all over the building, along with sign-up sheets for the various sports. A five-dollar charge covers the red or green T-shirt that represents one of the two randomly chosen teams.

The first event is the opening ceremony. At three o'clock, the 40 or so participants gather in the conference room that usually serves the senior staff meeting. They are a cross section of the organization: engineers, managers, secretaries, support staff. All are crowded around the long, shiny table, waiting. Suddenly the door opens, and Art, with a torch made of rolled-up computer printout and a crown of leaves on his head, enters the room and circles the table in slow motion. Those who have seen this before smile; the others look rather surprised. Art assumes his place at the head of the table and with a practiced motion flips on the viewgraph, removes the playful accoutrements, and gives a presentation.

The presentation lasts about fifteen minutes. The first transparency covers the history of the SysCom Olympics; the next one, the purpose; the next one, the rules; and the last, the administration. At this point, the event resembles a regular presentation, despite the red and green T-shirts, the unusual mix of people, and the crown of leaves on the table. Art, a technical-type manager, is clearly not comfortable talking. He follows the transparencies closely and seriously, uncovering one bullet at a time by lowering a sheet of paper. He calls on his secretary to give the administrative arrangements. She, straight-faced, replaces him and reproduces another perfect presentation with her own transparencies. Finally, Art sums up:

> "I want to say a few words. It's good that we are doing this. I'm glad you came. I know that things have been a little rough lately. There has been a lot of pressure. [Heads nod.] This will give you people an opportunity to relax and take your minds off things, to work off your excess energy, feel a little better about what's going on. Get a little more motivated. Also get to know each other, improve your morale. But remember. Nobody is

watching you. This is *not* a Tech event. So don't take off company time too blatantly. There is enough of that anyway. And don't get hurt. Benefits are great—but you're not covered on this one!"

Timeout fades back to timein. The ambiguous interpenetration of work and play and the significance they lend each other hang over the dispersing crowd, as people return to their daily routines. A departing engineer says to another: "I feel my morale improving already. How about you?"

Discussion: Talking Around

Compared with top management presentations and training workshops, work group meetings are less explicitly focused on delivering ideological messages. For the most part, they are ostensibly designed to accomplish work-related purposes, and talking ideology is an incidental activity. Nevertheless, it is here that members experience most acutely the pressures to express role embracement. This occurs for a number of reasons. First, work group meetings are perceived as more "real." Participants have salient and often conflicting interests, and they are constantly in the presence of those who are—or who might become—formally charged with evaluating their performance and allocating rewards. Second, the meetings take place on a regular basis and often in recurring configurations. Participants have extensive and ongoing ties with each other and will continue to serve as a relevant audience long after a particular event is over. Third, members experience the role of presenter most frequently at work group meetings. In any particular event a number of participants may share the role of presenter, and those in passive roles in one meeting are often active in another. Under these circumstances it is in the participants' interest to engage in what some refer to as "raising the flag": making oneself visible, creating an impression, and generally jockeying for the ideological high ground by positioning oneself as an agent of the ideology—a shining exemplar of the member role and a caustic critic of the failures of others.

However, the same features that exert pressure to express role embracement work in the opposite direction as well. The members' familiarity with each other, the need to maintain a semblance of order and harmony in the face of continued conflict and potential chaos, and the desire to preserve working relationships also result in extensive efforts to suspend and defuse conflict. More than in other gatherings, work group meetings are characterized by elaborate and highly structured displays of role distancing during transitional periods and timeouts—momentary and extensive, spontaneous and designed.

Thus, work group meetings are where members experience the contradiction between role embracement and role distancing most acutely. Consequently, these meetings are characterized by a studied ambiguity, a shared ironic stance, and frequent timeouts. The distinctions between "on-line" and "off-line" and between humor and seriousness, and the occasional need to achieve compromise or suppress deviance, become a central aspect of the ritual form. This dual significance is best captured in the use of ambiguous symbols such as the golden bull: a valued prize for company-approved technical accomplishment whose grotesque nature carries self-parodying connotations of "bullshit." Such ambiguity allows the ritual to take its course while also commenting on it and making available aspects of the submerged realities that rituals often obscure. Thus, the various meanings built into the ritual frame collapse into each other: the ritual is imbued with self-parody, ideology with common sense.

Conclusion: Ritual and Normative Control

Presentational rituals at Tech are an integral and ongoing feature of members' work lives. In one form or another they are a pervasive presence on the Tech scene and constantly make demands on the way members present themselves. Most generally speaking, the performance of the ritual—whether in large and festive settings or on smaller and less formal occasions—is a framing device: members, acting as agents of the corporate interest, attempt to establish a shared definition of the situation within which reality claims derived from the organizational ideology are experienced as valid. To this end, participants are presented with slogans and metaphors ("Tech is a bottom-up company," "We are like a football team") with which the complex reality that is Tech is to be expressed. In particular, a distinct and somewhat abstract view of the member role and its appropriate behaviors ("doing what's right," "working hard," "he who proposes does"), cognitions ("the importance of technological accomplishment," "the centrality of profit"), and emotions ("commitment," "having fun," "enthusiasm") is presented or implied, and, more crucially, specific instances of their correct application are dramatized, noted, and rewarded. In short, like all rituals, these occasions are used as vehicles for the exertion of what Pierre Bourdieu (1977) refers to as symbolic power—the power to define reality.

Tech rituals, however, have two distinct features. First, they are characterized by a decentralization of power. Symbolic power, as one might expect, is clearly possessed by those invested with formal authority and high status, and most effectively applied when the status gap between participants is large or the power of reward or sanction well defined. But in the context of ritual life at Tech, this type of power may accrue to those who possess other resources as well: the power of numbers found in the pooled resources and the concerted action of groups; temporarily assigned formal roles; acknowledged technical expertise or relevant experience; an open endorsement of the organizational interest; the threat that in Tech's open and shifting environment, reputation, status, and real rewards are in the hands of numerous, often unknown, others; and, if nothing else, a fluency in the language, mode of thinking, and style of ideological discourse.[21] In short, from the point of view of the individual participant, agents of control are everywhere: one is surrounded and constantly observed by members (including oneself) who, in order to further their own interests, act as spokespersons and enforcers of the organizational ideology.

Second, since the ideology is one of openness, informality, individual initiative, and real feelings, symbolic power is exerted, for the most part, quite subtly: overt, centralized control and forced compliance would belie the messages of the ideology. Nevertheless, its presence is revealed in brief episodes that resemble a small-scale version of what Turner (1974) calls "social drama." In Turner's view, a social drama is a fundamental and recurring part of the process of group life that unfolds in predictable stages: a public and dramatic breach or a challenge to the prevailing order is followed by a sense of mounting crisis and a series of attempts at redressive action, and culminates in either an unbridgeable schism between the opposed parties or reintegration and reestablishment of order.[22] At Tech, mini-dramas of control are an ever-present part of presentational rituals. Although they vary in length and intensity, these mini-dramas follow a predictable pattern: a challenge to the ritual frame causes the tension to rise, and members acting as agents for the corporate interest (in the rituals we have observed, these roles are widely shared by participants) use various techniques—Bourdieu (1977) refers to these as "symbolic violence"—to suppress or redefine dissent, silence the deviants, and gain the participants' support.[23] Thus, collective support for the ritual frame is bolstered by the organization's symbolic power, exerted through particular members.

The most dominant response to the exertion of symbolic power in the context of ritual life at Tech is the expression of role embracement: participants express their acceptance of the member role, including not only the prescribed behaviors but, more crucially, the beliefs one must espouse and the emotions one is to experience and display. This occurs to different extents in the various types of presentational rituals: it appears whole-hearted and festive in top management presentations; reserved and tentative in training workshops; and pragmatic, conflictual, and continuous in work group meetings. Despite the subtle and occasionally overt pressures to conform, many members, if asked, would claim that this stance—whether an expression of sincerely held convictions or a scripted role—is freely chosen. Such a response may reflect the participants' experience, but it is also consistent with the ideological depiction of the company: the open community, freedom of expression, "bottom-up decision making," informality, and so forth.

Whatever their causes, displays of role embracement may have a considerable impact on those who perform them. Public expressions of support for an ideological point of view may cause cognitive dissonance: members who, under pressure, publicly espouse beliefs and opinions they might otherwise reject tend to adopt them as an authentic expression of their point of view.[24] Moreover, as Arlie Hochschild (1983) suggests, when institutionally prescribed roles include definitions of appropriate emotions, they require "deep acting": the performer must try to "feel" rather than feign role-prescribed emotions.[25] Consequently, participation in ritual enactments of the member role at Tech—no matter how tentative—may lead to what she calls emotive dissonance: members are inclined to experience the emotions they display as authentic.[26] Over time, cognitive and emotive dissonance may blur the boundary between the performers' perception of an acted role and the experience of an "authentic self." This, in principle, should occur for all displays of role embracement, but it is probably more acute for sustained and scrutinized performances. Particularly susceptible in this regard are those members who perform the various spokesperson roles and those who act as agents of control, whether in their capacity as possessors of authority, as temporary volunteers, or as individuals recognizing the advantages of speaking for the company interest. The performance of such roles, Lewis

Coser (1974) points out, is a particularly effective mechanism for instilling commitment to ideological principles among those who perform them. Thus, extensive and ongoing participation in ritual life at Tech, may, as Mills (1940: 908) put it, induce people to become what at first they merely sought to appear.

There are limits, however, to the power of ritual to elicit the expression of role embracement. Some members—perhaps at some cost to their reputation—minimize their participation in ritual events. Others participate as a "secondary audience," excluded from the actual event but aware of it and participating after the fact through reports and reenactments. Such secondary participants may share in some of the potential for "deep acting" of the member role offered by presentational rituals. But in many cases their form of participation is also an indication and a demonstration of lower status, marginality, passivity, or lack of interest. Many members experience both primary and secondary participation at different times, and their effects might not always reinforce each other. More extremely, for many in support and service roles—mainly members of Wage Class 2 and temporary workers—such ritual performances make clear their status as what Goffman (1959) calls "nonpersons": individuals who are present in body only and not considered a relevant part of the scene. Here, too, there might be potential for deep acting, albeit of marginal or alienated roles.

More crucially, however, the ritual form itself contains built-in opportunities for temporary suspension of role embracement: transitional phases and timeouts that bracket and intersperse the ritual frame. These episodes resemble those stages of ritual that Turner (1969) has called "liminal": a relatively unstructured period that occurs between structured modes of relating where the participants' relationship is characterized by "communitas," a relatedness temporarily unmediated by social structure.[27] Liminal phases of ritual, Turner suggests (1969: 167), tend to highlight the most significant dimensions of a specific culture. For example, in his exemplary studies of tribal societies, liminality was shown to be the occasion for role reversals between subordinate and superordinate members: dramatized exchanges between up and down, strong and weak, having and not having authority (Turner, 1969). These he saw as variations on the theme of hierarchy.

At Tech, however, the liminal phases of ritual have a different flavor: not role reversal, but role distancing is their central attribute. These episodes are occasions for members to assume a reflective and openly self-conscious stance and to share a variety of dramatized and often structured commentaries on their condition and on the ritual frame. Thus, in the course of liminal episodes, a commonsense point of view that is sometimes at odds with the official one is expressed.[28] It includes less sanguine views of managerial ideology ("the bullshit that comes from above") and behavior ("the song and dance"), as well as a different view of member attributes: colorfully labeled behavioral scenarios ("setting up," "finger pointing," "midnight phone calls," "pissing contests," "backstabbing," "crucifying") and experiences ("hanging from shoestrings," "pain," "the fear of God," "burnout"), a cynical awareness of manipulative intents and disguised meanings (giving "Tech strokes," managing and exposing "hidden agendas," doing "rah-rah stuff"), or dispassionate "Tech watching." Expressed differently in the various ritual forms—subtle and controlled in top management presentations, aggressive and critical in training workshops, widespread and playful in work group meetings—the liminal mode provides an alternative reality: participants temporarily detach themselves from their performance of the member role, comment on it, and share with others the awareness, either cheerful or disdainful, of the theatrical nature of the proceedings. Thus, the liminal stages of Tech rituals differ from liminality as Turner depicted it: it is not the meaning of hierarchy (who is up and who is down) so much as the meaning of authenticity (who is "real" and who is not) and inclusion (who is "in" and who is "out") that is being enacted.

Although the centrality of these meanings to the participants' experience of the ritual would seem to undermine symbolic power by juxtaposing common sense and ideology, questioning the ritual frame, and contradicting expressions of role embracement, the reverse is often true. Controlled self-consciousness, appropriate and timely use of an ironic stance, and the ability to shift frames and stances are considered signs of elegance.[29] Members evaluate each other on their ability to express both embracement and distancing and to know when to stop. By structuring and defining as playful those occasions where commonsense alternatives to the formal ideology are pronounced—the shared interpretive routines, the more formally designed timeouts—real dissent is preempted. Moreover, a particular kind of "communitas" between members is fostered: not the one Turner seems to describe (and Kanter [1983: 203] attributes to employees in "strong culture companies"), but the communion of self-aware and talented actors commenting on their roles and performances.[30] These qualities of liminality are interpreted as further evidence of the benign nature of the company and its normative demands. Consequently, within very broad boundaries delineated by those incidents where deviance is openly suppressed, contradicting or escaping an adherence to normative demands is often difficult if not impossible. Participants may become mired ever deeper in a paradoxical normative trap within which whatever one does, thinks, or feels can be—and often is—interpreted as confirmation of ideological reality claims.[31]

Thus, ritual life at Tech is composed of a paradoxical, counterpunctual weaving of common sense, ideology, and the experiences associated with them that brings to the attention of participants a complex, multifaceted, and ambiguous reality. Participants are systematically presented with an explicit awareness of the dramatic mechanisms that underlie the process of framing reality, and an open acknowledgment of the manufactured nature of cultural categories and symbols, including those that are central to the ritual performance itself.[32] A self-consciousness that could be considered a fatal flaw in the ritual performances now becomes its central theme and is itself highly ritualized. This produces a potentially unstable balance between role embracement and role distancing that constantly calls into question the authenticity of the experiences associated with the member role precisely for those members who are the main targets of normative control.

In sum, presentational rituals are occasions for enacting, enforcing, and reinforcing the display of the managerially sanctioned member role and are thus a mechanism for mediating normative demands and normative responses. The mediating function of ritual, however, is not simple. The juxtaposition of "ideology" and "common sense," of subject and agent, of obligation and choice, of seriousness and humor, of affirmation and denial, of engagement and detachment, of being "in" and being "out," of work and play, of participation and withdrawal, creates a complex web of normative pressures. These pose the central dilemma of membership: to what extent is the enactment of the member role and its cognitive and emotional components the expression of a "real self"? To what extent are behavioral displays and presentations of self no more than scripts consciously enacted in response to organizational requirements? More deeply, to what extent do members control the differences between these modes and the different selves implied? And, ultimately, what is a real—or a false—self? These questions, seemingly inherent in normative systems of control, are explored in greater depth in the following chapter.

chapter 5

Self and Organization:
In the Shadow of the Golden Bull

> Has one not noticed that experiences have made themselves inde-
> pendent of man? They have gone onto the stage, into books, into the
> reports of scientific institutions and expeditions, into communities
> based on religious or other conviction, which develop certain kinds of
> experience at the cost of all others as in a social experiment; and in so
> far as experiences are not merely found in work, they are simply in the
> air. Who today can still say that his anger is really his own anger, with
> so many people butting in and knowing so much more about it than
> he does? There has arisen today a world of qualities without a man to
> them, of experiences without anyone to experience them, and it almost
> looks as though under ideal conditions man would no longer experi-
> ence anything at all privately and the comforting weight of personal
> responsibility would dissolve into a system of formulae for potential
> meanings. It is probable that the dissolution of the anthropocentric
> attitude (an attitude that, after so long seeing man as the center of
> the universe, has been dissolving for some centuries now) has finally
> begun to affect the personality itself. . . .
> And all at once, in the midst of these reflections, Ulrich had to
> confess to himself, smiling, that for all of this he was, after all, a
> "character," even without having one.
>
> —Robert Musil
> *The Man Without Qualities*

"**B**uilt right into the social arrangements of an organization," Erving Goffman (1961a: 180) says, "is a thoroughly embracing conception of the member—and not merely a conception of him qua member, but behind this a
conception of him qua human being." If this is true of all forms of organization, it is particularly true at Tech. Here, as we have seen, the managerially
sanctioned and enforced view of employees, which I have referred to as the

"member role," includes explicit, detailed, wide-ranging, and systematically enforced prescriptions for what members in good standing are to think and feel about themselves, their work, and the social arrangements under which it is performed. What forms of experience are shaped in the glare of this ideological spotlight and in the shadows of its darker sides? What meanings do people attribute to their experience as members of an organization with such definite ideas about its members' experience? How, in short, do members construct a sense of self in the face of attempted normative control?[1]

The nature of the relationship between the self—that ineffable source of subjective experience—and the social context within which it arises is, perhaps, the most enduring problem of social theory. If one generalization emerges from the enormous body of work on this issue, it is that self and society stand in a dialectical relationship: how one sees, thinks, and feels about the social world and about one's own place in it is the outcome of a continuing dialogue with the representatives of the social order into which one is born, its various forms of social organization, and the ready-made roles they offer.[2]

What is the outcome of this dialogue? As Goffman (1961a) suggests, a sense of self is formed both by the ways individuals identify with prescribed roles and the ways in which they distance themselves from them. In his words (p. 320), "the individual is best seen as a stance-taking entity, a something that takes up a position somewhere between identification with an organization and opposition to it, and is ready at the slightest pressure to regain its balance by shifting its involvement in either direction."[3] The self, then, is a social product, constituted not only from spontaneous internal responses but from the processes of self-awareness, self-management, and self-display in the context of social interaction. Underlying this definition is a belief in the inherent freedom of individuals to interpret and make meaningful their situation and to create and recreate their sense of self within socially imposed constraints.

In complex societies, self-construction occurs in a variety of social settings. Consequently, individuals may be seen as possessors of "multiple selves," each defined and brought forth for a particular region of social life and the roles it offers.[4] As Everett Hughes (1958) suggests, work life in general and organizational life in particular are central sources of self-definition.[5] In this sense, one might speak of an "organizational self"—the subjective meanings attributed to the self arising out of balancing acceptance and rejection of the organizational ideology and the member role it prescribes.

So defined, however, the organizational self is an elusive subject. At Tech, as elsewhere, self-referent meanings are not easily come by, nor do they lend themselves to straightforward interpretation. Some of the data are by definition inaccessible; the rest are often complex, context-dependent, and purposeful interpretations by members, and, as such, their meanings are rarely as self-evident as they are made to appear. To capture the subjective experience of membership at Tech, it is necessary to cast a wide net: a comprehensive interpretation requires attention not only to ritual events of the sort described in Chapter 4, but also to mundane occasions, routine settings, and private—and sometimes reflective—moments where an individual's sense of self is enacted. To accomplish this, a number of sources of data are used in this chapter: interviews in which members discuss their own experiences; observation-based descriptions of members' behavior; and analysis of self-display through the use of artifacts. It is worth noting that interviews are themselves a form of self-presentation, in this case to an audience of one—namely, the fieldworker.[6]

The focus is on Wage Class 4 members, who are most clearly both objects and purveyors of the organizational ideology and the member role it prescribes. However, to provide a more comprehensive picture, the experience of marginal members—Wage Class 2 employees and temporary workers— with regard to the organizational ideology is also described.[7]

The Full Member

Wage Class 4 employees are considered—and think of themselves as—full members of Tech, and are thus the main targets of the company's ideological formulations. Although distinguished along occupational and hierarchical lines, they all have in common the need to define themselves in the face of articulated and enacted claims against the self that are remarkably similar. The following analysis focuses on their common condition in relation to these claims: differences are highlighted only when they have a direct bearing on the discussion.

Managing the Organizational Self

The main theme of members' descriptions of their experience at Tech is the need to construct and manage an "organizational self"—first, by delineating the boundaries of a self relevant to the organizational context, and, second, by managing the organizational self's cognitive and affective responses to the requirements of the member role. The subjective meanings associated with each of these aspects of the self are analyzed in turn.

Managing Boundaries Work at Tech is experienced as making great demands on time and energy. Members describe heavy workloads, scheduling pressures, competition, and the possibility of working at home, and they perceive these as factors that combine to blur the distinction between work and nonwork. In response, members suggest, it is necessary to put considerable efforts into establishing boundaries to one's involvement in work. These take two forms: boundaries around time dedicated to work, and boundaries around the social relationships that develop in the context of work.

Time boundaries are established by designating segments of time as work-related and allocating them to the organizational self, while others are considered a respite from work. Members carefully distinguish time at work from nonwork time. Many make an effort to adhere to prescribed working hours. Says a marketing manager:

> "My boss puts in eighteen hours a day, and you should hear his wife complain. I do fifty hours a week, and then I have time for my real estate deals. Sometimes I'm tempted to work longer hours, to turn on the terminal at home. I have to remind myself—there is no rush! We just bought a second home. My wife is over in Marketing. There is a lot of free time there. So she manages some of the deals, and in a few years we should be independently wealthy. I still want to be a VP, but there's no rush."

Work time is portrayed as both contaminated and attractive. It is "shit" and "crap," yet engrossing nevertheless. Enacting the boundary between work time and nonwork time is described by a product manager as a daily ritual of purification.

"During the day, I'm 'on' all the time. No time to stop and think. I drive home thirty-five miles a day, slowly, on the right-hand side of the road, and play Mozart on the stereo. It sort of buffers me from the shit here. At home Tech doesn't exist; just turn it off. Look at those junior engineers: they don't know any better; they read journals like *Byte* at home. I don't. And I *never* use my terminal at home. I don't smoke or abuse stuff, I do a lot of sports. I want to retire at the age of forty, but in the meanwhile it's a good place to work if you keep in mind that it is a large company; so you put up with all the shit, all the talk about Tech culture."

Vacations are a longer period of nonwork time. These, too, are equated with purity. Yet, as one manager describes it, the boundary is often hard to maintain.

"I'm going to Club Med for a week. It's tiring, all this head work, all this politics. I need to wash the culture out of my hair. It's almost a physical thing. Here you just sit and talk all day. But even there you meet Tech people. Last year I wound up spending a lot of time talking Tech. We're having a reunion soon."

Members also take breaks in the course of their workday. Breaks vary in length and utilization of space. Short ones may be momentary and personal. One manager describes these as respites from "bullshit" and being an "asshole":

"You have to keep your sanity somehow. You gotta laugh. I go out for lunch, leave this building even for forty-five minutes with someone, talk about basketball. People just walk into your office here. You can't close doors or hide. Finding a few minutes for yourself is a problem. If I eat in the cafeteria, I'm caught up in business. People get caught up in this shit. It's not only the power. Maybe the growth. The times I want to leave are when there are too many things happening that are out of control.

I can't take too much bullshit even though I'm paid to be an asshole."

Lunchtime leisure activities offer more extended communal breaks: daily basketball games, running, "Trivial Pursuit," bridge. Says one engineer:

"Without my daily bridge game I'm a wreck. Look at all those runners. What do you think they're running from?"

More extended breaks may be accomplished by defining "off days." As one manager describes it, this requires a considerable effort.

"The most important thing is keeping a boundary. Prioritize. You can't do everything. That is what I tell my people. My terminal is often shut all day and I don't take any calls. When I want to hide, I go sit in someone else's office. It takes a lot of energy to separate yourself. Discipline. People are after you all the time. Before you know it, your calendar is full. Luckily I don't get too much pressure from home, and the secretary has orders to let my wife through whenever she calls. Most people I know are just-married or divorced. It is incredible how many divorces there are. You can tell by looking at someone's calendar what the state of their marriage is."

Time segmentation may also be accomplished by constructing images of the more distant future and past. Hope and memory offer a fantasy of limits to involvement. One option is to see a future end to one's career at Tech. Many speak hopefully of the day they will leave—a benchmark beyond which the organizational self will cease to exist, thus making way for other forms of experience. Such images of future disassociation often carry overtones of purification. An engineer says:

"You have to take a lot of crap here. It's rough, it's crazy. I want to slow down. It's not worth it, all the Tech crap. I've been considering leaving—maybe to a new discipline altogether: carpentry, plumbing. Take a cut in income—but kiss Tech goodbye. Perhaps when my kids grow up and go to college."

One often-posed alternative for the future is "meaningful work." A group manager, reputed to be highly successful and very involved with his work, nevertheless says:

> "I give myself five more years before I go back to teaching art. That was my major in college before I got caught up in this. It's still my first love, although I don't have too much time for it. But I promised myself that I was going to go back."

Another frequently mentioned alternative is affluent leisure. A thirty-one-year-old product manager, currently on the fast track, has clear plans:

> "I'm planning to retire at the age of forty. I had it all planned when I was still at school. By then I will be independently wealthy. I'll live on my yacht. By then I will have deserved it."

The past, nostalgically remembered, offers another time boundary. The company's early days, for those who can claim to have "been there," are recollected as purer, a time when, unlike the disappointing present, heavy involvement was justified. Says a product manager:

> "In the early days loyalty was real and strong. We had less than 20,000 people. I worked my butt off to make it a success. I believed in the company. It was a moral force. People were behind that. You worked for a company that didn't deliberately lie to customers, you worked to keep commitments. We worked hard. Now that it's big, people are more concerned with their own welfare. With 20 people you can have a company spirit. In '72 we did. My badge number is 13705. There were 10,000 people then. I could call up a vice-president—there were only two or three. I could go around my boss and his boss. Today the open-door policy is not nearly as open as it is alleged to be. I can do it with my boss, maybe, but many others can't. And in '72 *they* would have been going around to speak to us."

In sum, most members find that work, by its nature, is not limited to a time or a place. Consequently, the construction of time boundaries for an organizational self is essential. In the recurring imagery, work is impure and crazy; nonwork is pure and sane. Work is at once seductive and repulsive; nonwork time must be protected. Maintaining a time boundary between the two is considered important and difficult and is thought to require discipline and effort: one has to combat both the company's demands and one's own impulses, not easily distinguishable, to allocate more time to work and to the organizational self that is formed in its context.

Also crucial for the maintenance of a successful organizational self is the active management of social relationships. This is considered necessary because of the frequent overlapping of work and nonwork relationships. As a development manager describes it, this may occur when nonwork relations are pulled into the sphere of work:

> "They needed a lab manager here and asked me if I knew anybody. I recommended a guy I sort of knew socially. It didn't work out. He couldn't operate on his own. He was making rules, you had to go fight and scream to get anything. He turned into a little czar. It just didn't work out. I still saw him socially. I helped him get another job because I felt responsible."

More often, work encounters offer the opportunity for socializing. A project supervisor says:

> "Socially there isn't much going on here, but there are connections. My two best friends work for me. It happens that these are the people you run into."

Consequently, work relationships often become personalized. For some—particularly those farther up in the hierarchy—this serves instrumental goals. Says a senior development manager:

> "Over time you develop a series of personal/professional relationships. It is based on trust and can take years to develop. Without it, nothing can work for you. It requires a lot of work, including socializing."

Similarly, another manager mentions the importance of having Tech "confidants":

> "You need someone you can trust, someone you can do reality
> testing with about what's going on. A lot of people have confi-
> dants: an ex-boss, a friend from somewhere else. Without reality
> testing, you can go crazy."

This potential for overlapping relationships is for many members a cause of considerable tension. Some attempt to separate, at least conceptually, different types of involvement with the same people. Thus, after-hours socializing with work acquaintances is labeled by some as work, as a duty, or as a political necessity that should be kept to a minimum. A development manager says:

> "At Silicon I worked eighty hours a week. That's two weeks in
> one. Then I realized that you can walk away from your job but
> not your family. I decided that my family comes first. I've been
> married for twenty-two years now, and I keep my life *totally*
> separate. Look around and you'll see how unusual that is. We
> do no socializing. Nothing. It's an ironclad rule we have. I go
> to my boss's party every year, but that is work. I only socialize
> when it is political."

Many who do socialize with colleagues take care to distinguish a work relationship with someone from a social relationship with the same person. Thus, a supervisor says of her relationship with an engineer who reports to her:

> "We go out together sometimes. But after work we have a rule
> never to talk about work. Every Thursday after work we drive
> to a ceramics class together. The company sponsors it. They are
> very good at that type of thing. We very consciously don't talk
> work. Once when there was a crisis, I said: 'I'm breaking the
> rule now because I forgot to tell you something, but it will never
> happen again!' "

Conversely, there are limits to the degree to which "personal" issues are allowed to surface when working. Another supervisor says of his engineers:

> "I'm willing to listen to some of their problems. They come with all kinds of stuff. Some supervisors listen, but when it gets too personal I send them to EAP—the Employee Assistance Program—free-lance shrinks the company hires. That's what the company pays them for."

An extreme case of overlap occurs when two members are married or live together.[8] This requires a continued effort at social segmentation that is both public and private. Says one supervisor, married to an engineer who works at the same facility:

> "My husband works here too. We work on separate sides of the building and try not to see each other. I don't want to hear his voice. And I don't want any finger pointing. People might not trust you if they know you have a special relation. Some things you might not hear. I know my boss is sometimes concerned about information flow. I ride home with my husband. But some things I just wouldn't tell him."

On the whole, however, work and nonwork aspects of social ties are experienced as hard to separate, requiring constant definition and redefinition and never fully resolved. Consider the following description of a manager's relationship with his boss:

> "His wife is unhappy. She complains a lot about his work involvement. I had them over one evening. You learn a lot that way. She is a potential ally. I should invite them again. But it is because they are OK. My wife likes them. It would never be only for politics. I would never do that! Social is separate from political—you have to draw the line. Somewhere. . . ."

In sum, members consider the management of social relationships an important complement to the management of time in creating and sustaining well-defined boundaries to an organizational self. It is not so much the success or failure of these efforts but the perceived importance and difficulty of engaging in them that is indicative of subjective experience. Drawing boundaries is experienced as a struggle to limit self-involvement in the face of organizational and internal pressures to merge work and nonwork aspects of life and thus to expand organizational influence over private experience.[9]

Managing Role Responses   Members also construct an organizational self through the active management of thoughts and feelings prescribed by the member role. Such role responses, frequently enacted in the rituals described in Chapter 4, take two forms: role embracement and role distancing.[10]

Role embracement—expressing identification with aspects of the member role—is a widely shared and often-recurring feature of self-reports. Generally referred to as "being a Techie," role embracement is reportedly experienced as a general orientation to the company, a combination of beliefs and feelings glossed by the label "loyalty." A typical explication is offered by an engineering manager.

> "You know, I like Tech. I don't think of leaving. People might say that the culture swallowed me, but there really is a feeling of loyalty I have. We have a lot of that in the culture. We like working for Tech. It is a positive company. You get really involved. I get a real charge when Tech gets a good press. Or when people I knew from this other company were dumping on Tech, I was offended. I didn't like hearing it. They made millions with us! Because of us they got rich! They get all this free knowledge from us and say it with impunity! My husband works for Tech and he feels the same way. We spend time with friends talking about work; we're worse than doctors. I guess you can call me a Techie."

Note in particular the pervasive imagery of incorporation—"swallowing" —that underlies the language used to describe the relationship of self and company. (The habit of preempting criticism by referring to "what people might say" is discussed in the following section.)

Many members also acknowledge the validity and applicability to their own experience of specific aspects of the prescribed member role. An engineering supervisor combines beliefs and feelings in his acceptance of "individual responsibility and ownership"—a fundamental and oft-repeated ideological principle (see Chapter 3):

> "I'm a slow cultural learner. It took me two years to learn mainly that 'it is your own ownership.' You can do anything you want, but you have to push. The idea is that you are a professional and responsible. You gotta *feel* the ownership. Don't sit and wait. You're a grown-up. The onus is placed on you to live up to expectations. Don't bitch about problems; go do something about it. I buy that. You know, I'm trying to get my son into Tech—that should tell you something."

Role embracement is typically associated with Tech as a whole rather than with functional subgroup affiliations. Groups, if anything, are conceived of as stepping stones, temporary arrangements that do not require loyalty or identification. For example, a manager who thinks he is about to lose his job in one of the unfunded staff functions is openly disturbed and worried about his future. He is angry with his boss and his peers, whom he blames for the failure. He sees his commitment to the company, however, as overriding the commitment to the specific group.

> "I'll never leave Tech. I'm a Techie! But I want to leave this group; I came because I wanted to learn and watched it crumble and fall apart. I was insulted; I got upset and stayed home. My boss is crazy; he's nuts! The worst boss I've ever worked for. I have my resume out, and I'm speaking to all my friends. People come and go. Organizations change here. But you'll meet again if you're around for a while." [11]

The meaning of role embracement may be gleaned also from the ways members discuss the experience of others in the company. This allows members to present themselves implicitly, by way of contrast, as possessors of culturally appropriate selves, or at least reveal their adherence to standards to which they—or others—might hold themselves. Hierarchical relations are a frequently observed basis for such contrast. Senior managers present themselves as agents of the company, "the culture," and its demands. They identify themselves through contrast with subordinates whom they wish to change "for the company's good." A senior vice-president says reproachfully of his "direct reports" (who, under different circumstances, might make similar claims about their own subordinates):

> "They come to the staff meetings and want to know what is in it for them, not for the company! That kind of responsibility does not exist. It is a question of maturity. Not everything is always immediately relevant, but what about the company good? They don't have it in their gut! I have to keep pounding away at them; I have to keep painting a vision. I told them I was at the executive staff meeting and I sat in on stuff that didn't concern me. I made a contribution for the company good! That is the mindset we have to create."

Embracing the member role, then, is seen as a developmental matter—a question of "maturity"—but this view of the self also carries connotations of a religious experience: conversion, total commitment to "the larger cause," and self-sacrifice. This is evident in a senior manager's views on his role in motivating people:

> "You know the old anthropological maxim: Get them in a survival mode. Convince them that survival is at stake, that there is a threat to survival, then make them see the light. I'm a missionary. I articulate the vision. Sure, careers can get hurt. It's often more than they bargained for. But they help others in getting the religion. Give them the resources and point them in the right direction. They'll kill themselves."

Middle managers often assume a more pragmatic, macho style. The images of intense involvement and strong motivation are the same, but the explanations are less lofty. A development group manager says of a peer who is "in trouble":

> "She's in the problem employee mode now. You saw the signs. She's an alcoholic. That is the nature of the industry. Constant

change, high pressure, motivation to achieve. It results in burnout. That is the 'old Tech.' Sam has one primary criterion:
success in the marketplace. Nothing else counts, no institution
at Tech is holy. We'll try different things. Sociologists tell us
the price is high. Bullshit! Get people really involved and motivated, and 20 percent burn out. But 80 percent work. And there
are countless start-ups to employ people. I worked at Data Corp,
and it was exactly the same."

Standards for evaluating appropriate embracement of the member role
might be applied to one's peers and managers as well. For example, a lower-
level manager says of her supervisor, with whom she has been feuding:

"He's a loser. He just can't handle the ambiguity. He wants
someone to tell him what to do. He doesn't go out and get it
done. Gets all scared when he doesn't get clear direction. You
know the kind. He was out sick for a few days after one emotional meeting. A wimp. It doesn't work in the Tech culture." [12]

Role embracement, then, means submitting to the company's definition
of one's self. Such submission, however, is typically presented as a form of
voluntary exchange with the company. A number of different attributes of
the company are often cited as facilitating such an exchange. One is the
image of the president, who has come to symbolize the "philosophy" and
everything that is unique about Tech. A positive view of Sam Miller is frequently heard, particularly at middle and lower levels (more senior managers
often tend to be critical; it is a sign of the insider to be close enough to know
"the real story"). For example, a mid-level manager, speaking, as many
do, in the first person plural, acknowledges his belief in the validity of the
ideology, identified with the president. Emotional attachment is presented
as a fair exchange:

"Maybe I've swallowed slogans, the party line, the whole Sam
Miller 'do what's right' thing. But I *do* believe that Tech 'does
what's right.' We don't lay off, even though some people deserve
to be laid off. So you feel loyalty back. Sam Miller believes in

'taking care of your people,' and he gets paid back with loyalty. They've never done wrong by me."

A similar exchange is apparent in an engineering supervisor's description of the impact of a speech by Sam Miller:

> "I trust the man. He means well. There is a lot of honesty at the top and the bottom of the company. I don't know about the middle. But he really means it when he says it's the company's duty to take care of employees and customers. I've never met him, but I've seen the videotapes. He can be very powerful. I got excited when I heard him say: 'It's our moral duty to give the customers what they want.' *Moral* duty!"

Frequently heard from engineers is support for "Sam Miller's philosophy":

> "You can tell he's an engineer. His philosophy is give the workers the tools and they will do the job. He believes that their goal in life is not to rip off the company. That's the way it should be!"

A second factor facilitating the exchange is the perception of the company's positive treatment of its employees (often in comparison with other companies). Thus, an engineer compares Tech's tradition of job security to its competitors' approach:

> "Tech is good because they grow to your weakness; other places, they milk your knowledge dry and then kill you. At Data they pay great, but they fire you as soon as the downturn comes. This company keeps people and retrains them. I just love this company. I would die for it! There is a tradition of job security here: you can have your neck chopped off and it'll grow back again. You take your risks and you're not hurt too bad. Take Henderson's group: they were responsible for Jupiter and now they're back again. 'Fail and you're history' is just hype."

Similarly, an engineer whose project is sinking is nonetheless positive:

> "I don't want to leave Tech. I like the environment. These things happen elsewhere too. I wouldn't want to be at some other place. You know the stories, you've heard them so often. Some old engineers working on obsolete technology in the basement of Corporate. The project was canceled, and the company sent them to school for six months; they went on to become the biggest fans of the company. That's why I basically like it here; I certainly don't want to go into supervision, and I'm keeping the headhunters at bay in the meanwhile. It'll take time to evaluate—maybe a year or two—to see if the product makes money."

Many value the relative security of working for a large and stable corporation. Compared with the high-risk life at start-ups, Tech is seen as a haven of stability. A consulting engineer says:

> "In the start-ups and the small companies, things are much worse. I worked at one where the bank auctioned off the company and the paychecks were held up. In comparison, here the pressure is fairly low. The whole industry is high-pressure. Time is important. You've got to get things out before the competition. But in the small ones it is much more competitive. I tried a start-up for a while. The headhunters got to my head. It was a big mistake! Things were crazy there. I burnt out. Had to see a psychiatrist. I really needed help. I was lucky they took me back. I called my old boss. Except for a few 'I told you so's,' there was no problem."

Members also cite Tech's "corporate culture" in explaining their positive orientation to the company. They contrast its "informal environment" with beliefs about other companies. A manager says of his reasons for joining:

> "I didn't want Chiptech. I have an irrational dislike of them. Suits, pinstripes, the whole corporate clown thing. And because they unfairly and unjustly dominate the market. They just don't

deserve the sales they have. It's not right! It's only because the purchasers are morons. I took a lateral to come here and also lost some pay."

Another manager points to the freedom and opportunity he feels is characteristic of the company:

"When you join the company, people convince you that it is different, that it is a unique place: there is a lot of freedom from higher up; you have to be self-motivated in your work; and there are a lot of opportunities. It's partly true! You *can* be creative; I've seen cases where you can convince people; it *is* more open; they allow people to transfer freely in the company; they spend money on employees; I've done a lot of training. Even the fact that I was offered this position shows that they prefer to develop people. That's why I like it here."

Engineers often portray Tech as "a good environment for engineering," a "country club" or an "engineers' sandbox" where engineers who are supposedly addicted to their work and emotionally attached to their projects can "play." An engineer in Advanced Development explains:

"Tech has the best engineers. I'm an engineer, and I want state-of-the-art technology. At Chiptech they develop what Marketing tells them. I'm happy as long as you keep me away from marketing types. Tech caters to engineers. Its reputation in the industry is a country club for engineers. It's laid-back. Overall there are less fires, less stupid deadlines. They allow people to transfer freely, they put a lot of money into training, they give inexperienced people opportunity. Learning is the most important thing to me. If I gave it up, I'd become comatose. Right now I'm learning chip design. A totally new area for me. Some engineers love houses, others cars; engineers like details, how things work. I like to learn. And the environment here is open enough to let you get involved in anything you like."

Similarly, many engineers acknowledge attachment to Tech's technology, which they view as unique, and through that to the company. Says one:

> "Once you've worked with Tech products in a Tech environment, it's hard to go to anything else. They are just so much better. It's an engineer's dream—if he's into technology."

Finally, some depict Tech's business practices and moral stance as worthy of one's commitment. Tech's way of doing business is often contrasted with the less than honest approaches presumably found elsewhere. One project manager contrasts Tech with "sleazy defense contractors"—the companies that develop products for the Department of Defense:

> "I worked for a while for a company that was built on those contracts. I worked on the ABM radar. It's not so much that I mind what the products end up doing. No. But all the dishonesty—the excessive costs, the stupidity, the unnecessary work—it really got me down. The norm was: hide the basic specs, follow the letter of the law and produce garbage, then get another contract. Disgusting stuff. Like telling reliability engineers to cook figures. At Tech at least we give customers an honest product. They get what they pay for. Most of the time. I feel good about that."

In sum, role embracement is a recurring theme in members' description of their subjective experience. The rhetoric of role embracement is built around the imagery of immersion, incorporation, psychological maturity, and religion. The organizational self is presented as tightly coupled with the company: the "mature" self is bound by ties of belief, strong emotions, and even religious fervor, all of which, members seem to imply, are quite authentic. At the extreme, self-definitions merge (at least temporarily) with the shared definitions of the culture, suggesting the collapse of the boundaries between self and organization.

Unqualified role embracement, however, is felt by many to be undignified. This is evident in the self-conscious quality of the descriptions, and in the emphasis on a fair and, more crucially, on a controlled exchange with the company. Thus, members claim the right to control the extent and the degree to which role demands are embraced. This capacity for role distancing—one that we have seen enacted in the course of organizational rituals— is often made explicit and elaborated with regard to both the cognitive and the emotional dimensions of the member role.

Cognitive distancing—disputing popular ideological formulations—is manifested when one suggests that one is "wise" to what is "really" going on. Being "wise" implies that despite behaviors and expressions indicating identification, one is also fully cognizant of their underlying meaning, and thus free of control: autonomous enough to know what is going on and dignified enough to express that knowledge.

One frequently encountered mode of cognitive distancing is cynicism. This is usually expressed as a debunking assertion, cast as a personal insight, that reality is very different from ideological claims. For example, an engineer questions the meaning of Tech culture:

> "It's like a religion, a philosophy that the company expounds; Sam Miller says, 'Do what's right,' be on the up and up, satisfy the customer, do the right thing by them. He's a weird bird; pushes all this morality stuff. There is a whole Sam Miller subculture. His memos circulate on the technet. It's like a kind of morality thing. You can go into Sam's office if you're not happy about a supervisor. I've heard of someone who has done it. Of course, nothing might get done. In this group, 'do what's right' means 'make your manager visible.' [Laugh.] Aren't all organizations like that?"

A second mode of cognitive distancing is that of detached theoretical observation, often referred to as "Tech watching." Its essence is the ability to interpret Tech reality and view it with scientific detachment; observations are frequently cast in the language of various social scientific disciplines. Tech watching not only expresses a point of view that is distinct from ideology; it also reverses roles: members who are often the subjects of organizational research become knowledgeable students of organizations (and of organizational researchers).[13] A senior manager who has since left the company says:

> " 'Tech culture' is a way to control people, to rationalize a mess,
> to get them to work hard, and feel good about it; it is really an
> ideology. Like all other ideologies it is part truth and part lie."

Similarly, a personnel manager, just promoted and viewing his success as
related to his "understanding of Tech," explains his perspective:

> "Look at the 'Engineering Guide,' look at the values in it. It is a
> uniquely American value system, grounded in, almost straight
> out of, the Puritan tradition, out of Emerson, Thoreau. You
> know, the Protestant Ethic, Weber, and all that. Now this will
> *really* interest you: Sam really wants a 'Christian company' with
> 'Christian values'! When I heard him say that at the forum, I
> turned around to look at some of the Jewish managers. Won-
> dered what they were thinking. You'll find this an interesting
> place, but you really need a few years to begin to understand it
> all. I've been here seven years now."

Tech watching often takes the form of cultural commentary. Says an engineer, possessor of an undergraduate degree in sociology and a fan of Erving
Goffman:

> "The company may appear informal, loose. Open offices, first
> names. But there is a *very* distinct status system here. People
> always ask who you work with. They won't ask you your title or
> your rank, or look at the size of your office. Once they have you
> placed, they will treat you accordingly."

Most Tech watchers, however, are more familiar with the style of analysis propagated by management theory and the popular business press. A
development manager says:

> "I have a mixed reaction to layoffs. Sam Miller says things
> like 'moral obligation' to employees, but it isn't consistent with
> American culture. American culture is individualistic. No lay-
> offs are suited to the Japanese. It's consistent with their culture:

paternalism, traditions. It's a long time coming getting rid of poor performers. The question is: is it worth betting the company? He feels it is big enough to absorb the slack. He feels he has responsibility; I respect him for that. But I respectfully disagree. Making a profit and carrying the deadwood don't go together."

Similarly, a manager says of a consultants' report on the problems in a well-known project:

"There was nothing surprising about the report for anyone who has been here for ten years. Every book will tell you the same thing—*Soul of a New Machine* or *Mythical Man-month*: you have to be careful not to mix cultures, not to have just one technical guru. So we proved them right again—there is nothing specific to Tech about all that."

A third mode of cognitive distancing is the reference to "common sense," presented as a body of practical knowledge that describes the social attributes of Tech, yet is not part of the formally prescribed ideology. In some cases the difference between ideology and common sense seems more stylistic than substantive. A group manager distances himself from "the culture stuff" and contrasts it with independently gained pragmatic knowledge:

"They are making more out of this culture stuff than it's worth. You have to laugh. It's an instance of self-consciousness. 'Look at us enjoying ourselves, being good guys.' I never read that stuff, maybe see it in passing. It's the same nauseating stuff they print in *Business Week*. They have this intro course for new employees. They talk about culture, but I will never send anyone to it. It leads to circular thinking. It's a waste of time. You have to know how this place really works, how decisions get made at Tech. You pick it up as you go along. I tell my people how to get things done. We know that we want consensus, that power plays lose. I don't know what it's like at the top, how the big guys fight, or what they do. But the people who work for me, I brief them: 'Be tactful, don't beat 'em up, don't piss 'em off.'

> I train them explicitly and show them how. I'm a development engineer. I don't buy all that theology. If it works it's good; if it makes money it's good. Everything else—everything!—is bullshit."

In other cases the substance of commonsense knowledge differs from ideology. A project leader, challenging the ideological claims concerning Tech's uniqueness, describes what "everyone knows":

> "I don't buy all that 'we are unique' song and dance. There is nothing unique about Tech. Constant reorganization is a way of life in this industry. Everyone knows that—unless their head is up their butt. That's the way it is, particularly in this kind of changing technology. Every company is like that; at Data Systems I had eight bosses. Nothing is unique here, except, perhaps, for Sam Miller's influence; like everyone else we're good at product development, bad at marketing. I've been around, and I can tell you that all companies like to feel that they have a culture, that they are a community. It makes them feel different: kinda special, unique. At Data Systems people sat around crying into their beer that they didn't have a corporate culture. It's an intangible force. It helps identification, gives a sense of belonging, and extracts a little extra loyalty."

The three modes of cognitive distancing differ (no doubt influenced in part by the speaker's perception of the interviewer), but all demonstrate the felt ability and freedom to reflect on the validity of ideological reality claims and to offer alternative formulations. This is manifested in the rich terminology used to refer to the managerial point of view: "religion," "philosophy," "song and dance," "ideology," "theology," and "bullshit."

It is not just in the domain of ideologically prescribed beliefs that members claim the right to some autonomy. Distancing also occurs with respect to the feelings prescribed by the member role or associated with the organizational self. Three types of such emotional distancing are apparent in members' discourse: denial, depersonalization, and dramatization. Denial is accomplished by presenting one's motives for membership as purely instrumental. The relationship with the company is construed as contractual and economically driven, and its emotional aspects denied. For an engineer, this means not only avoiding the "people and the politics," where "emotions" are likely to be found—a typical response—but also a denial that one "loves one's work." An engineer says:

> "I wanted the security of working for a big company—no excitement and less pay. I don't identify with any organization. Those things are circles within circles; they come and go, but the job remains. I get green dollars, I do my best, I know my worth. I work flexible hours but *never* more than eight. Technology is *not* my hobby. I have no terminal at home, and I keep my social life separate. I'm a private person. I don't go to the workshops or to the meetings. That's for those who want to make an impression, those who want to get ahead. They can have it. None of the 'addicted to your work,' 'ego-involvement' bullshit. I do my job. All the weird political aspects of the project don't bother me. They fight all the time. They are defensive and paranoid. There is an 'ain't it awful' attitude. Finger pointing. Accusing each other of screwing up. But I stay away from all of that emotional stuff."

Managers, too, may engage in emotional denial. Says a group manager, considered a hard worker:

> "Loyalty—they make a big deal about that—is old school. What is important is work. Some people feel a sense of belonging, but in my case it's not strong. It's a nice company, but it isn't my mother. I'm not a joiner; I never liked organizations or clubs. I just don't feel that way about organizations, even though I bust my ass here. Others get some satisfaction in belonging. 'Techies'! [Laughs.] At social gatherings they will talk about Tech, say: 'We do it this way, we do it better.' Some of them don't even work at Tech any more. Some started fifteen years ago, felt part of what was happening. But it isn't the same any more. Some moved on. Tech is just a thing. I find it amusing when I hear all that talk."

In both cases, denial of emotional involvement in work is contrasted both with recognized ideological role demands and with a caricatured depiction of those who accept them.

The second mode of emotional distancing is depersonalization. Here, the emotions experienced as part of the organizational self are presented as distinct from other aspects of emotional life and at some remove from one's "authentic" sense of self. Specific codes for such emotions are widely used in everyday discourse. The word "emotion" often refers to a recognized part of work-related interaction, a form of experience that is used to explain behavior but is isolated from other facets of one's emotional life. "Pain"— sometimes accompanied by a tap on the stomach to illustrate its location— refers to negative "emotions" of this sort. One manager describes a stormy staff meeting:

> "It was an emotional meeting. We went through a lot of pain. But we did reorganize. Bill lost quite a bit of his project work, and Jim is going into a career-examination mode—he took the heat for the slips. But everybody took it professionally—you can't let those things get to you. Go home and forget about it till tomorrow."

Similarly, a senior finance manager makes use of the terminology of emotions when speaking of his role with regard to his boss.

> "My job is to read and interpret the numbers. I keep track of them all, and then I whisper in his ear when to get angry. People start getting midnight calls. We put the fear of God in them. It spreads the pain through the system. Nail a few people to the wall and drive a spike through their heart!"

Terms for positive emotions also exist, as this comment by a manager illustrates:

> "I'm very excited about the second-quarter figures! When they see the profit numbers and read the reports coming in on this project, management will get the warm fuzzies."

Successful depersonalization is seen as requiring a constant effort, captured by the recurring images of "ignoring crap" and "developing a thick skin." Says a development manager, temporarily on a staff assignment after his project was "unfunded":

> "I've learned here that you can do your own job, but you have to let the waves flow over you; ignore them or you'll go crazy. There is a lot of shit coming down, people wandering around, consultants, studies; that's the way it is, but it isn't a bad place. On a scale of ten it's maybe a six or a seven; but they really stuff ten pounds of shit into five-pound bags. I have a Russian immigrant friend who says it reminds him of the USSR; all this shit about Big Brother."

In a similar fashion, a product manager, considered by many to be highly successful, explains his success:

> "In this job we are self-motivated, internally driven. But you have to have a thick skin to survive. You must depersonalize; it's a rough environment. Take all this stuff professionally, not personally."

And a marketing manager says of himself:

> "Sometimes it's like here is Jim doing all this getting involved, getting excited, jumping up and down, yelling and screaming; and here is Jim watching. I have to keep reminding myself it's a game. I should watch it and enjoy it."

Depersonalization, then, requires that one control and even suppress personal and spontaneous reactions to the work environment, thus purging them from the organizational self and leaving only appropriate "emotions." Failure to do this is noticed in others. A group manager says of a peer:

> "Rick gets too emotional; he takes it too personally. He's a good manager, but he gets carried away with his stuff. It's not bad, but sometimes I think he overdoes it, loses control. It's not

professional, and it can harm you. Personally, and also career damage. Someone should tell him."

In the third mode of emotional distancing, dramatization, emotional expression is viewed as strategically driven: it is contrived and calculated in order to accomplish goals, and the authenticity of performances is therefore regarded with suspicion. In a typical statement, a development manager describes his view of members' underlying motivations:

> "Techies. We're all Techies. The whole goddamn industry. It's a type of individual who is aggressive and involved, looks loyal, puts in a lot of time, but underneath the surface is self-serving and owes allegiance only to himself. They are mobile and choose the projects as they see fit."

More specifically, a supervisor refers to the ability to manage and interpret the display of emotions as "people skills":

> "I'm developing a thick hide. Before I take anyone's advice, or react to yelling and screaming, I think about what their agenda is. The people skills are important here; I learned that the hard way. I'm suspicious. All of a sudden my boss is being a good guy, being nice. He's learning to put on that act. That means I have to be even more careful now."

Similarly, a manager of one of the staff functions suggests that emotional expression is a game that many recognize:

> "We went to this off-site meeting. A consultant led a session on 'how we feel toward each other.' People were talking. But it's not real. It's just an opportunity to see how you handle yourself in that kind of session. The only one who believed all that California bathtub crap was the consultant. I'd believe it too for fifteen hundred bucks a day."

Members often describe their own displays in a strategic light. For example, a supervisor reveals her approach to a discussion with her boss in which they reviewed her performance and decided on her future responsibilities:

> "Before I had a one-on-one with my boss, I read some advice in *Things They Never Taught Me at the Harvard Business School*. Good stuff. It says: 'Never show them that you're feeling anything; keep a straight face; confuse them.' It's exactly what I did. Worked, too."

An engineer says of his campaign for a promotion to senior consulting engineer:

> "I didn't get the promotion. Maybe my boss didn't support me enough, or maybe someone on the promotion committee was playing some game. So I'm in a career-evaluation mode now. I'm angry. I haven't signed on to any new projects. I'm too depressed and angry. The EAP therapist type—I met her at a workshop on stress—says I'm too dependent on external approval and should change jobs. I'll show them dependency."

And a development manager says of his plans to generate support for one of his projects:

> "I'm gonna go into that meeting and put on my dumb-engineer act. Ask them for help with the people issues, the politics, ask for advice. [Opens eyes wide, parodying the performance.] 'Gee, I dunno. . . .' And be very grateful. 'Thanks guys!' By the time I'm through, they'll recommend I do what I've already done. And with Sam—well, he is very manipulative, but I've learned the most effective way to deal with him. I'm totally naive. I say: 'I don't understand, Sam. Didn't you say that. . . . I thought that. . . . Explain it to me, Sam.' It disarms him. And he isn't used to it. Everybody is so afraid of him! And in the meanwhile I'm positioning Paulson to be the proponent for the X-101 strategy. I slap him on the back on every opportunity, tell him how great he's doing, how excited we all are with what he is doing—and I'm distancing my organization from the project.

So when it blows up, you know damn well who Sam is going to turn on!"

Inability to dramatize, and the ensuing perception of loss of control, is viewed as a serious problem, worthy of managerial attention. A development manager says of one of his project leaders:

"Jim has a people problem. He is gruff with people and says exactly what is on his mind. He gets angry in meetings. I want him to control himself. Next year he is going to be evaluated on that. I'm watching him. He knows it."

And a project manager says of a supervisor:

"He's a good manager, but a complainer. He's too negative about the company and constantly complains about too many levels of management, fucked-up decision making, and all that. It's a bad attitude."

In sum, cognitive and emotional distancing reflect the felt necessity of maintaining a controllable distance from the beliefs and feelings prescribed by the member role and displayed as part of the organizational self. A ludic metaphor underlies members' attempts to convey this experience: the construction of an organizational self is seen as drama or as a game. Notions of performing, playing a game, watching oneself, strategically designing roles, and, ultimately, assuming a calculative stance toward the management of one's own thoughts and feelings are deeply ingrained in experience and explicitly articulated by members.

Speaking of the Self The organizational self is that part of the sense of self that individuals associate with membership in the organization. The organizational self is commonly experienced as an arena for two types of self-definitional struggles. First, members attempt to delineate and control the boundaries of an organizational self in the face of experienced organizational pressures, as well as one's own impulses, to expand self-involvement; and, second, members seek to control both cognitive and affective responses within the bounded organizational self. Thus, embracement of the member role is presented as a limited reality; it is balanced by cognitive and affective distancing, which represent members' attempts to assert control over beliefs and feelings perceived as threatened with outside control. Distancing then, is a declaration of autonomy, an emphasis on free choice and open exchange, a hint that the self behind the role is not coterminous with the role, despite the claims of others—and, perhaps, one's own suspicions—that it is. The successful organizational self, then, is seen as capable of strategically controlling these contradictory elements by managing a shifting balance of role embracement and role distancing. How this is accomplished in everyday life is the topic of the following section.

Successful Selves: Controlled Displays

The organizational self is routinely displayed to other members of the organization. Two main types of self-display are evident: behavioral displays that occur in the course of work-related social interaction, and artifactual displays that are part of the workspace.

Behavioral Displays   Work, for many, consists of a series of encounters with others, and every interaction contains, explicitly or implicitly, a view of the self that one wishes others to accept. We considered in the previous chapter large-scale, managed, formal, and festive encounters that occur as part of organizational rituals, and their implications for the self. In these events, as we have seen, the balance of role embracement and role distancing is structured and prescribed; consequently, members may discount the significance of self-displays, whether of role distancing or of role embracement, by attributing their own (and others') behavior to the rules of the situation. It is in informal interactions between peers, acquaintances, and those most directly related to one's work—situations experienced as more spontaneous and less rule-bound—that the active construction of an organizational self is more suggestive. Such chance encounters in the course of the workday—in the office and in the lab, during lunch, in the corridors, even over the technet—provide a stage for momentary, seemingly insignificant, yet continuous instances of self-presentation.

Role embracement is perhaps the most frequently observed response in the casual interactions between acquaintances. It finds its expression—seemingly automatic and natural—in the skillful use of company shorthand, terminology, clichés, and slogans conveying conventional wisdom in reference to one's own activities, in settings that appear to exert no pressure to conform: informal gatherings where the language flow is considered natural and many non-Tech topics are discussed. A group of engineers gathered around a cafeteria table for an informal lunch are representative. After some small talk about the Celtics' run on the basketball championship, one of them, in response to a question, begins to talk about his latest project:

> "I need to get people to agree. The general philosophy has agreed that it is the right thing to do, but a philosophical buy-in is different from an implementation buy-in. I'll put together a straw dog proposal and send it to most development managers and consulting engineers in Lyndsville. Let them push back. Then we'll go off and make it happen."

After some questions, someone asks if Larry Bird—the Celtics' star—is going to "make it happen." The discussion flows almost imperceptibly back to the NBA playoffs.

Many such displays are accompanied by self-conscious commentary that allows the protagonists to create a sense of ambiguity around the significance of the displays and their implications for the self. For example, one manager, recognizing my lunch partner at a popular restaurant just outside Corporate, walks in and sidles over to our table. Standing beside us, his eyes also tracking new arrivals and others walking by on the sidewalk outside, he exchanges greetings:

> "How are you?"
> "Super! Super!"
> "Haven't seen you since—when was it?"
> "Last year at the management forum."
> "Yeah. I'm over with Poseidon now."
> "Super! Super!"
> "It's really neat. They're going to wheel it into Sam's office pretty soon. He's gonna see the performance numbers and love it."
> "Super! I hear it's tough getting anything through Corporate these days."

The conversational moves continue as they discuss the specifications of the project in the same tone of clipped excitement. When the manager leaves, my partner turns to me and says: "He's vicious! He'll eat you alive! But I heard that he's still a fifty-fifty. Not clear if he's a win or a lose."

Chance encounters between closer acquaintances or confidants often elicit more elaborate displays of role distancing. A member of a staff organization walks by a peer's cubicle. He stops and looks in. The inhabitant turns from her computer screen, an invitation to enter. Her eyes are red, the ashtray is full: signs of hard work. He enters and sits on the table, and the following exchange ensues:

> "Howya doin'?"
> "Surviving . . ."
> "That's the name of the game. [Both laugh.] Just let the shit wash over you. [He runs his hand over his body.]"
> "Hug me."
> [He offers hand; she gets up and hugs him.] "Don't forget its a game—all a game."
> "I'm going on a vacation. Gotta get outta here for a while. Can't take much more crap."

They briefly discuss vacation plans. The tone changes when he asks a work-related question.

> "You workin' for X-101?"
> "I offered my services, but . . ."
> "Did you finally get funded?"
> "It's hard to know."
> "It's crazy, you know, they want us to cut headcount and not lay off anyone."
> "How is X-101?"
> "They're committed to crazy schedules. But they have no real commitment. It's a myth. I've shipped enough products in the company. They'll never do it. [Pause.] But guess what: I'm a grandfather! Yup, a girl. One week old."
> "That's wonderful."

He gets up, winks, and leaves. She turns back to her screen and lights another cigarette.

Communication over the technet also offers an opportunity for self-display and an ambiguous combination of role embracement and role distancing. Here, too, the theme is strategic self-management. A development manager sent the following message to a product manager responsible for one of the products being developed in his group. The product manager had sent out a memo complaining that group members were not cooperating in the meetings he had called. The memo was regarded by some as a "flame-o-gram," an incendiary and inappropriate communication. The response emphasizes "diplomacy" as the appropriate mode of self-presentation.

> To: Frank
> From: Bob G.
> I'm frankly unhappy with this memo. You obviously are more concerned with covering your own ass than being a part of the team. It was not necessary to laboriously reveal your personal feelings on this. This certainly does not promote feelings of trust with the people you need to work with. I will not show it to anyone else on the design team since I believe its content would doom your effort to work with them. Dealing with the meetings was my problem to work. Please try in the future to deal in diplomacy rather than negativism and defensiveness. Come and talk to me if you so desire.

The ability to engage in controlled displays and manage ambiguity is recognized in others. Speaking of a newly arrived manager from across the ocean, a manager refers to expressions of role embracement as an acquired language skill:

> "This guy is a Brit, but he speaks the culture. With a *British* accent. He started talking and I recognized "Corporate" immediately. People recognize it. He said to me: 'I speak Tech culture.' He knows all the catch phrases, all the idioms."

A particular behavioral style associated with the use of such language routines is recognized as appropriate, as being a "Techie":

"We're Techies. We network, we break the rules, we are less formal. I went to this conference, and most of us were out of the lecture room, in the halls. We 'do what's right,' we speak of 'dying' and 'killing,' 'winning' and 'losing.' We're all aggressive. The first rule is 'Notice me!' You 'put up the flag,' call attention to yourself."

These brief examples, drawn from the ebb and flow of everyday interaction, illustrate what is considered a crucial theme in the appropriate construction and presentation of an organizational self: controlling an ambiguous balance of role embracement and role distancing by engaging in diplomacy, talking the culture, doing it seriously, remembering that it is a game. In short, it is very serious acting. A similar balance was observed in the organizational rituals described in Chapter 4. Here, however, there are no formally prescribed modes of acting; rather, members appear to have internalized the rules of self-presentation and draw on their own resources to construct and display an ambiguous organizational self that will further their purposes.

Artifactual Displays A second stage for self-display is the office. Tech's "open office" approach to space is designed to maximize communication, exposure, and face-to-face work, while minimizing status differences. Offices are small and simple, with little in the way of concrete boundaries, and with no elaborate furniture or decorations (see Chapter 2). How members transform this standardized, impersonal space into their own territory reveals aspects of the self that they wish to convey to themselves and to others.

Offices typically have a number of "regions" of self-display: the ways in which boundaries are constructed; the work-related artifacts that indicate the occupant's work activities; a personal region, where nonwork aspects of the self are displayed; and, finally, statements about the company, conveying the occupant's views, ideas, and feelings with regard to the organizational ideology.

Boundaries are to a large extent symbolically constructed from available materials. (The descriptions given in this section are excerpts from fieldnotes.)

Many offices have bookshelves placed against the entrance to narrow it. More extremely, one office has an entrance maze constructed out of a number of bookshelves and filing cabinets that force a circuitous route on the visitor. A large picture of a threatening Rambo conveys the message on another. One manager, away on a two-day vacation, sealed his office with a strip of tape across the entrance.

Members often respect symbols of privacy. It is customary, for example, to indicate one's presence at the nonexistent door by saying "knock knock." Similarly, members pretend to ignore easily overheard private conversations. Nevertheless, office conversations often occur with an unspoken awareness of an audience. A manager was telling me a project-related story he thought was "sensitive." Suddenly he smiled and mimed pulling the pin out of an imaginary hand grenade and tossing it over the partition, indicating the designed impact of his words on his neighbor. "Real privacy," if needed, is found away from the office.

Artifacts in the work region combine to convey the impression of intense effort. For engineers, these include extra equipment, piles of tapes, and computer output. Managerial offices are often stacked high with paper: reprints, the trade press, and proposals. The blackboards are covered with the visible output of thought processes: diagrams, calculations, and formulas. Desktop computer terminals are typically on all day, and they provide a constant background noise of high-tech work: quiet humming, spurts of keyboard squeaks interspersed with beeps of arriving and departing electronic mail, and the unpredictable bursts of the guttural, driving sounds of printers.

The personal region contains aspects of life beyond work. It is a downplayed reminder, a hook to the other, non-Tech world out there, a manifestation of the distinction between the two worlds and the boundary between them.

> Over the desk are pictures. Mike has the standard loved ones arrangement: pictures of wife, wife with kids, Dad with kids. Fireplace. Idyllic. Hobbies are also depicted: water skiing, mountain climbing. Self against the elements. Bob, in the adjacent office, isn't married and has a picture of a haloed Jesus

and some inspirational words semi-hidden over his desk in the same place, along with a copy of *Do Black Patent Leather Shoes Really Reflect Up?* Hip high-tech Catholicism.

The boundary, however, is not always clear. For some, organizational attachments have invaded this region too, and the balance between the organizational and the personal is swayed:

> Mary is unmarried. Over the desk, where others keep family, there is a glossy picture of her at a trade show with colleagues. A row of ribbons and name tags from various such events is pinned to the wall next to it. Above it is an "I LOVE TECH" bumpersticker. On a shelf there is a golf section with a few trophies. "Most Improved Golfer" from *Golfer's Digest*, and a Tech trophy. Next to it a color print of a sailing boat with a large Tech logo on the billowing sail. An orderly row of beer bottles, and mugs with a Tech logo, all with their handles facing left.

The ideological display region contains statements that reflect the stance of the occupant toward the surrounding reality. Statements of role embracement are constructed with available company and industry materials: newspaper clippings, company advertising, and the myriad artifacts through which the company identity is—intentionally or not—stamped on physical forms:

> Steve is a product manager. The decoration is almost entirely company-oriented. On the wall are Tech posters. One proclaims in large letters: "Help overcome competition." Another, fairly popular, depicts Tech as a truck about to run over a bicycle rider representing the competition. A third provides a family tree for all Tech products. Outside the entrance are clippings from the press with disparaging comments about the competition yellowed in. The space is very orderly. Piles of trade journals as well as copies of *Business Week* and *Fortune* are on the table, and a few xeroxed copies of a *Harvard Business Review* article. The bookshelf has a few Tech technical publications, the "Engineering Guide" and *In Search of Excellence*.

Displays of role distancing seem to become more common at lower levels and at greater distances from Corporate. In the vicinity of a vice-president's office, for example, only formal company material is displayed. Engineering facilities, on the other hand, feature an abundance of this type of corporate art. Humor plays a central role in such displays—a defused and legitimate expression of dissent. Many expressions are standard and ready-made: comic strips bemoaning the stupidity of organizations, clever sayings posted on walls, ironic takeoffs on slogans ("There is unlimited opportunity at Tech— for inflicting and receiving pain"; "I'd rather be dead than excellent"). More elaborate expressions are also available. At one facility, the "management model" was constructed anonymously and incrementally:

> On a filing cabinet just outside the entrance to the office some- one has placed the "management model." It is a plastic toy in which little penguins appear to be climbing up a mountain. It could be activated by pouring water onto the penguin track, which would make the little penguins move slowly up the moun- tain and then slide down in an endless circle. Above it a large sign says: "Management model. Makes a lot of noise, climbs Heartbreak Hill, and gets absolutely nowhere." To that someone has added: "I know. But don't you just love to watch?" There is space for more comments.

Less humorous and more critical materials are more likely to be found around engineers' offices. Willing to be labeled a dissenter, one engineer posted company materials with commentary attached at the entrance to his cubicle:

> Prominently posted in front of the office is a personalized form letter from a senior vice-president thanking the recipient for contributing to the success of a sales event. The recipient, an engineer, adds in a scrawl: "What kind of nerds run this com- pany? I was only there for a few hours. No wonder Tech stock is down!" Posted next to it is a copy of a recent Engineering newsletter. On the front page is a lead article by a VP calling for excellence. It has been circled and a yellow note attached: "Tech's answer to Chiptech's Journal of R&D."

This is a safe and often ambiguous outlet, one that may be interpreted also as a form of role embracement: the angry author is hoping for a better Tech, finding senior people to blame, and announcing it loudly. Criticism of this sort—often just as platitudinous as ideological formulations—is always present. The displayer must strike the exact right tone or risk being labeled "negative" or "burnt out" (unless, of course, one desires the label). It should not be overly public, and should have "constructive intent."

A repeated theme is the relationship of the individual to the company. The catchy insights that decorate office spaces reflect the image of the organizational self that their residents wish to convey. Such statements combine role embracement and role distancing. For many, the image is that of a strong individual surviving in a hard, competitive, often irrational world: it is at once the manifestation of the entrepreneurial spirit prescribed by the member role and a criticism of the company and its way of life. One young and promising ex-engineer who has chosen the managerial route put more effort into this image than most:

> His office is in the corner, behind an enclosed secretarial space. It is dominated by a large chart with colored markers depicting his projects and their stage of development, and a board for calculations. Over the desk is a page borrowed from an advertisement in the *New York Times Magazine*: simple, elegant white letters against a black background: "The race goes to the swift." It is not one of the ready-made ones that decorate many similar offices. Next to it a clipping from the *New Yorker*: A manager holding a "smoking" club saying to an employee, on the ground, just clubbed: "That should take care of any more ideas from the right side of the brain." On the left, a card depicting a lonely fisherman on a small, icy island, fishing. All around are sharks: a graphic portrayal of the frequently heard metaphor for life at Tech. Next to it is a card with one word: "WINNER," and another with a sketch of one violinist playing in front of a row of flailing, uncoordinated conductors.

In a nearby cubicle, a less imaginative peer conveys a similar, if less classy, message, typical of many offices:

Facing the entrance is a large poster with a mean-looking alley cat staring out over the caption "No More Mr. Nice Guy." Next to it is a framed reminder: "When running with the herd never fall down; getting up can be a bitch."

Ambivalence—a central theme—is carefully displayed. Ed, a development manager just awarded the "golden bull" trophy, has moved with his project team to a new location. They are now clustered in about ten cubicles in the new office space, having taken with them what they consider essential:

> On a message board hanging next to the entrance to Ed's office are two xeroxed pages. On the left is a computer printout with a status report on the project he is managing. Certain lines are yellowed in, indicating pride in the technical achievements: "new high levels of speed performance—metrics on performance." On the right side, next to it, is a Pogo strip. This one is worn and was one of the few decorations to move with him when he moved into a new space. In it Pogo says: "They say if you is patient and tolerant, you gits covered with glory." In the next frame he is deep in a hole, digging. Another character is pouring garbage over him. "My sakes, what are you doing in the garbage hole, Pogo?" he is asked. The response, and the punchline: "I'm gittin' covered with glory!" In the cubicle next to his, Bill, the project leader, has competitor equipment wired up, connected to cables from the ceiling. The equipment is in various stages of dismantling. Against one partition he has arranged about 500 empty cans of Coke in a pile, left over from many long nights. In the other corner, on the table, is the "golden bull," garish, funny, sticking high into the space over the cubicles, visible from anywhere in the building.

Thus, the office space contains numerous clues to the inhabitants' stance toward the organization. These artistic depictions of the self are a collage constructed of a variety of materials; together, they may be seen as carefully composed renditions of successful organizational selves. By juxtaposing the contradictory elements of experience, they reflect—indeed, they flaunt—a profound ambivalence and a carefully constructed ability to manage it.

Displaying the Successful Self Routine display of the successful organizational self is a complex accomplishment. Dramatic and artifactual displays differ in a number of respects. Behavioral displays are designed for
a specific audience and setting. They are time-bound: once accomplished,
they exist only in memory and gossip, and the performer is free to move on
to other performances. Artifactual displays, on the other hand, are less public; they are frozen in time, a standing exhibit, so to speak, in one's private
space for guests and passers-by. If in drama one can choose aspects of the
self for particular display, art encompasses the entire statement.

Taken together, these displays illustrate how the main elements of the
organizational self are routinely assembled. Both suggest that self-construction is difficult and requires constant efforts: successful organizational selves
are founded on control of the balance of role embracement and role distancing and the ability to maintain and display an air of ambiguity that allows
multiple, occasionally contradictory, interpretations of one's stance.

The centrality and importance of self-control in the construction of a successful organizational self is underscored and further explicated in members'
views of what can go wrong.

Failing Selves: Burning Out

Members are acutely aware that the successful self is in constant danger
of failure, or "burnout"—a widely recognized, frequently discussed, and
often-applied label for specific experiences considered an integral part of life
at Tech.[14] Members typically consider burnout a serious condition. Stories of
alcoholism, divorce, psychiatric breakdown, and even suicide are told publicly and openly: they are consistent with images of exciting and dynamic
high-tech organizational life. More routine cases of burnout, often referred
to as "not being able to handle it," are considered a private experience. An
engineer who regards himself as a veteran offers a typical definition:

> Burnout is when you can't handle it any more. It's so intense,
> and you need a vacation; emotionally you just can't handle it.
> You need private time. It's easy to burn out. It's happened to me
> a number of times. I just couldn't handle things any more. So
> you learn to manage yourself—when to quit, when to go home.

One symptom of burnout, most members agree, is the public loss of self-control. Says one manager:

> My girl friend is a technical person working for Tech. She got burnt out. I mean really burnt out. You know, fighting, screaming four-letter words, the whole route. Well, she had a nervous breakdown. She is emotional about work as it is. She started shaking in the morning, couldn't face going in, got hives. I did too.

And an engineer says:

> "I was burnt out. Doing twelve-hour days. I couldn't sleep or listen to anyone. I only managed 50 percent of the work. You know the signs. I didn't care. I got tired. One day I just stopped, broke down, and called the EAP guy. He told me what to do, what to say. They have a lot of experience with it. He coached me: 'Get up, go have a glass of water, go home, don't talk to anyone on the way out.' Then people said: 'Dan is burnt out,' and started avoiding me. So I took a job here. It's more relaxed and I don't work so hard. I watch it, though. In business it's tough, it's a jungle. Don't make friends, don't trust anyone. Just let your boss know that your work is your work."

Burnout is generally thought to result from a loss of the required capacity of self-management: maintaining boundaries and managing role distance. In the members' view, this may occur for a number of reasons. The first of these is managerial pressure to perform. Says an engineering manager:

> "I'm burning out. Burnt out. I've got a wife and three kids who want attention. Some nights I'm up all night working problems, as long as the mind works. Even when I'm asleep, I dream about work. My terminal at home broke. I'm thinking I shouldn't fix it! They say that some supervisors watch who is logged on to their home terminal at night."

Similarly, a product manager describes a burnout episode in his past:

> "I worked all weekends and on New Year's Day. I gave 150 percent. You get recognition for it—especially technical people like us. Being a Techie took over my life. There is more work than you can handle and a hiring freeze. My boss put it in print. He said: 'If you work nine to five you get an average job review.' "

Peer pressure may be a second cause of burnout. The Tech environment is perceived as highly competitive, hard, merciless, and dangerous. Evaluations are quick. Everyone is said to have a "press," a reputation based on past performances that determines his or her current credibility. It is easy to become a "loser," as one manager explains:

> "Reputation in this company is based on the last performance. They are out to get you, sharpening the knives. You are a violinist, and if the string breaks, that is it; you've had it. You are as good as lost. Burnt out. This is like primordial soup. The intensity in Engineering can't be compared to other functions. It is so much greater. Over there, I never lost any sleep. Here there are people nipping at your heels, holding a gun against your head."

Under such conditions, life is a struggle, and failure can lead to burnout. An engineer gives his impressions of a group he has just joined:

> "I was warned that they would eat me alive before I came here, that they would burn me out. This is a rough place. A lot of head butting. It took me a while, a few problems and some beers after work, to learn my work."

Association with a failed project, as one engineer suggests, can be the kiss of death:

> "I survived Neptune. It was a circus. Living hell. A bunch of them burnt out. Some left the company. I took this job for a while to relax."

Moreover, a person's burnout may be intentionally caused by others. "Setting up"—deliberately causing someone to fail—is a well-known and often-
used tactic in the political battles between peers. A manager warns his staff
about a senior manager in another group:

> "He will not be highly successful. We will help him but keep our
> distance. If he goes down, he might drag us down too. He has
> no credibility. A lot of unspoken stuff around him. The strategy
> is to make him such a bastard that everything goes around him.
> Either he burns out or he leaves. So if he calls you, don't do
> *anything* until you've checked with me!"

Burnout is also linked to members' internal drive. Says a project leader:

> "You get carried away by the complexity of the problems. There
> is so much stuff it boggles your mind. I know two cases who are
> going to burn out. I say: Slow down, take some time; you have
> to decide. They want to develop the perfect design. Sooner or
> later it will take all you've got to be good, to be a genius. Did
> you read *The Soul of a New Machine*? When a project is over,
> they have a tremendous need to dedicate themselves to some-
> thing. You have no other identity. 'I'm an engineer' versus 'I'm
> Joe.' They are intense people."

"Addiction to work" and the ensuing burnout are often explained as a response to the company's seductiveness. Thus, a development manager with
a reputation for long hours and emotional intensity says:

> "This is a real seductive organization. You wanna do more and
> more. I work seventeen, eighteen hours a day. I get a few hours
> done in the early morning, then I take the kid to school, spend
> the day here, and work in the evening. It's family and work.
> That is it. It's hard. A lot of burnout. Maybe because of 'he who
> proposes does.' It's not like Silicon or Chiptech. They say Tech
> encourages divorces. They promise you a lot, make it lucrative,
> give you more and more. It's not just Tech; it's this whole in-
> dustry. People get addicted to work. I look around and I see

weird things. I see screwed-up marriages, I see fucked-up kids.
I thought Ben had problems: alcoholism, a depressed wife. So I
found him another job. But now his replacement has just left his
wife and kids himself."

The internal and external pressures that cause burnout are frequently seen
as related, as part of the "burnout spiral" that drives members "deeper
into the hole." Says a development manager associated with a major failed
project:

"I'm in a hole right now. Most of my group no longer reports
to me. I just want to get out of the hole. I asked myself how far
along I was to burnout. I don't know. I've never been burnt out
before. I work eight to twelve every night on top of the regular,
trying to save this project. It might be too late. There might
be some career damage. I might look for another job. I have a
daughter, and I should protect her."

There is more to burnout, however, than a painful personal experience in-
duced by external or internal pressures; it is also a meaningful and complex
display, a distinct and elaborate message that people send. Such displays
may be artifactual. One development manager, for example, has been held
responsible for an extended and very visible fiasco that caused months of
delay on an important product. It has attracted the attention of senior management. He has been relieved of most duties and, in a temporary staff
position, is working full time on salvaging the project. His future is unclear.
It is common knowledge that he is burnt out. A little plaque on the front of
his office says: "Before I came here I drank without a reason; now I have a
reason."

Displays of burnout may also occur in interactions with others. An engineer describes an incident involving his recently departed manager:

"Our manager burnt out. He was in over his head to begin with.
But his wife and he and their teen-age son are also alcoholic.
They tried to get off the stuff and things got really bad. One day
he stood up and told us that he was going to a detox center with
his son for two weeks. In the middle of our crunch. He didn't

have to tell us. Some people were quite upset. Keep that kind of shit to yourself or tell the EAP advisor. He's gone now."

Displaying symptoms of burnout is one way of sending signals to one's superiors. It is a sign that one is heavily invested in work, proof that one is allowing one's experience to be dominated by the requirements of the member role, evidence of commitment and self-sacrifice, and from this perspective, a call for some respect, a declaration that one has become a casualty. Says a manager, slumped in front of a terminal, his desk overflowing with documents:

> "I can't take it any more. I'm leaving; I'm dropping out. I'm getting real burnt out. I don't get along with my manager, and he is really going to screw me in performance appraisal. He is the biggest obstacle for me. I went to his manager's secretary and told her I need a padded cell. He'll get the message from her."

Burnout is also a recurring topic in group meetings. When the problem is discussed at a staff meeting of a development organization, a solemn air of shared acknowledgment of overwork accompanies the statement by the concerned-looking group manager:

> "I want to say one more thing. I know we are all flat out. That is the way it is. We are flat out, and it becomes a way of life. I want you to think about it. I want you to think what it means. Think about your health and about those around you. Every spare resource will get sucked up. Some people are getting funny. Even in this room! [Personnel manager nods.] I want to place an action on Personnel. In one month lead a discussion on the issue. What can we do with ourselves to ensure survival?"

Someone says, "Take drugs," and all laugh. The manager pauses and continues:

> "Seriously. Being flat out is a way of life. How do you survive without serious damage? Even physical. With the junior people it is different—they are just overworked. But at the higher

levels, with what we put up with, burnout, you start getting silly behavior."

One of the managers comments: "People on my projects are approaching borderline." Others nod in agreement. The group manager looks at the solemn faces around the table and adds:

> "There are some things we can do. We can't send them to the Bahamas or even to Boston. This is not a lecture, but when I was a project manager I knew their names, their wives' names, some of the kids. I knew who was sick, who was pregnant. I want you to do the same. I don't want to feel responsible for someone's collapse or damage. It's selfish too. We need them for a long, long time. I'm worried about them. I'm worried about you. I'm worried about myself and about Carpenter too. I spoke to him. I told him."

Burnout is an extreme condition, a drastic outcome that exposes the often hidden or tacit meanings associated with constructing an organizational self in everyday work life. On the face of it, burnout is a failure of self-management: a loss of control over role responses and the boundaries that separate and protect the self from the demands of the organization, and an inability to sustain the facade of controlled ambiguity characteristic of the successful self. Yet even in burnout ambiguity permeates the members' experience. On the one hand, burnout is considered both demeaning and difficult, evidence of a personal failure and dramatic proof that despite their promised benefits, the sirens' call for identification with the organizational demands may have dangerous, painful, and potentially disruptive consequences. On the other hand, many members feel some pride in surviving burnout or living with its threat. It is a battle scar, a purple heart, a call for respect, a sign of belonging and of willing self-sacrifice, an indication that one's heart is in the right place.

Burnout, with its connotations of both degradation and elevation of the self, captures the ambivalence that is the essential experience of full members—the Wage Class 4 employees who are the targets of normative control. The following section examines the very different experience of other members of the organization.

The Marginal Member

Tech has two distinct marginal categories. For Wage Class 2 employees, the membership role is mixed. Much of the organizational ideology supposedly applies to them, but it is less rigorously and systematically enforced, so that an organizational self is formed in response to the very uncertainty of its applicability. Temporary workers are assumed to be exempt from membership's demands (and benefits). For them the challenge is to form an organizational self in the face of exclusion.

Wage Class 2: On the Sidelines

Most of the Wage Class 2 employees in Engineering are secretarial and clerical workers. Although they are considered full members, the ideologically prescribed role demands were largely formulated with others in mind. Consequently, many in this group have an openly instrumental relationship with the company. Tech is seen—and referred to—in the third person plural. "They" are seen as capable of giving or withholding rewards, usually of the economic sort. Beyond instrumental concerns, the experience of membership is shaped by ambiguity concerning the degree of their inclusion in the culture. As one secretary explains, "getting in" is important:

> "I always wanted to work here; I grew up around here and have a lot of friends and relatives at Tech. A friend brought me for a day as a temp. Most secretaries tag for a while, but I lucked out—got in just before the freeze. The tag program is OK; you get the same pay but no benefits. But you could be out the door if they don't need you."

Inclusion is typically interpreted as the right to participate in certain aspects of "Tech culture," primarily the economic security it is perceived to offer. Another secretary says:

> "The best thing about being an employee here is the no-layoff policy. Other companies also had it but lifted it when times got rough. Here they are still sticking with it. My brother—he's a technician over at Lyndsville—was terminated. That means he

> has six months to find another job at Tech, and in the meanwhile he's on full pay."

The degree to which other aspects of the ideology apply to members of this group is a matter of some debate. For many, the exchange is the standard one: employment, benefits, and guarantees in return for prescribed efforts; beyond that there is open detachment. Time boundaries reflect this. Wage Class 2 work is strictly nine to five. Part-time and flexitime work is a privilege of Wage Class 4. Similarly, Wage Class 2 members rarely participate in the kinds of rituals described in Chapter 4. Most often they are in the background or on the sidelines, helping or coolly observing the staged dramas.

The spatial organization of secretarial work is also indicative of their status. Most secretaries sit at desks in the open spaces in front of offices, or in partly enclosed areas that lead into managerial space. Secretarial space is usually not adorned (this is particularly true for secretaries of senior managers). At lower levels, decoration reflects detachment. One secretary—one of the few blacks working in the facility—has a poster of Martin Luther King, Jr., and next to it a large calendar with a picture of a partly unclad, extremely well-built black man; the image stands out in the predominantly white and very nonphysical environment. Others display semivisible and easy-to-ignore versions of the "secretary's lament": poems, comic strips, and sayings that depict the annoyances and grievances of secretarial life. Few, if any, exhibit materials that suggest a positive orientation to the company.

For those who appear to be reconciled to their station, the expression of low involvement seems congruous, and potential enlargement is seen as a burden. Thus, a secretary says of her boss's attempt to increase her responsibilities "in line with Tech culture":

> "My boss gives me some of the easier technical assignments, like running computer tests and correcting documents. He says that is the way to do things at Tech, that is the culture. But I get all the stuff the engineers hate doing. I'd rather read a novel and answer the phone, like some of the others. That's what I'm paid for."

Those with more ambition might aspire to a promotion within their wage class. A long-time secretary considers promotion for its economic advantages:

> "I've been here fourteen years. Grew up here. I'm a two, but I want a promotion to administrative secretary. The biggest difference is that you stop being an hourly and become a salaried worker with overtime. You need a degree or minimum years service. I have the years. But there is also a committee, and you have to take a test. Like it's serious, y'know."

Those who seek increased involvement wonder about the applicability of the organizational ideology. Beyond the promise of inclusion, security, and economic return lies a gray area. Their current status is uncomfortable and frustrating. Work is often boring and occasionally humiliating. A secretary who is openly interested in advancement says, as she absent-mindedly separates documents:

> "This is mindless work. I hate dealing all day with managers and their inflated egos. They want things done they can't do themselves. And all those brilliant people—all they can do is numbers."

The rhetoric of the organizational ideology is a potential resource for her. Recognizing and identifying role demands is a first step:

> "They say they don't hold you back here like some other places. I'm a college graduate and I want to get in and interact with customers, maybe something in sales. (Definitely not anything technical!) I can do it. I can be just like those Techies—running around, taking initiative. Sometimes I feel like them anyway."

However, the feasibility of making a status transition is in question. A secretary who has just been accepted as an employee after a few months of "tagging" is enrolled in a community college, often spends her lunch hour with management textbooks, and has an updated resume ready on her work station. Nevertheless, she has doubts:

> "I went to a career management seminar. 'Taking charge of your own career at Tech.' I often think it's just lip service when it comes to us. I almost walked out on the first day when I saw that it was mainly the Wage Class 4 people there. Then I said: 'Fuck them! I'll keep pushing!' I look at the job book every day. There is a copy in the library, and you can pick one up at Personnel. I like the marketing and sales, not the technical stuff. I'll bring my resume, get some phone numbers; I'm persistent. I'm going to make it. But in the meanwhile I have to stay here for at least a year in this job. That's the policy—and they won't count my tag time for the year. I hope Gary, my boss, will help me and let me leave. Some managers want to keep you. People have a mindset against the secretaries. I know someone who made the shift. She was a secretary for seven years, and now she's a product manager. She encourages me, but I think they still keep her down. They won't forget she was a secretary."

For Wage Class 2 employees, then, membership is a mixed bag. The degree to which the ideologically defined member role is applicable to them is not entirely resolved. For many, the choice is between responding to the occasional opportunities to enact it and maintaining open detachment. As the following example illustrates, this mixed membership role is frequently displayed in the course of daily interaction.

A number of managers are standing around after their staff meeting in the common space between the offices, which also accommodates the group secretaries' desks. Anne, the most senior secretary, who is hoping to be promoted to administrative secretary, participates in the animated discussion from her seated position. Jill, a temp at the adjacent desk, is quiet, apparently daydreaming between phone calls as the discussion swirls around her. The political implications of the group's planned move to another facility are discussed with breathless excitement. Knowledgeable interpretations of the move are offered, complete with the first names of the various senior managers involved. Anne, from behind her desk, adds her perspective as one of the group and then, as if the incongruity of her stance is too obvious, smiles suddenly and adds: "But what do I care? I'm just a peon!" A moment of silence follows. The conversation resumes but quickly runs out of steam. The managers are soon off to their various lunch engagements, leaving Anne and Jill at their desks. As she turns her attention to the unfinished document on the screen of her terminal, Anne says to Jill: "They come, they go. I'll cover for you. Take a lunch break."

In sum, the organizational selves publicly enacted by members of this group are shaped by the question of partial inclusion. Either they want in, or they don't care that they are out. The more ambitious might experiment with the applicability of the ideology, but at the foundation the relationship is openly economic. In low status and low self-involvement there is apparent congruity, as Anne seemed to indicate. The organization is "they," and the status of "peon" (including the insight to recognize that status) is apparently more comfortable than attempts to adopt Wage Class 4 roles.

Outsiders: The "Extra-Culturals"

Unlike Wage Class 2 employees, temporary workers are fully exempt from membership and its deeper implications. Although physically present, they are not expected (or allowed) to become full-fledged participants in the organization or subjects of its ideology. In the managerial view, temporary workers are present in body and activity only and are not expected to share the experiences that members are assumed to have. The relationship is defined as economic, and there is no managerial attempt to encompass or penetrate the self. A commonsense understanding of this is pervasive. An engineer says:

> "Well, you can't expect too much from them. You'll find uncooperative behaviors and no loyalty. That is true for all contract people: it's true for temps and it's true for freelancers. They're just not Techies."

What is *not* expected from temporary workers suggests what *is* expected from others: an exchange that is more than economic.

Temporary workers move through the organization without much friction with the ideology and its agents. In many cases their activities are separate, unnoticed by regular employees, and frequently dirty: late or early cleaning, kitchens and dining rooms, night shift security. The worker's inner experience attracts no managerial attention: since the body is replaceable, leverage of the soul is deemed unnecessary. In relation to full members and the organizational routine, their scope for self-expression is very narrow. Interaction with Wage Class 4 members is typically minimal and limited to the actual services performed. For example, only a minimal self is displayed when a security guard and a senior manager briefly cross paths at the main door of an engineering facility.

It is a few days before Christmas, 6:00 p.m., dark and snowing. Jim, the guard, is at the front desk, ready to start the night shift. He is in uniform, equipped with a transistor radio for later use. The last of the daytime people are leaving the building. He is telling me:

> "They gave out turkeys today but only for the employees. Heck, I don't need a fucking turkey. I can go out and get one for myself!"

A senior manager hurries out. He is carrying a large brief case and extra documents under one arm. In the other hand is his Christmas turkey, frozen and packed. He nods absent-mindedly at us and stops to put on a dark fur coat, peering out the window past his reflection, looking for his chauffeured car. Jim, who has been talking about his efforts to get a full-time job at Tech, stiffens, and the following exchange ensues:

> "Good night sir. Careful. Its slippery out there. We had an accident on 131 a few hours ago, sir."
> "OK. I'll tell the chauffeur to be careful. Good night. [He turns to leave and adds an afterthought as he passes through the door.] And Merry Christmas."

When he is gone, Jim relaxes. "Boy. A chauffeur *and* a turkey! Some guys have it all." He laughs. And then he adds seriously, as he turns on the radio: "He's a pretty important guy, y'know."

Like many others, such interactions are smooth and scripted, the roles clear and acknowledged, the attributed meanings tacit and private. Yet lurking close to the surface is the question of inclusion and exclusion in the organization, and the associated feelings.

The minimal self may occasionally seek public enlargement. When this occurs, aspects of the self beneath the organizationally prescribed one are displayed, the smoothness of the interaction is broken, clear behavioral rules are temporarily suspended, and participants surface private meanings and comment to themselves and to each other as they strive and negotiate for recognition.

Such "enlargement dramas" occur most frequently in settings where the more rigid rules of organizational reality are relaxed and otherwise ignored aspects of the selves of marginal members may be displayed and attended to. For example, a company-sponsored softball game is an occasion for Joe, a stockroom helper whom most of the managers and engineers present recognize but few know by name, to make his presence felt. He is a local boy, large and muscular. He arrives suited up. His outfit stands out; most of the others are casually attired. He volunteers to pitch. The opposing team, busy on their batting order, stop to watch him warm up. He seems oblivious as he takes the ball and delivers a professional-looking fastball to the rather startled catcher. Others pause to watch the performance. After a short warm-up, the game starts, and Joe delivers the usual high, slow pitch with an air of boredom, lazily fielding the first dribbler to the mound and putting away the slow-running engineer. For a brief moment, he is at center stage.

Another example occurs after hours. It is nine thirty in the evening. Only the dedicated, the overworked, and the cleaners are still around. John, a project supervisor, is in his office working on a document, deep in thought in front of his terminal. For him it is crunch time. Mike, a cleaner, is making his routine way from office to office, collecting the leftovers of the day from the wastepaper baskets. He is a temporary worker, about twenty-five, clad in jeans, sneakers, and a baseball cap. The edge of a tattoo shows on his upper arm. He is wearing an apron with a Tech insignia and has a temporary name tag—a removable paper label that is fixed to the shirt at the beginning of the shift and peeled off and discarded at the end. As he moves to collect the plastic bag under the table, John turns and throws in his plastic coffee cup. Their eyes meet. "How ya doin'?" Mike asks automatically. "Shitty!" exclaims John. The scene freezes. John, noticing the surprise, says: "What do you want me to say? Great?" Mike straightens up and says more conversationally: "I dunno. All these people here—real professional-like, y'know." He imitates their exclamations: "Great! Super! Have a good weekend! Merry Christmas!" Both laugh. A brief silence. Mike turns and on the way out says: "Well, have a lousy Christmas." John calls after him: "Hope your New

Year stinks." The mutual recognition is a brief—and atypical—break in the routine enactment of practiced selves.

Self-enlargement also occurs during more formal occasions. This typically happens quietly, on the boundaries of the event. Barney, a fifty-year-old cleaning man pulling a little wagon with boxes of wastepaper, encounters a crowd of engineers overflowing from a seminar room. They are listening intently to a senior manager who is making a public presentation inside. Instead of walking through them like a shadow, as many of his status do, he chooses to make his presence felt. As he maneuvers through the edge of the crowd, he says to no one in particular: "*Gee*-sus! Standing room only!" Some heads turn, but quickly turn back. He slows down and says to the last person in the crowded doorway, a young engineer who is straining on tiptoe to see inside the darkened room: "Are you *getting* something out of this?" The man, looking slightly deflated and no longer on tiptoe, smiles sheepishly, indicating, perhaps, that a similar question was crossing his mind. After a brief pause, Barney goes on with a final emphatic "Gee-sus!" Pushing through the outer doors, he stops to chat with the security guard in the lobby. The engineer turns his attention back to the presentation and assumes his earlier stance. Barney appears neither angry nor envious. Instead, he presents himself as questioning the display of earnest involvement on the part of the Wage Class 4 audience. For a brief moment his stance is acknowledged by one member.

Temporary secretaries—"temps"—are a more problematic case. In their case, the membership boundaries are open to some negotiation. While some appreciate the part-time nature of the work and soon disappear, for many the goal—not always easy to achieve—is to become a permanent employee. During routine work life, they are indistinguishable from other secretaries. They often spend their time with regular employees and frequently perform similar duties. Except for the different ID card they wear, they could pass for full members. Events that publicly highlight their different membership status might be occasions for enlargement dramas in which the feelings associated with exclusion are thrust into the public domain. An example is the question posed by the temp during the career workshop described in Chapter 4. Her challenge to the comfortable order that ignores the situation of marginal members creates a sticky moment. It is quickly suppressed by other participants anxious to preserve the appearance and emotional tone of routine interaction. A secretarial supervisor describes another scene that occurs when the Christmas turkey—a Tech tradition—is distributed. Computerized lists of employees are the basis for the distribution—a policy made, from the point of view of development organizations, "somewhere in Corporate."

> "Things got very uncomfortable today. The turkey slips arrived, and we each got one with our name on it so we could pick it up when the truck came in the afternoon. As I was putting them in the mail slots, Faith—she's been tagging here for two years—started crying. I don't know why they're so mean. *You* can have one, *you* can't. And they give the leftovers to charity. I mean, shc's like almost one of us, does the same work. Would it hurt them to give her a turkey?"

In sum, the role attributed to temporary members implies a minimal organizational self. In the course of routine interactions with full members (particularly those in Wage Class 4), these people tend to engage in the prescribed behaviors that reflect this narrow view. Their presence, when orderly, serves as a defining contrast for others, who presumably are what the minimal self is not. Enlargement dramas are breaks in the routine order. The situation of the minimal self is put on display and brought into question, followed by a self-definitional struggle that temporarily disturbs the order and often has emotional overtones.

Enlargement dramas of this sort are revealing. They offer a temporary suspension of practiced organizational selves, an opportunity for negotiation, for enlargement, perhaps a cleansing moment of truth. In acknowledgment and interpretation there is dignity and perhaps the only form of camaraderie possible: actors commenting on their roles. But these temporary breaks in the order reveal its true nature: the minimal scope it routinely grants to the organizational selves of those engaged in temporary work.

Conclusion: The Unstable Self

The organizational self is formed in transaction with the ideologically prescribed member role and the demands it makes on the members' experience. By omission or commission, thought, word, or deed, participants explicitly or tacitly choose a stance toward what is attributed to them; in this process,

they define, interpret, and display their understanding of the social environment, their personal experience, and the relationship between the two.

In this regard, Tech poses a distinct contrast between the experiences of
marginal and full members. Marginal members—temporary workers and
Wage Class 2 employees—are not subjected to all the demands of the member role. Temporary workers are completely exempt from the organizational
ideology and are limited to a minimal self, and Wage Class 2 members
are only partially and ambiguously the target of its prescriptions. This may
not always be a comfortable or a desirable condition—indeed, attempts at
self-enlargement occasionally occur—but for members in both marginal
categories there is a certain congruity between low status and few demands
on the self.

For full members, in contrast, the extensive demands of the member
role pose a fundamental dilemma. By seeking and accepting higher status,
greater opportunity, increased centrality, and more rewards, Wage Class 4
members have also exposed themselves to the organizational ideology—
the codification of "Tech culture" and its cognitive and affective correlates.
They are the targets of its formulations, "overlaid worlds," and attempts
at mind and emotion description, prescription, and control. By choice they
have entered into a contract that is more than economic, one that must contend with overt external claims on self-definition. Behavioral conformity
and evidence of a vaguely defined "loyalty" are not enough. A demonstration of "incorporation" of the culture, of adoption of an organizationally
defined and sanctioned self, is required. Consequently, the appearance of
personal autonomy—a condition naturally (and ideologically) associated
with the high status they seek—is threatened. Although it is not immediately apparent, the price of power is submission: not necessarily to demands
concerning one's behavior, as is typical of low-status work, but to prescriptions regarding one's thoughts and feelings, supposedly the most cherished
belongings of autonomous beings.[15]

In short, inherent in a system of normative control is a contradiction between the requirements of internal and external control of the self. This
causes members to experience what Merton (1957: 6) refers to as "sociological ambivalence"—a condition that results from "incompatible normative
expectations of attitudes, beliefs and behaviors assigned to a status or a set
of statuses in society." Sociological ambivalence is manifested in numerous
ways. It is articulated as confusion between the attractiveness and repul-

siveness of the company and its demands, between the seductiveness of increased involvement and the desire and need to maintain personal autonomy. It is artistically expressed in office artifacts and publicly displayed in such central symbols as the "golden bull" and the "management model," which contrast "shit" and "glory." Perhaps its ultimate expression is found in the double meaning of "burnout" as both elevation and degradation—the contrast between being a casualty and engaging in self-sacrifice, between becoming a loser or a hero.

The organizational self that is formed under conditions of sociological ambivalence is founded on the carefully cultivated ability to control and manage an appropriate and often ambiguous or shifting balance of role embracement and role distancing. This balancing act may be observed in the ironic stance that permeates ritual performances and social interaction; in the self-consciousness that infuses the members' discourse; in the humor that at once highlights and denies ambivalence; in the rapid frame shifts in the course of presentations; and in the qualifiers that precede many statements and the escape clauses designed into them. More tellingly, perhaps, it is evident in the pervasiveness and centrality of the metaphor of drama in the construction of experience, and the oft-repeated and widely shared insight that things are never as they seem.[16]

These qualities of the organizational self under normative control seem to challenge traditional views of member-organization relations. Self-involvement in the organization has long been viewed along a continuum ranging from attachment to detachment or from positive to negative emotional orientation (Dubin, Hedley, and Taveggia, 1976; Etzioni, 1961). At one extreme, ideological claims are affirmed and acknowledged: members are "engaged," "satisfied," "motivated," "self-actualizing," "morally committed," and so forth. At the other, the self is felt to be safe—or alienated—from the demands made on it, the validity of the explicit claims against it are denied, and members experience a variety of negative emotions. The traditional scheme proposes that employees find an equilibrium point along the continuum. This view of the self in organizational settings, in fact, lies at the very heart of the concept of normative control: normative control is designed to induce a wholly positive, "authentic," and structurally stable emotional orientation to the organization (see Chapter 1).

The validity of this view must now be questioned. When people face engineered cultures of the sort found at Tech, it becomes apparent that the relationship of members to the organization is not one-dimensional, and that equilibrium is difficult to sustain. For many individuals in Tech's Wage Class 4, both attachment and detachment are evident, positive and negative emotional orientations are simultaneously expressed, and constructing a self is a problematic and disjointed endeavor. The organizational self becomes an active and artful construction, a performance, a tightrope walk, a balancing act of organizational reality claims, fluctuating between contradictory modes of relating to the organization and always faced with the threat of burnout, or the exposure of its own illusions.

We have come full circle. If the attempt to engineer culture and accomplish normative control is aimed at defining the members' selves for them, this very attempt undermines its own assumptions. The engineers of culture see the ideal member as driven by strong beliefs and intense emotions, authentic experiences of loyalty, commitment, and the pleasure of work. Yet they seem to produce members who have internalized ambiguity, who have made the metaphor of drama a centerpiece of their sense of self, who question the authenticity of all beliefs and emotions, and who find irony in its various forms the dominant mode of everyday existence.[17] In short, when the contested terrain, to use Edwards' (1979) term, is the self, the terrain itself is transformed and perhaps deformed: the unremitting glare of the ideological spotlight degrades that experience which, perhaps, can flourish only uncontested, in the dark.

chapter 6

Conclusion

Indefatigable boozers, and you, thrice precious martyrs to the pox, while you are at leisure and I have nothing more important on hand, let me ask you a serious question: Why is it commonly said nowadays that the world is no longer gormless? Gormless is a Languedocian adjective, signifying unsalted, saltless, tasteless and flat. Metaphorically it means foolish, simple, devoid of intelligence, and cracked in the upper storey. But would you say, as might logically be inferred from this, that the world which was once gormless has now turned wise? What conditions, and how many, did it require to make it gormless? And what conditions and how many, were necessary to make it wise? Why was it gormless? And why should it become wise? By what signs did you recognize its former folly? By what signs do you affirm its present wisdom? Who made it gormless? Who has made it wise? Which were more numerous, those who loved it when it was gormless, or those who love it now that it is wise? For how long was it gormless? For how long will it stay wise? What did its former folly spring from? What are the roots of its present wisdom? Why did its ancient folly come to an end at this time and no later? Why did its present wisdom begin now and not before? What harm came of its former folly? What good can we expect of its present wisdom? How can its ancient folly have been abolished? How can its present wisdom have been restored?

Now answer me, if you please, and I'll use no stronger entreaties on your reverences, for fear I may disquiet you, my worshipful fathers. . . . I swear to you by the great Hurlyburly that if you don't help me by the solution of the problem I've propounded, I shall shortly be sorry that I ever put it to you. Indeed I am sorry already. But I'm in a great quandary, as if I held a wolf by the ears and had no hope of assistance.

—François Rabelais
Gargantua and Pantagruel

This book set out to explore, describe, and evaluate the reality behind the rhetoric of corporate culture. The idea of developing strong cultures, I argue, is the latest stage in the historical evolution of managerial ideology toward an emphasis on normative control—the desire to bind employees' hearts and minds to the corporate interest. To examine the practical and moral implications of such an ideology—whether and how it is implemented, and what it does to people—I undertook an ethnographic investigation of the engineering division of a high-tech company considered an exemplar of successful culture management. In this chapter I review and critically interpret the main findings concerning Tech's engineered culture and its significance for those subjected to it.

The Management of Culture

All the evidence suggests that the ideology of Tech culture is a very practical matter: Tech management takes the implications of its own rhetoric seriously and invests considerable energy in attempting to embed the rules, prescriptions, and admonitions of the culture in the fabric of everyday life in the company. The preceding chapters illustrate in some detail the main ways this is accomplished.

First, management pays a great deal of attention to developing, articulating, and disseminating the organizational ideology for internal consumption. With the strong support of senior management, a large group of internal ideologists, acting as lay ethnographers of their own culture and making extensive use of the work of academics, consultants, and journalists, have created a systematic and full-blown theory of Tech culture.[1] This ideology, analyzed in detail in Chapter 3, portrays the company as a morally sound, organic, undifferentiated community and defines a member role founded on the internalization of appropriate beliefs and emotions along with abstract and rather ambiguous behavioral prescriptions. Managerial spokespersons, guided by the principle of endless repetition, and claiming the authority of experience, of expertise, and of scientific and journalistic objectivity, use a variety of media, communication channels, and educational techniques to disseminate these ideas to members.

Second, ideological principles are embodied in specific managerial policies governing the members' work life. These policies, reviewed in Chapter 2, are designed to minimize the use and deemphasize the significance of traditional bureaucratic control structures—hierarchical and functional differentiation, economically motivated performance—and to elicit instead behavior consistent with cultural prescriptions. Thus, Tech's job-category and compensation systems, perceived by members as no different in principle from competitors', are grounded in the unchanging bedrock of traditional employment practices. However, they are complemented by additional policies specifically designed—at considerable cost to the company —to encourage extensive employee involvement in both formal and informal aspects of work life, to maximize a sense of ownership and security, to generate commitment to the organization rather than to any particular subgroup, to remove functional and hierarchical barriers to communication and internal mobility, to enhance the members' exposure to each other, and to remove some of the symbols, and realities, of status, supervision, and formal control.

Finally, the practical and symbolic deemphasis of traditional bureaucratic control is complemented by practices that encourage and enforce adherence to the member role. As Chapter 4 illustrates, structured gatherings that have the quality of ritual are a central feature of work life.[2] These frequently occurring interactions—both large-scale and minute—are not only occasions for the generation and expression of role-prescribed collective belief and emotion, but also the stage for a very pronounced form of face-to-face control that is pervasive at Tech. In traditional bureaucratic control systems, one's role performance, defined largely in terms of required behaviors, is supervised mainly by immediate superiors. Here, there is evidence of a decentralization and a deepening of control: performance of the member role, and particularly of the extensively articulated beliefs and emotions it prescribes, is "supervised" by a broader group of control agents—practically anyone who is a member of the organization. Management, as it were, sets the stage, provides the rhetoric, and reserves the right to the final word in these interpretive struggles, but most of the work is done by the members, in whose interest it is to continuously reinforce in each other and in themselves overt adherence to the member role. This type of control is usually manifested in very subtle forms of group pressure; occasionally there are more dramatic outbursts—the social mini-dramas of Chapter 4. The ideology of openness, flexibility, and tolerance notwithstanding, these are occasions for what Bourdieu (1977) calls "symbolic violence": expressions of deviance are silenced, and adherence to official versions of reality is enforced.

In sum, Tech's engineered culture appears to be a pervasive, comprehensive, and demanding system of normative control based on the use of symbolic power. Its essence is a managerial attempt to corner the internal market on the power to define reality, to prescribe and control the expression of the members' beliefs and emotions, to enlist members as agents of control, and, ultimately, to expand that aspect of the members' selves that is determined and defined by corporate interests.

As John Van Maanen and I have suggested elsewhere (Van Maanen and Kunda, 1989), systems of managerial control build on, rather than replace, one another.[3] At Tech, despite the managerial commitment to normative control, management clearly does not relinquish the use of what Etzioni (1961) termed utilitarian control: the use of managerial power to allocate material rewards designed to appeal to the members' calculated self-interest. On the contrary, it appears to reserve the right to balance cultural management with the optional use of the traditional bureaucratic methods of management associated with this approach. Thus, the engineered culture may be seen as an additional overlay of control that complements other means of eliciting compliance. Under these circumstances, it appears that some of the more overt trappings of bureaucratic control systems and managerial power are relaxed, disguised, or reinterpreted. However, the enhanced flexibility, structural ambiguity, looser behavioral controls, and less rigid supervision of work behavior that are prescribed and often implemented by the designers of the culture are balanced by management's relentless efforts to define and impose the member role. The essence of bureaucratic control—the formalization, codification, and enforcement of rules and regulations—does not change in principle under a system of normative control; it merely shifts its focus, at management's discretion, from the organizational structure to the organizational culture, from the members' behavior to their experience.

As a managerial aspiration, normative control is not new; but at Tech the platform has been transformed into practice. This, the evidence suggests, is made possible by a strong and long-term managerial interest in the implementation of such ideas, the availability of technology and resources for its accomplishment, the climate of managerial and perhaps public opinion that provides a degree of legitimacy to such efforts, and, not least, Tech's continuing long-term economic viability.[4]

Culture and the Member

What are the consequences of a designed and managed culture for the people who must live with it? Two stand out. First, members are differentiated by their stance toward the organizational ideology. Specifically, a three-tier system is evident that reflects not only hierarchy, but cultural inclusion: Wage Class 4, Wage Class 2, and temporary workers. Wage Class 4 comprises full members, citizens in good standing of the corporate community. As such, they are clearly both subjects and agents of normative control and primary participants in Tech's cultural life and the rituals associated with it. Members of the other two groups regard the applicability of the organizational ideology to themselves with some skepticism. Despite the prevalent rhetoric of normative control, there appears to be a clear contradiction between the reality they live with and its ideological representation. Wage Class 2 employees are subjected to a system of utilitarian control based mainly on economic incentives, while temporary workers work under conditions closer to what Etzioni (1961) referred to as coercive control: they are subject to immediate termination and possess no rights as employees. Thus, one consequence of the managed culture is a polarization of central and marginal members: the former must accept or limit an extensively defined organizational self; the latter must live with or seek to enlarge a minimal one.[5]

The second consequence involves the impact of normative control on its main targets: members of Wage Class 4. As Chapter 5 shows, their experience is characterized by "sociological ambivalence": as members move in and aspire to increased centrality and higher status, they are also increasingly subjected to normative control and threatened with a loss of personal autonomy. Responses to this dilemma, described in detail in Chapter 5, are based on the attempt to balance self and role under conditions where equilibrium is hard, if not impossible, to sustain. Thus, the central experience of membership is not only that which the ideology seeks to instill, but also the experience of struggle with it. In this sense, members have internalized the "problem of control" that lies at the heart of organization, and the private selves of members have become part of the "contested terrain."

If the idea of normative control is founded on the hope of offering members a stable self grounded in a morally sound organizational community, the opposite is produced. Among full members, we find an ambivalent, fluctuating, ironic self, at war with itself and with its internalized images of self and other. And among marginal members, we encounter estranged participation in a community that makes promises and creates expectations, but withholds full membership. In both cases, "loyalty," "allegiance," and "commitment," to the extent that they may be said to exist, are dramatically mediated; and in the theater, authenticity is always in question. In this sense the attempts to implement the ideology of a "strong corporate culture" seem to contribute to its demise.

What, then, have the engineers of culture created? If the story I have told suggests that there is a culture at Tech in the true anthropological sense of the word, it is certainly different from the ideological claims made in its name.[6] The culture I have attempted to describe is founded on self-awareness, reflection, and articulation in the service of a struggle for control. Consequently, it is a culture riddled with contradictions between ideological depictions and alternative realities: where democratization is claimed, there are also subtle forms of domination; where clarity of meaning and purpose is attempted, there is intentional and deeply ingrained ambiguity; where an overarching morality is preached, there is also opportunistic cynicism; and where fervent commitment is demanded, there is pervasive irony. These contradictions are perhaps inevitable in any authoritarian system, but they become all the more acute when the culture becomes its own object, when the seemingly objective, scientific concept of culture is expropriated and drawn into the political fray by culture engineers and their various helpers in the service of corporate goals.[7]

To the extent that the engineered culture in fact serves managerial purposes—and many, if not most, members indeed appear to work hard and long—its success must now be seen in a somewhat different light. At Tech, corporate management maintains and enhances its power not by imposing ideological clarity, but by creating and selectively applying and interpreting ambiguous definitions of reality. Under such circumstances, many members find that their work lives are enmeshed in an ever-accelerating vicious cycle. The race to meet corporate standards of accomplishment, get corporate approval, and procure the pecuniary and personal rewards the culture promises becomes the only way to find stable meanings and compensate for a sense of confusion, lost authenticity, and inner emptiness; but it is a self-defeating exercise, one that recreates and reinforces the very circumstances it seeks to correct.

Tech management, in short, has and extensively uses the power to profoundly affect the work environment and the experience of its employees. It is to a critique of the social consequences of this power that I now turn.

Culture and Corporate Power

The evolution of managerial ideology toward normative control was accompanied by a continuing moral discourse only occasionally (and usually thinly) concealed by scientific or technical terminology. As Chapter 1 shows, at the heart of the debate is an attempt to evaluate the impact of corporate power on individuals and society. On the one hand, we are afforded apocalyptic visions and dark warnings of tyranny, domination, and oppression. On the other hand, we find images of utopia and promises of an organizational society without discontents: a "you can have it all" world that fulfills the dream of release from the constraints of limited opportunity. What light does this study throw on these concerns? How is one to evaluate the complex reality I have attempted to document?

On the face of it, the argument for tyranny would seem to have some merit. In its attention to the formulation and dissemination of ideology, Tech management indeed resembles Big Brother (as some members point out). Similarly, the widespread use of rituals, the importance attached to group testimonials, and the face-to-face control they allow are reminiscent of brainwashing techniques.[8] Moreover, members report feeling intense pressure, an invasion of their private life by corporate requirements, and, in many cases, considerable personal suffering, manifested in burnout and associated forms of despair. Together, these facts seem to support the critics' claims that the modern corporation is fast becoming—if it has not already become—a monstrosity that "bosses not only our working hours but invades our homes and dictates our thought and dreams" (Bendix, 1956: 339).

Overextending the use of such analogies, however, might contribute, inadvertently or not, to the trivialization of tyranny. Economic enterprise must be seen in a comparative light for the purpose of evaluation. Tech is more open to investigation than a South African gold mine or a Cuban sugar refinery, not to speak of more sinister forms of organization. To state the obvious (occasionally a necessary antidote to overstated analogies): within economic constraints that in many cases are not too pressing, membership is voluntary, members are free to associate with alternative groupings, and they have some recourse to external and independent agencies of regulation and control. In such an environment, as the evidence suggests, members are far from reaching that state of "ritualization of belief" which Schein (1961) sees as the ultimate success of normative control; perhaps the best proof of this is the members' continuing involvement in reflective discourse and the widespread ironic stance, manifested in cynicism, humor, and analytic insight. Moreover, the economic rewards and benefits of membership are not insubstantial, and employment, in many cases, is regarded as desirable and personally rewarding. In short, Tech members experience such freedoms and rewards as capitalist societies offer; and despite certain resemblances, and perhaps managerial fantasies, the company is still far from becoming what Goffman (1961a) calls a "total institution": an establishment that has full control over all aspects of its members' lives and extensive power to enforce its views.

But how far? Taken literally, the metaphors of condemnation fall short of the mark. But, as metaphors are wont to do, they also capture underlying truths that challenge the veracity of the idyllic images and benign rhetoric offered by proponents of strong cultures—a challenge that is particularly important in an age when the crumbling edifices of totalitarian regimes in some parts of the world are held up as evidence that all is well close to home. This study raises three specific concerns regarding the extent and impact of corporate power within the context of a pluralistic, democratic society.

Consider first the impact of corporate power on its central members: professional and managerial employees. For these members, Tech culture is not a prison, and its managers are neither jailers nor tyrants in the simple sense of the word, but it does, nevertheless, represent a rather subtle form of domination, a "culture trap" combining normative pressure with a delicate balance of seductiveness and coercion. As Goffman (1961a) suggests, personal autonomy is found in the interstices between social institutions and their requirements. At Tech, these interstices are systematically filled with the rhetoric—backed by the authority and power—of managerial ideologists. The evidence suggests that though many members maintain a sense of freedom, they also experience a pull that is not easy to combat, an escalating commitment to the corporation and its definitions of reality, coupled with a systematic and persistent attack on the boundaries of their privacy. Their seeming cooperation with the corporate interest and the apparent benignness of the corporation's goals with regard to its employees must not disguise the fact that phenomenologically, if not concretely, people over time are submerged in a community of meaning that is to some extent monopolized by management: a total institution of sorts.[9]

This monopoly has a different impact on different members. Some, as

critics have warned, allow corporate definitions of reality to serve as unquestioned criteria for their self-definition and their world view. In most cases,
however, the culture trap works in more insidious and perhaps more dangerous ways: the corporation does not necessarily "capture the soul," but
systematically undermines its foundation. Thus, for many at Tech, the authenticity of their own (and others') experience is simultaneously prescribed
and cast in doubt; life as theater becomes an all-encompassing reality; and
the ability to establish a life and a self independent of the corporation's influence is diminished. In short, in the name of humanism, enlightenment, and
progress, the engineers of Tech culture elicit the intense efforts of employees not by stirring their experiential life, but, if anything, by degrading and
perhaps destroying it.[10]

The second concern this study raises is the contribution of corporate
power to the marginalization of members. Specifically, it is necessary to
understand the fate of the "extra-culturals"—those who become, in terms
of the culture's categories, "nonpersons." (This is a question that not only
Tech, but the larger society as well must face.) The temporary work force
is clearly a rising phenomenon.[11] As the evidence suggests, these people
are in a position to be truly marginal—belonging neither to home nor host
cultures, governed by few regulations, often invisible, yet an increasingly
necessary feature of corporate life. In this sense, "the extra-culturals" are
equivalent to the homeless, forced to depend on the kindness of strangers.
One might argue that these people are free of the corporate tyranny of the
mind and heart, but their invisibility also defines them as possessors of minimal selves and leaves them with little protection from a tyranny of the body.
The ideology of organizational culture and its various forms of implementation seem not only to contribute to the evolution of this state of affairs, but
to obscure its reality.

Finally, the findings of this study must also lead us, with some license to
generalize, to question the impact of corporate power on society. To the extent that the world view and the values implicit in strong corporate cultures
permeate the larger culture, and to the extent that corporate communities of
the sort described here become the main form of association for many individuals, we have cause for concern. What, we must ask, is the strength of a
moral order based on the assumption and the promise of abundance, a view
of life as a search for "fun," and a tenuous, dramatically mediated commitment to collective goals, where the distinction between theater and reality

is not clear, but the performance is often all-encompassing? Such a perspective is, arguably, suitable for economic activity in times of prosperity. But shaping citizens by such an ethos might, in the long run, undermine the foundations of collective action. How, we must ask, will these corporate products behave in different arenas of social action and association—family, community, politics—if their fundamental conceptions of themselves and their relationship to others are shaped in the corporate image?[12] And, more crucially, what will happen to the theater of reality and its elaborate props when, or if, times change and assumptions no longer hold?

At the same time, the ostensible personal incorporation of organizational goals—whether dramatically mediated or not—leaves them unquestioned. The well-known specter of the organization man who has no questions looms in the background: deprived of an autonomous self or a sense of "authentic" experience, and driven instead to strategically design an organizational self governed by the standards of corporate profitability and its rewards, such people lack the foundations of a moral framework that would enable them to evaluate corporate activities.[13] At Tech, indeed, analysis of the role, use, and social consequences of the company's technology was conspicuous by its absence; rather, such issues are glossed over by words like "innovation," "productivity," "profit," with their connotations of inevitability and rightness. Is this typical of engineering organizations? Of the high-tech industry? Of all bureaucratic organizations? Perhaps. But the system of normative control and its anticipated and unanticipated consequences described here seem both to enhance and to disguise this effect, in an industry that claims a major role in shaping not only the technologies of the future, but also the people who make and use them.

These are serious concerns. How might they be addressed? It is not my intent to offer solutions or even to suggest that there are any. But the logic of this book does suggest two concluding prescriptive lines of thought. The first concerns the personal stance of those who must live with corporate pressures of the sort described here. In his now-classic *The Organization Man*, Whyte (1956) documented the ills and dangers of corporate power in an earlier and more naive period, and called on members of organizations to recognize that there will always be a fundamental conflict of interest between individuals and organizations. The organization man, Whyte says, "must fight the Organization . . . for the demands for his surrender are constant and powerful, and the more he has come to like the life of the organization the more difficult does he find it to resist these demands or even recognize them" (p. 404). It is good advice, but perhaps not sufficient.[14] Faced with what Coser (1974) calls "greedy institutions," it is necessary not only to fight back in an attempt to make them "more responsive" or "more humane"—this study documents the traps in that strategy as the sole method of response— but to remember that organizations are instruments of social action and not ends in themselves, to fortify and bolster those boundaries that are the target of corporate ideologists who would convince us otherwise, and to rediscover and cultivate alternative arenas for self-definition.

The second prescription is addressed to the practitioners of social scientific analysis of organizations. The struggle between organizations bent on normative control and individuals subjected to it is over the definition of reality, and it is a difficult one, for meanings both personal and collective have become part of the contested terrain. It is inevitable that social science will enter the fray. Unfortunately, it is fighting predominantly on one side: in this book I document the ways in which scientific efforts tend to serve those in positions of authority by providing—sometimes for a fee, at other times unwittingly—the rhetorical weapons they need as well as the moral justification they seek. Thus, rather than end this book with a call for more research—this will no doubt occur, regardless of exhortation—I will recall for students of organizational life Erving Goffman's (1983: 17) view of the sociologist's charter: the "unsponsored analysis of the social arrangements enjoyed by those with institutional authority—priests, psychiatrists, schoolteachers, police, generals, government leaders, parents, males, whites, nationals, media operators, and all the other well-placed persons who are in a position to give official imprint to versions of reality."

appendix

Methods: A Confessional of Sorts

> Jesus! I've t'ought about dat guy a t'ousand times since den an' wondered what eveh happened to 'm goin' out to look at Bensonhoist because he liked duh name! Walkin' aroun' t'roo Red Hook by himself at night an' lookin' at his map! How many people did I see get drowned out heah in Brooklyn! How long would it take a guy wit a good map to know all deh was to know about Brooklyn!
>
> Jesus! What a nut he was! I wondeh what eveh happened to 'im, anyway! I wondeh if someone knocked him on duh head, or if he's still wanderin' aroun' in duh subway in duh middle of duh night wit his little map! Duh poor guy! Say, I've got to laugh at dat, when I t'ink about him! Maybe he's found out by now dat he'll neveh live long enough to know duh whole of Brooklyn. It'd take a guy a lifetime to know Brooklyn t'roo an' t'roo. An' even den, yuh wouldn't know it all.
>
> —Thomas Wolfe
> *Only the Dead Know Brooklyn*

This study belongs to the genre known as "ethnographic realism."[1] This identification says much about presentational style, little about the actual research process. The descriptive style of this genre presents an author functioning more or less as a fly on the wall in the course of his sojourn in the field—an objective, unseen observer following well-defined procedures for data collection and verification. It requires no great insight, however, to recognize that ethnographic realism is a distortion of convenience. Fieldwork, as all who have engaged in it will testify, is an intensely personal and subjective process, and there are probably at least as many "methods" as there are fieldworkers.

It is the task of the methods section to balance the potentially misleading implications of the realist style as adopted in the text with a backstage glimpse of the actual research process. Often reading like a confessional, the fieldwork account emphasizes (along with proof of one's intimate familiarity with the subject matter) shortcomings, potential for bias, and the random nature of fieldwork. Such a discussion serves a number of purposes. First, it conforms to the conventions set by more stylistically scientific genres. The methods section provides the reader with procedural information, and, for the more sophisticated, it introduces the issue of observer subjectivity into a consideration of the scientific process and its limitations. This, it is hoped, should allow a qualified reading (replication having fallen on bad times, even in experimental circles).

Second, and more interestingly, a methods confessional serves to establish a kind of ethnographic credibility; here self-criticism not only exposes weaknesses and qualifies assertions, but allows a demonstration of the breadth, depth, indeed the relentlessness, of an ethnographic incisiveness seemingly so powerful that it is applied most scathingly to oneself. Thus, although it reads like a confessional, it is in fact a self-application of one's scientific tools, a "realist ethnography" of the research process.[2]

However, as an ethnography of ethnography, a confessional—no matter how dramatic, how insightful, how excruciatingly honest—falls short, a victim of its own interpretive logic. One is writing of oneself; and beyond the human conventions and constraints of self-presentation, one runs afoul of a basic epistemological dilemma inherent in interpretive logic: how is one to know oneself? Techniques for verification, for introducing multiple voices, for turning the object of meaning around and repeatedly lighting it with evidence from apparently independent sources (what the more mathematically minded would refer to as "triangulation") are not applicable. Self-analysis has opened the writer to the criticism of informant knowledge that is the essence of the ethnographic enterprise: it is only "experience-near"; it is only "first-order"; it lacks the distance required of a valid interpretive effort. The question, then, looms large: how is one to break through the vicious cycles of one's own interests, distortions, and misperceptions?

There is no clear answer.[3] Nevertheless, since I believe that such contextual information may be helpful and perhaps interesting to readers, I will offer some observations and comments on the background of the study, the nature of my activities in the field, and the process of data analysis and writing. What follows should be regarded primarily as an informant-produced text; as elsewhere in this study, it is offered with the recurring caveat: let the reader beware.

Why Fieldwork? The original research for this book was done in 1985 as part of a doctoral dissertation at the Sloan School of Management at the Massachusetts Institute of Technology. In retrospect, it seems that a number of factors—above and beyond the theoretical justifications specified in the preceding chapters—led me to do fieldwork at Tech. For my thesis I wanted to study a large business corporation. I had experience as a researcher in public sector people-processing organizations (Kunda, 1986) and as a participant in military, psychiatric, and educational institutions in Israel. I had little firsthand knowledge of the business world (though I was in a school of management), and there were few secondhand sources that seemed trustworthy. I felt that an extended sojourn in this world was necessary for a student of organizations.

My personal background seems to account, in part, for the specific directions this study took. As an Israeli who had come to the United States in order to pursue graduate studies, and therefore a foreigner (albeit one in a rather accelerated process of assimilation, and, but for the accent, almost perfectly bilingual), I was already in an ethnographic mode. "Learning the culture" was a real-life experience. Formal "fieldwork" seemed an opportunity to discover more of America, and particularly to observe some of the manifestations of its power. In Israeli slang, "America" stands for everything that is advanced, powerful, comfortable. Things American carried (and still do) an ongoing fascination for me, whether found in Fenway Park, on Route 128, or wherever I chanced to stumble, like Thomas Wolfe, with my map. In some sense, they came to represent an authentic cultural source of the secondhand artifacts that flood and tantalize the rest of the world. For an Israeli, growing up in a premeditated and designed culture, "authenticity" was a never-ending quest.[4] For many Israelis, moreover, "America" is both a dream and a threat, representing an option not taken by one's grandparents, and always posing the dangerous temptation either to "Americanize" Israel or, more drastically, to commit the ultimate betrayal and emigrate.[5] As a resident alien in the United States, I was already suspect on both counts. Ethnographic exploration of corporate America was an excuse to follow the sirens, examine them up close, and in the process turn the tables on the historically one-sided anthropological enterprise.

Another factor was my (somewhat militant, at the time) stance vis-à-vis methodological debates in the field of organization studies.[6] I wanted to do "qualitative research," "see for myself," get involved firsthand, test my methodological beliefs concerning the importance and feasibility of interpretive methods, and challenge what I took to be the dry and unexciting procedures (and findings) that characterize much of the research on formal organizations. I was armed with much (perhaps too much) previous reading and some ideas about culture, ideology, identity, and interpretation; the specifics of high-tech engineering never really attracted me—and they still do not, although I did develop an advanced layman's working knowledge of some of the technical issues (having succumbed to and overcome an addiction to computers in the days of Fortran, punchcards, and anxious overnight waits for output), as well as an ongoing curiosity about the social worlds built around them and a grudging respect for the skills involved. But, ultimately, I was after a generic business corporation as an American microcosm and as a methodological proving ground.

My background seems to have influenced my theoretical preferences as well. Those familiar with Israeli culture will understand my preoccupation with the relationship of ideology and the self: it is a central and salient part of the experience of my generation. Israel is the product of Zionism, an ideology that held, and still holds, a central place both in public discourse and in the private concerns of Israelis.[7] Zionism not only defines the Israeli collective but also makes heavy demands on its members; interpreting and coming to terms with its significance in the various arenas of social life is an ongoing and often intense activity. As those who follow the news from the Middle East are well aware, the historical interpretive debate over Zionism is far from being resolved, and, for those whose lives are affected, the outcome is often experienced as a matter of life and death. Upon rereading this study, it seems to me that it may be read also as an allegorical discussion of certain aspects of my own society: the theoretical edifice that I erected—such as it is—can quite easily accommodate the tension between the demands of Zionism and the emergence of an Israeli identity. In this sense, doing ethnography is also a process of self-exploration and discovery.[8] I do not recall thinking of these matters at the time, but looking back, they seem to account for a good deal.

Finally, I might add that there are solid, rational reasons for taking an interpretive approach to research. Of central importance is the fact that the subject matter is elusive and highly context-dependent, inseparably intertwined with the way people understand their reality and reflect on it. Research requires some intimacy in order to access conscious constructions, and close observation of behavior to uncover tacit ones.[9] However, many interesting but fruitless methodological debates have convinced me that there is more than rationality at stake in methodological preference. These rationales become clichés hurled back and forth. The best one can do, then, is to let the work speak for itself.

In the Field   Fieldwork was characterized by continual ambiguity with regard to my role vis-à-vis the company and its employees. The first contact was made through MIT. I was approached by members of a staff organization seeking consulting help. Intrigued by the idea of combining and perhaps comparing ethnographic and clinical approaches to research, I decided to explore this possibility.[10] How and why it failed is another story—one about which I have only partial data. In essence, the staff group had completed a study documenting the shortcomings of a specific engineering project and wished to introduce me to an engineering development organization to help "implement" some of the conclusions. The engineers, however, were clearly not interested, viewing this as a political move by the staff group, for whom they had little sympathy and no respect. Nevertheless, one of their managers was willing to accept my presence as "an MIT sociologist" interested in "the culture." In return I promised to make a presentation about my findings.[11] "I am interested in what you write, but I want you to know that it might also make this group look good to have someone like you," he told me, with the bluntness that characterized many managers at Tech. He was the new manager of a group that in the past had been seen as "closed" and "paranoid." I, presumably, was to be one of his "signals" that times were changing.

As my role as a passive observer in the development group emerged, my fortunes with the staff group changed. In the course of my entry, I had established good ties with a number of the members of the group, some of whom became valued informants. Nevertheless, when the nature of my role became apparent—an unstructured observer rather than a free management consultant—the staff group manager considered asking me to leave. By then, however, my ties with the engineering group were established, and rather than make waves, he chose to tolerate (at arm's length) my presence in his group as a participant-observer and as someone vaguely associated with the "SysCom space." Consequently, I wound up with access to both the staff group and the engineering development group referred to as SysCom in the previous chapters.

The staff group was located at corporate headquarters. It consisted of twenty to thirty people encompassing training (both technical and behavioral), communications (the various publications and newsletters generated in the organization), some technical consultants, and marketing research. It also had a number of "individual contributors," including Ellen Cohen, the full-time "culture" expert. The manager of the group reported directly to Dave Carpenter, the vice-president. The group had relatively low status (as do most staff groups) but was quite central. Through this group I gained access to the various training affairs and also got a bird's-eye view of the entire organization and particularly of senior management. I was given my own office space, a computer terminal with access to electronic mail, whatever administrative assistance I needed, and a free run of headquarters.

SysCom consisted of about six hundred people housed mostly in the Lyndsville facility (see Chapter 2). Here life was harder. I was given grudging access to three projects (one of which was considered to be "in bad shape"), temporarily vacant office space, another terminal, and permission to initiate interviews with anybody, with the understanding that they had permission to refuse.

Once formal access was negotiated and my presence became relatively legitimate, I was left to my own devices. In the staff group my role evolved into that of an "individual contributor" functioning in my own "meta-space" (a role that, as in progressive mental institutions, evokes much overt tolerance and just as much covert backbiting). I also possessed some credibility as an academic with a perceived specialization in "management." In SysCom I was "overhead," with what some considered the redeeming features of an uncharacteristic and rather wild-eyed thirty-second appearance on *Eyewitness News* resulting from my private political involvement in Middle Eastern matters, an inexplicable (to many) MIT affiliation, and a last-minute overtime goal (also uncharacteristic) in the SysCom Olympics soccer game.[12] But to many, my true motives and the exact nature of my work remained unclear. This was caused not only by my own vagueness, the tension between the two groups with which I was associated, and the general air of high-pressure ambiguity that characterizes Tech, but also by the widespread suspicion of the consultants and academics who are a familiar— and to many not always a welcome—sight at Tech.

Between January and June of 1985, I was a full-time participant-observer in the staff group, averaging three to five days a week. I participated in all public activities and a variety of private ones, and established a number of informants as well as various acquaintances. During this time I also used the group's help in gaining access to SysCom.

Between June and December I spent most of my time at SysCom, working the same three- to five-day schedule, but spending a day a week with the staff group. At SysCom, I began by initiating rather extensive interviews (one to two hours long) of the sort known as conversational.[13] First contact would usually be made at my initiative, by requesting permission to talk. In reserve I had a note from the group manager suggesting that "it was all right." Responses varied dramatically, from friendly acceptance to a complaint to the personnel manager that my request constituted harassment. From these initial interviews, I developed a number of informants and friends, formed many casual acquaintances, and learned of many people who seemed to consider my presence there a problem. I made an appearance at all public activities: talks, group meetings, summer sports, training sessions. I enrolled in anything that indicated open enrollment: workshops, sporting events, and so forth. I also managed, with the help of friends, to get invited to a number of more private affairs: staff meetings, design meetings, review meetings, and the like. Although some participants seemed to find my presence disturbing, others were quite willing to share their thoughts and concerns about the proceedings. Over the last months of my fieldwork, I initiated day-long observations of managers and engineers with whom I had established relationships. They would choose a day, and I would tag along, going to meetings, having lunch, asking questions when possible, and disappearing when necessary. On some occasions I offered myself as a driver; several interesting discussions took place on the road with a captive informant beside me.

In between scheduled events, there was much free time. I spent these long hours in a variety of places: in the library, poring over trade journals, in-house publications, and company videotapes; in the cafeteria, eating and eavesdropping, sometimes feeling lonely and at other times relieved that, unlike most members, I could easily disengage from the pressures of corporate life; in front of my computer terminal, exploring the public files or reading my technet messages and mail; or wandering aimlessly through the labyrinth of cubicles, trying to present myself to those whom I encountered as someone with a purpose in mind (on the way, I read and memorized the various signs, decorations, comments, and comic strips adorning the offices). It was during these walks that I established ties with members of Wage Class 2 and temporary workers, many of whom seemed curious about my activities, friendly, and eager to talk.

Toward the end of the year, I stepped up my staff activities again, largely because contact with the staff was easier, and my role of observer–confidant–interesting guy seemed to work. The group was undergoing a rather painful disbanding, and a friendly ear seemed to be appreciated. There is nothing as seductive for the fieldworker as being made to feel like an insider, like someone with something to contribute, particularly in an environment where "value added" is the ultimate measure of a person's worth, and worthlessness is very unsubtly communicated. I responded to invitations eagerly and developed what often seemed a quasi-therapeutic consulting role with a number of people.

Studying a formal organization surfaced two major concerns that stayed with me throughout my fieldwork. First, the problems for ethnographic work posed by a hierarchical system. As was to be expected, the extent of my access was inversely related to hierarchical level. One indicator of power is the ability to preserve privacy, and my interactions with the pinnacle of power were limited to some interviews, observation of presentations, and continuous and often frustrating contact with protective secretarial gatekeepers. A number of senior managers took an interest in my work and made themselves somewhat more available. Toward the end of my fieldwork, the vice-president responded to a request I made in a moment of recklessness and surprised me by inviting me to observe some of his activities. I sat in on a few of his staff meetings, wondering what had held me back earlier.[14] Most of my contacts, however, were engineers and managers in the middle range and in my age (thirty-three, at the time)—and possibly status—group. With them, my main goal was to transcend their suspicion of my ties with more senior managers or with other groups, and avoid colluding with whatever organizational purposes they might have. In addition, those who were somewhat different, or marginal, seemed to find their way to me: minorities, especially those with an interest in my Israeli background, those who were failing, unhappy, or "burnt out," and those who wanted to distance themselves from the "nerd" and "Techie" images. I have no way of evaluating my success other than by intuition and "clinical" skill and the fact that people seemed interested in talking and thinking about their experience, even when it was apparent that doing so involved no benefit—and might even involve some danger—for them. For people at the lower organizational levels, I seemed to be a curiosity, an anomaly, someone close to having a Ph.D. yet marginal in organizational terms. My marginality seemed to attract some of the disaffected in this group, while I also appeared to represent an easily accessible (even openly grateful) contact with the class of people from which members of Wage Class 4 hail.[15]

Second, my access to the dense social network and the informal aspects of life at Tech was limited. Some of the events that were of interest to me occurred in inaccessible places: off-site meetings, private, after-hours discussions, secret one-on-ones, and so forth. My access was further curtailed by the nature of my involvement. By limiting myself to relatively standard working hours and to the main working facilities and their close environment, I restricted the range of events that were accessible for direct observation. This decision reflects the difficulties inherent in the research process, the rather segmented social lives many people at Tech lead, deficiencies in my "networking" and socializing skills, and, to some extent, my own family constraints. Consequently, participation in certain kinds of events was relatively rare. I was invited to only three homes over the course of the research, and I did not travel with members, many of whom spent considerable time in airplanes, hotels, and conference centers. For what transpired outside my view, I pieced together hearsay, gossip, and stories.

Despite these constraints, I was swamped with information. Throughout my year in the field, and despite the advice I frequently received, I did not consciously define what I was after. Everything was interesting, and my discussions, interviews, and observations usually focused on whatever was occurring at the time and on the particular interests and concerns of the people involved.[16] In the course of this process I generated thousands of pages of fieldnotes and interview transcripts (produced each day from the fragmented notes hastily scribbled during and between events and interviews), collections of archival material, computer output, newsletters, papers, memos, brochures, posters, textbooks, and assorted leftovers. Internally produced statistical evidence landed in my lap on a number of occasions, along with explicit caveats or dark hints about their "political" nature, "sensitive" quality, and questionable validity. I also made some informal counts through the interviewing process (educational background, personal background, employment status, and so forth). As it should be clear by now, however, the strength of my argument does not rest on data of the quantitative sort.

Writing It Up Ethnographers describing their craft, and I am no exception, often cultivate the aura of heroism associated with their activities. In comparison with the armchair efforts of their tamer colleagues, fieldwork, they claim, is an adventure. Ethnography's tribulations however, are found not only in the unknown jungle, tropical or corporate, but also, I submit, in the seemingly unexciting task of analyzing and reporting one's findings.[17]

Having returned to safer shores, I discovered that, chained to a desk like the mythical hero, I was forced to relive the essence of the dangers and pain of the field adventure over and over again: facing the unknown, the incomprehensible. Masses of facts, stories, vignettes, numbers, rumors, and endless pages of fieldnotes documenting the observed trivia of everyday life—their sheer volume offered daily testimony to the seeming impossibility of making any valid statement at all. And, ironically, the more conscientious one is as a fieldworker, the more impossible one has demonstrated one's task to be. Moreover, the less adventurous and closer to home the field experience, the more difficult the secondary one, for one is not the sole owner and interpreter of the particular culture one has studied. Everything, it often seems, has been said; all is already known and, if anything, overdocumented.

I began the analysis and writing during the last months of my fieldwork, and completed the thesis close to a year later. The first step was reading and cataloguing my fieldnotes, creating, combining, redefining, and discarding numerous categories and groupings. It was in the course of this process that the main analytic categories—ideology, ritual, the self—emerged. Next, I wrote a short ethnographic description of Tech as part of a co-authored paper (Van Maanen and Kunda, 1989). This became the basis for a rather frenzied, apparently directionless, yet satisfying process of writing descriptions that I engaged in after the fieldwork was (arbitrarily) terminated. The final version of the thesis emerged after repeated writing and rewriting, and under pressure from readers to move from pure description, with occasionally disguised theoretical insinuations ("illustrated diatribes," in the words of one advisor), to an explicit analytic framework. This transition, the heart of the ethnographic procedure, is also the stage most difficult to specify. In my case, this difficulty reflects not only the inherent problem of generalizing from ethnographic data, of combining the general with the specific, but also my own deep suspicion of any general theoretical statement. A careful reader might detect in the book the traces of a struggle with standard presentational requirements and accepted forms.

Responses to the thesis from Tech were limited—largely, I believe, because of my preference for a low-key withdrawal from the field and my decision to reduce my general discomfort with my role and its implications by severing contact with the company. My promised feedback session never materialized, forgotten or considered unnecessary by management, and gladly ignored by me. There were no responses to the copy I sent by mail about one year after I left, and I did not stay in touch with any of the people I had worked with in the field. The only formal response was from a senior manager in the Human Resources Department, who had received a draft from one of my advisors and who sent a note back indicating that the findings could be used to help plan whether and how to spread Tech culture to foreign subsidiaries as the company became increasingly multinational. Tech employees who read various drafts generally confirmed the validity of the findings and added comments ranging from "Yes, but why the negative tone?" to "You should really let them have it!"

Transforming the thesis into a book occurred over three years of intensive reanalysis and rewriting. Some of the empirical data were discarded, others added; the theoretical sections were rewritten and the analytic framework restructured and sharpened. During this period I did not return to the field, nor did I contact any of my informants. I did, however, follow the company's fortunes closely. Writing the book occurred under conditions of personal flux, as I was making the decision to leave the United States and return to Israel, and during the first two years of my return; throughout I was troubled by the implications of my choice in light of recent events in the Middle East and continuously concerned with my own identity, my responsibility to my family, and my stance toward the ideological underpinnings of my own society. Whether and how these concerns are reflected in the book, and whether these are at all relevant questions, I leave to the reader.

I regard this study as far from finished. Each completed sentence represents, to paraphrase one of Max Weber's biographers, "a tenuous victory
over the infinite complexity of the facts." Such victories are short-lived, and
the battles must be fought again. If, as Thomas Wolfe, himself a student of
detail, suggested, "only the dead know Brooklyn," then the living can only
continue to sketch and follow their own maps.

notes

Chapter 1: Culture and Organization

1. I will use the term *member* to refer to all the people employed by the company. (See Chapter 2 for a discussion of the various categories of membership.) The concept of "role" has been extensively used by social scientists to understand the link between individuals and social groups (Rosenberg and Turner, 1981). *Role* refers most generally to sets of prescribed activities associated with particular institutionally defined positions. Typically, the analytic focus has been on the *behavioral* aspect of the role. Yet, as Berger and Luckmann (1966: 77) suggest, "To learn a role it is not enough to acquire the routines immediately necessary to its 'outward' performance. One must also be initiated into the various cognitive and even affective layers of the body of knowledge that is directly *and* indirectly appropriate to this role." Few, however, have heeded them, and, as I will attempt to show, this is a very significant omission. It is Berger and Luckmann's broader definition of *role* that I will use to analyze the "member role."

2. "Culture" is a notoriously complex and ambiguous concept. For reviews of the definitional debates that have raged between anthropologists, see Harris (1968), Kroeber and Kluckhohn (1952), and Kroeber and Parsons (1958). For a sharpening of the cultural anthropologists' (somewhat arcane) debate about whether culture is found in the "minds and hearts of men" or located in public systems of signification, see Geertz (1973) and Goodenough (1981).

3. The definitional debates surrounding the concept of culture have been replicated by students of organizations. See Allaire and Firsirotu (1984) and Sanday (1979) for a conceptual overview and Ouchi and Wilkins (1985) for a review of research on organizational culture and related concepts. The precise boundaries of the culture-bearing collective are also the subject of considerable debate. Some theorists assume they coincide with the formal boundaries of the organization; others have focused on specific subgroups (managers, occupational groups, and so forth) that often extend beyond the formal boundaries; and others yet have left the boundaries undefined or considered their location an empirical question. See Louis (1983), Schein (1985), and Van Maanen and Barley (1985).

4. Organizational effectiveness is usually conceptualized by students of organizations from a managerial perspective. In this view, effectiveness is coterminous with the attainment of managerially defined goals, and is defined in terms of quantitative measures of innovation, productivity, survivability, and profitability. An alternative formulation is found in the Human Relations tradition, where effectiveness is defined in terms of human outcomes: worker satisfaction, organi-

zational climate, turnover, and so forth. However, these too are framed from the perspective of managerial concerns and are conceptually linked to other measures of effectiveness; the underlying assumption is that happy workers are productive and that harmony in the workplace is a precondition for profit. For reviews of various approaches to the concept of organizational effectiveness, see Cameron and Whetten (1983). For reviews of the relationship of culture and effectiveness, see Ott (1989) and Ouchi and Wilkins (1985).

5. Some of the theoretical issues raised by the concept of culture have in the past been addressed by such notions as "organizational climate" and "organizational character" (Ott, 1989). Those who cater to the managerial mind are, it seems, forever looking for innovative formulations. Thus, the popularity of social scientific concepts in the corporate world has a faddish quality: "hot topics" come and go at a seemingly accelerating pace. Given the managerial appetite for new terminology and the academic requirement of constant innovation, the future probably holds more metaphors for the same old story.

6. See Barley, Meyer, and Gash (1988) for a discussion of the transformation over time of the concept of culture to suit the practical concerns of consultants and managers.

7. See for example *Business Week* (1980) and *Fortune* (1983).

8. The distinction between "emic" and "etic" is the anthropologist's way of distinguishing concepts used by the people being studied and those used by the people doing the studying. Others have used the terms *first-order* and *second-order,* or *experience-near* and *experience-far.* This distinction might be easy to maintain during temporary visits to illiterate and isolated societies; however, as Giddens (1976) points out, the complexity of interactions between social scientific discourse and natural language makes a clear distinction close to impossible.

9. As Jackall (1988: 142) points out, Kanter's work is a good example of how this genre tends to expropriate and recycle the language of the 1960s New Left ("let a thousand flowers bloom," "grassroots empowerment," and so forth) and systematically introduces quasi-radical jargon into managerial ideology.

10. Similar texts in this genre have focused on selling an idealized (from the managerial point of view) version of Japanese management systems (Ouchi, 1981; Pascale and Athos, 1981). It is interesting to contrast these mythical representations with the careful ethnographic work of Rohlen (1974). See n. 21 to Chapter 3.

11. See for example Ouchi's (1981) glorification of Hewlett-Packard, Peters and Waterman's (1982) discussion of excellent companies, and Deal and Kennedy's (1982) conceptually similar analysis of corporate cultures.

12. Examples include Davis (1984), Kilmann et al. (1985), Pfeffer (1981), and Trice and Beyer (1984). This literature ranges from the serious consideration of sym-

bolic management in corporate settings to such titles as *Myth Making: A Qualitative Step in OD Interventions* (Boje, Fedor, and Rowland, 1982). See Barley, Meyer, and Gash (1988) and Kunda and Barley (1988) for a review of some of this material.

13. Etzioni (1961) classifies organizations by the type of power management attempts to exert over the membership (coercive, remunerative, or normative) and by the type of member involvement in the organization (alienative, calculative, or moral). The three main forms of organizational control occur where there is a congruency between type of power and type of involvement. These are: (1) the use of coercive power over alienated members; (2) the use of economic power over calculative members; and (3) the use of normative power over members who form a moral attachment. Although most organizations contain elements of all three, according to Etzioni, they tend to cluster around a particular type. Work organizations, in his view, typically fall into the second category: members contribute time and effort to the organization in return for economic rewards in a contracted exchange that requires little or no personal involvement. Etzioni's typology is a useful tool for comparative analysis, but it provides little in the way of explanatory power. Although Etzioni views the three main types as equilibrium positions, Perrow (1986) points out, quite rightly, that as a dynamic explanation of the emergence of particular forms of control, this scheme is tautological: coercion produces alienation and vice versa. To the extent that Etzioni's goal was not explanatory, the criticism is overstated. Where Etzioni does fall short, however, is in his failure to exploit the dynamic power of his framework, and specifically in the lack of analysis of noncongruent positions.

14. The self, most broadly speaking, is the locus of an individual's subjective experience of the world. In commonsense usage, it is loosely defined and is typically thought to encompass the entirety of the individual's psychological structure and psychic mechanisms. Such a view of the self is often associated in Western tradition with the right to—if not always the actual enjoyment of—a measure of personal autonomy for adults; and it is precisely this autonomy over one's own experience that is challenged by corporate attempts at normative control. Social scientific attempts to categorize, organize, and explain the components of the self have spawned not only a variety of concepts and theoretical perspectives, but whole disciplines. These efforts have not necessarily contributed to clarity, and the "self" remains a poorly defined concept. See Chapter 5 for a review and discussion of the different perspectives on the self and its relationship to the social contexts within which it emerges.

15. Bendix (1956: 2) defines managerial ideology as "the ideas espoused by or for those who exercise authority in economic enterprises, and which seek to explain

and justify that authority." These ideas focus on the nature of the enterprise and the people it employs. See Chapter 3 for a further discussion of ideology in corporate contexts.

16. See Brandes (1976) for a review of "welfare capitalism," and Chandler (1966, 1977) and Pollard (1965) for a history of the evolution of the American corporation and its business practices. See Kunda and Barley (1988) and Perrow (1986) for a review of the developments in managerial ideology since the 1950s.

17. The first extensive sociological analysis of "bureaucracy" was offered by Weber (1947), who used it to refer to the manifestation of rational-legal authority in the sphere of administration. Weber's view is by now well enough known to require no lengthy description; for a review, see Gerth and Mills (1948) and Perrow (1986). Generally, in Weber's view, the defining features of the ideal type of bureaucracy are: a hierarchy of offices with clear specification of authority; a division of labor based on training and expertise; a system of rules and records; a separation between person and office; impersonality in the performance of duties; and graded, salaried careers for officials. In this sense, the bureaucratization of industry in the twentieth century is almost self-evident. Chandler (1977) provides a historical analysis of this process in the American context. In his view, one of its main features is the emergence of managerial capitalism: the separation of ownership from control, the replacement of market mechanisms with administrative regulation, and the rise of a class of professional managers who control the administrative apparatus of the business enterprise. Like other powerful concepts, however, "bureaucracy" has been appropriated by commonsense users (as well as by various critics of the human condition), who tend to emphasize its negative connotations. Here *bureaucracy* has come to mean everything from unnecessary red tape to the kind of inhuman machinations captured in Kafka's work. As Perrow (1986) suggests, however, the criticism is at the very least overstated and ignores, or takes for granted, some of the potential benefits of bureaucracy.

18. In addition to Weber's influence, much of the work in this tradition is influenced by Durkheim's (1964) classic *The Division of Labor in Society*, in which he foresaw the breakdown of solidarity and social integration as a result of the increased differentiation and specialization of labor. However, empirical research in this tradition, particularly in the United States, has been concerned for the most part with correlating various quantitative indicators of bureaucracy with each other and with measures of efficiency—thus constructing sophisticated quantitative models but ignoring the underlying dynamics whereby solidarity is created or normative control accomplished. See for example Blau and Schoenherr (1971).

19. "White-collar workers" are the managerial, professional, and clerical workers who filled the expanding middle levels of large organizations both as agents of coordination and control and as production workers themselves. Generally, white-

collar work evolved from the delegation of activities traditionally associated with ownership and from the increasing professionalization of organizationally based work (Hall, 1968; Mills, 1956; Wilensky, 1964). Compared with lower-level industrial work, these tasks involve more discretion, less predictability, and less possibility of routinization, measurement, and evaluation and are thus harder to monitor and supervise directly. Moreover, since this is a salaried work force, the motivation presumably associated with ownership is no longer a relevant factor. Thus the problem of control: how does one generate and keep the commitment of workers to tasks that call for heavy investments of time and effort and yet are difficult to prescribe, program, and monitor?

20. Barnard's reflection on his own experience as an executive at New Jersey Bell has provided an inspiration to many organizational theorists (Perrow, 1986). However, Barnard's major theoretical impact has been on those who concern themselves with the remunerative-calculative aspects of organization and leadership, while his views on the normative side have been largely ignored. Thus, it is from Barnard that such concepts as "satisficing" and "inducement/contribution ratio" were borrowed and developed into theories of economic decision making under uncertainty (March and Simon, 1958; Simon, 1976). Yet, although crude by today's standards, Barnard's views on indoctrination have proved to be prescient. With the exception of Selznick's (1957) treatment of administrative leadership, it is only recently that the role of corporate leaders in shaping and designing cultural variables has come under scrutiny. See Pfeffer (1981) and Schein (1985).

21. Edwards is extending and modifying Braverman's (1974) argument concerning the control of the labor process under capitalist modes of organization. He identifies three basic forms of control: simple control is manifested in face-to-face coercion; technical control occurs through mechanical control of the labor process; and bureaucratic control embeds control in the social structure of the workplace. Edwards suggests that contradictions and conflicts inherent in each form of capitalist control cause a new form of control to emerge gradually. The new forms of control are manifested in the more innovative industrial sectors of the time, while earlier forms are still found in other sectors.

   With regard to the Marxist perspective, Edwards adds a valuable view of the impact of bureaucratic processes, a much neglected issue in this brand of theorizing. However, the focus is almost entirely on the lower levels of organizations: blue-collar production workers and the lower rungs of the white-collar world. Here, it is possible, his argument is valid. But what of the higher levels? It is increasingly untenable to view them as "agents of the capitalist" and thus a vaguely evil entity that requires no analysis except in their role of agent/expropriator. Equally untenable is the attempt to view managers and professionals as a new proletariat (Zussman, 1985). Thus, Edwards ignores the more important question of the control of this rapidly increasing population, a question that is the theme of this book.

22. See Emery and Trist (1966) and Perrow (1986) for a discussion of organizational environments. It is worth noting that the postindustrial conditions faced by the white-collar and professional labor force in developed countries depend on (and perhaps facilitate) the continuing existence of industrial and even preindustrial working conditions in other parts of the economy. These, to some extent, are made invisible by using a secondary labor force or by exporting some industries and types of work to more amenable foreign shores (where authoritarian control of the labor force is funded, critics might suggest, by the resources controlled by postindustrial economies, and supported by their political power).

23. Questions regarding the nature of the ties between individuals and social institutions have come to be regarded as increasingly urgent. As Durkheim (1964) pointed out, the modern era is characterized by a breakdown of traditional forms of authority and the rise of increasingly differentiated, segmented, and fragmented social groupings. He saw the maintenance of social integration and order in the face of these developments as a crucial problem for any society. Under such circumstances, the tension between individualism and collective action comes to the foreground of consciousness and becomes an issue, a question, a problem, a debate. This (quite celebrated) condition has been referred to as the "crisis of modernity" (Berger, Berger, and Kellner 1974) and in an American context has been most recently revisited by Bellah and his colleagues (1985), who attempted to reexamine the themes of individualism and commitment in American life first raised by De Tocqueville (1961). Interestingly, they focus on arenas other than work and work organizations.

24. See Perrow (1986) for a review of the various strands of Human Relations theory and research.

25. Bendix (1956) claims that the relationship of rhetoric to practice is, at best, tenuous, and suggests that the Human Relations ideology was rarely implemented. More recently, others have questioned the impact of the various programs designed to create the conditions for normative control (Perrow, 1986; Strauss, 1969).

26. See Beyer (1981) for a review of this literature.

27. Most case studies of explicit normative control in organizational settings have focused on "people-processing" organizations, where various combinations of coercive and normative control are often the explicit social function of the organization. The underlying model they share is that of a relatively captive group of inmates and a faceless group of agents. For example, studies of professional education (Becker et al., 1961; Light, 1980), mental health institutions (Goffman, 1961a; Strauss et al., 1964), prisoner-of-war camps (Schein, 1961), police

organizations (Manning, 1977; Van Maanen, 1976), schools (Illich, 1971), and prisons and reformatories (Street, Vinter, and Perrow, 1966) illustrate the conflict between normative organizational demands and individual needs, and the ensuing struggle to define and shape member experience from two different perspectives: the organization (often presented as oppressive) and the individual member (frequently cast as a victim). Empirical examinations of these issues in business and industrial organization focus, with few exceptions (Dalton, 1959; Jackall, 1988; Kanter, 1979; Rohlen, 1974; Rosen, 1984), on lower-level workers. See n. 5 to Chapter 5.

28. Goffman's (1961a) conceptual framework is illustrated in the context of a mental institution, where inmates "make do," "work the system," find escape worlds, engage in ritual insubordination and ultimately attempt to demonstrate (to themselves, if to no one else) that they have some personal autonomy. Although he focused mainly on patient life in a psychiatric hospital, he also ranged far and wide through literature (in both the academic and the artistic senses of the word), and engaged in speculation and perhaps—dare one say—introspection, in order to generalize the problem of the self in normative organizations beyond the walls of the mental institution, or to expand those walls to include other types of organizations. While openly speculative, Goffman pushes the conclusions as far as he can, with an air of authority whose force, certainly not derived from data, must derive from the reader's experience—the ultimate validity test for an interpretive method.

29. The perspective on culture that I take in this study is informed by what is usually referred to as an interpretive approach, represented, in particular, by the work of Geertz (1973). According to Geertz, culture "is not a power, something to which social events, behaviors, institutions, or processes can be causally attributed; it is a context, something within which they can be intelligibly—that is, thickly—described" (p. 14). In this view, then, culture is located in the symbolic expression of the various interrelated systems of meaning created and maintained by a group, and it is the analyst's task to identify, understand, and interpret them. With this in mind, it is necessary to distinguish the etic use of culture as an overarching analytic concept from its emic significance—"culture" as defined and used at Tech (see n. 8 above). This is not always easy, since there are many intricate connections between the two types of concepts, something I attempt to document and explain in the following chapters, along with an analysis of other cultural phenomena that lie beyond the members' own conception of "Tech culture."

Chapter 2: The Setting

1. The necessity of maintaining a disguise requires the distortion of some of the facts and figures used in describing the company. All descriptive statistics in this chapter have been rounded or changed. Where relevant, relations between the numbers have been maintained in order to illustrate analytic points. All names are, of course, fictitious.

2. See Chapter 1 for a review of the historical context within which these ideas evolved, and Chapter 3 for an extensive analysis of the company's managerial ideology in general and Sam Miller's ideas in particular. From its foundation, Tech management employed as consultants some of the leading academics of the time, including key figures in the Human Relations movement. This association was more than purely theoretical; in the best tradition of Human Relations, senior management conducted frequent off-site meetings in which business issues were dealt with along with intense and often emotionally loaded examinations of personal issues and group dynamics. Observers of the company and veterans of Tech's early days see a connection between the confrontative style of these early group sessions—now part of the company mythology—and the norms governing meetings of the sort described in Chapter 4.

3. The matrix is a type of complex organizational structure in which an attempt is made to balance a number of organizing dimensions. A typical matrix has a standard structure organized by functional groups—Research and Development, Marketing, Manufacturing, and so forth—overlaid by a project- or product-oriented structure based on cross-functional groups dedicated to working on a particular product or project. Thus, one of the central principles of bureaucracy—clear lines of authority—is broken. People find themselves reporting to two (or more) managers—a functional manager and a project manager. See Davis and Lawrence (1977) and Galbraith (1973) for a review of the matrix, its advantages, and its problems.

4. Annual plans are a central part of the budget cycle. Managers compose their plans, including the resources they need and the "deliverables" they promise; these, after many rounds of "wordsmithing" with peers and managers, are folded into their group proposals and presented by their managers in additional rounds of the process. Thus, annual plans make their way up the hierarchy and are accepted, rejected, or modified. Once accepted, the promised "deliverables" are used as a criterion of managerial success.

5. It is important to note that the domain of each technical area is a highly politicized topic and is subject to continuing conflict, negotiation, and debate. Reorganizations and redefinitions of areas of responsibility occur relatively frequently as senior managers attempt to carve out their "space" and define the company's

direction under conditions of considerable uncertainty with regard to technological developments, the competition, and the nature of the market. Sam Miller
prides himself on the company's flexibility and ability to adapt to the rapid and
unpredictable changes that are characteristic of the high-tech industry. His critics
in the company suggest that he also tends to take personal credit for some of the
past successes in predicting technological developments and organizing the company appropriately—a process, they suggest, that may be seen as rational only in
hindsight.

6. This group was one of my main research sites. See the Appendix.

7. "Dotted lines" are the alternative, overlaid authority channels typical of a matrix,
weaker and often not fully specified relations that are added to one's regular reporting lines (see n. 3 above). Connoisseurs of the matrix can distinguish different
types of dotted lines.

8. Product managers fill one of the quintessential "matrix roles" and are often the
victims of matrix problems. "Lots of responsibility, no authority" is how many
characterize their work; it is therefore, one often hears, "a one-way street to
burnout."

9. Most members of the Wage Class 2 population at Tech are found in the Manufacturing Division. They will not be discussed here.

10. Throughout its existence, Tech has maintained two policies that define its relationship with its employees: the principle of "no layoffs," and the open internal labor
market. Job openings are publicly posted, and employees are encouraged to make
internal transfers and seek promotion at their own initiative rather than through
hierarchical channels. The company also offers its employees a broad array of
benefits: a credit union, education, stock options, health insurance, childcare.
These are seen by many as "golden handcuffs" designed to lock employees in.

11. For a discussion of engineering's status as a profession and a review of the relevant
literature, see Zussman (1985).

12. Management may informally encourage these projects or turn a blind eye to the
time and energy they demand. It is rumored that many a successful Tech product started off as a midnighter, occasionally even using company funds somehow
made available. Real midnight projects are, apparently, becoming less frequent.
Some see this as a loss of the creative spark the company possessed when it was
smaller. Others, particularly managers, welcome the normalization. Students of
engineering work use the term "bootlegging" to refer to similar phenomena (La
Porte and Wood, 1970).

13. In his now-classic examination of engineering, Gouldner (1957, 1958) categorized engineers by the degree to which their orientation was "cosmopolitan"
(oriented to the professional world) or "local" (oriented to the company and its
concerns). Later work, however, suggests that this dichotomy is not tenable and

that most engineering work is characterized by some measure of both orientations. Zussman (1985) asserts that a dual orientation is inherent in the nature
of engineering work. In this view, no clear boundaries divide the technical aspect of engineering work from the administrative side; moreover, business con-
siderations and the parameters and constraints they impose are the very stuff of
technical work.

14. The data in Tables 1 and 2 were collected from a variety of internal and external
sources, and, as is true of all statistical data, the context of their production must
be questioned. At Tech, statistics of this sort are considered "sensitive" and their
accuracy is often challenged. The reader is warned.

15. Shenhav (1988) reviews sociological studies of researchers' transition to administration in Research and Development and discusses the dual career ladder.

16. This, of course, creates misleading statistics. It is merely one example of the
systematic distortions that are built into company-sponsored statistical data and
analysis.

17. Tech's compensation policies are fairly standard for the industry. The company
conducts ongoing surveys of the pay policies of its competitors—large and established high-tech companies—and attempts to offer comparable compensation.
Within these general guidelines there is of course much room for maneuver-
ing: each level has a defined pay spread, and people may receive raises at the
company's or their managers' discretion. Moreover, stock options are regularly
awarded in a secret process to members considered "outstanding performers";
here, too, there is room for managerial discretion. Exceptional offers may be
made to specialists in highly desirable technologies. But, overall, it is the company's policy to offer competitive monetary compensation, with nonmonetary
benefits and "a good working environment" as an added attraction.

18. An additional managerial group consists of the functional managers (personnel,
finance, marketing, and so forth). While some have technical training, many do
not, and are therefore considered second-class citizens within the managerial
ranks. Functional managers who are nontechnical are often viewed as "overhead," as "product preventers," or at best as a nuisance to be tolerated. Those
in Engineering are aware of their status. They are in service roles, and for them
engineers and their managers are a group to be understood, dealt with, often
pampered, and just as often criticized. Functional managers in finance and personnel develop careers within the function. For many, the career path leads out of
Engineering.

19. The policies guiding managerial compensation are similar to the ones for engineers. A comparison of Tables 1 and 2 suggests that there is some basis to the
claim that the managerial track offers an advantage over the technical track in
terms of one's chances for improvement over time in basic compensation. How-

ever, the many ways fixed pay scales can be circumvented and the systematic distortions of such data make it hard to draw firm conclusions.

20. Managers take pride in their budgetary achievements. Some of those who hold a "business perspective" seek to reform the company by introducing professional management processes and mechanisms. They regard the "engineering mentality" in a critical light. A typical view of engineers is offered by one manager: "They are arrogant know-it-alls with an 'only way' mentality. They just throw the product over the wall. No conception of the customer or the market." The compliments are of course returned.

21. Managers evaluate engineers on their ability to "drive a stake in the ground"— that is, to settle on a well-defined piece of work and produce it in a reasonable "time frame."

22. To address this phenomenon, and to prevent what management viewed as "a misuse of the company's commitment to internal mobility," a policy requiring managers to remain in a position for at least two years was established during the period this research took place.

23. At the time of this research, no freelancers were employed in the groups I studied. One who had just left told me that one of the advantages of his position was that he did not have to speak to people like me. Although it is an interesting role, it will not be discussed further.

24. Temporary work is used by creative managers to circumvent budget and head-count freezes, and is therefore the subject of manipulative statistics.

25. See Chapter 5 for a further discussion of the office and its use.

Chapter 3: Ideology

1. Like *culture, ideology* is a loaded term carrying multiple meanings. Yet it has proved to be an indispensable analytic concept. Early Marxist perspectives defined *ideology* as a system of thought used to legitimize relations of domination and hegemony (Marx and Engels, 1947). Mannheim (1936) attempted to retrieve it from narrow Marxist use for scientific purposes by formulating a nonevaluative general concept of ideology as the basis for a sociology of knowledge. Merton (1957) elaborated this view by defining ideology to include all systems of thought analyzed in terms of the social context within which they arise, while suspending (and ultimately not addressing) questions of validity. Berger and Luckmann (1966) extend this perspective to include not only formal bodies of knowledge but also its everday, commonsensical, and taken-for-granted forms. Despite the various usages, ideology has remained, to a large extent, a concept favored by those who seek to relate ideas to the underlying interests of those who formu-

late and propagate them. See Giddens (1979: 165–97) and Thompson (1984) for critical reviews.

2. Geertz (1973) narrows the concept of ideology to explicit, highly articulated, and logically coherent systems of ideas that attempt to make sense of the social reality faced by a collective. In this sense, ideology is a subset of culture and refers to that aspect of a society's meaning system that is self-consciously and authoritatively articulated, as opposed to other aspects of culture—like common sense or tradition—that are implicit, taken for granted, and often less systematic. The substance of ideology, Geertz suggests, consists of meaning-conveying symbols, and these must be understood in their own terms prior to the analysis of their role in social processes. This is not to say that ideology does not have social causes and consequences, but these must be identified and proved rather than assumed a priori. In Geertz's view, ideology arises during times of symbolic strain: historical periods characterized by a lack of clear and coherent images that provide a satisfactory shared understanding of society and of social processes.

3. In organizational analysis, ideology has been used in a variety of forms. With few exceptions, analysts leap to causes and consequences, with little attention to meaning. For example, in a review of the literature on ideology in organizational contexts, Beyer (1981) defines ideology broadly as "all ideas that create loyalty and bind people together . . . explaining the environment in terms of cause and effect." These she relates to traditional organizational variables, not asking what "loyalty" is and how people are "bound together." Thus, the definition precludes what is perhaps the most interesting empirical question. A few studies have attempted a contextualized and detailed examination of the nuances of organizational and managerial ideology, most notably Bendix (1956), Kaufman (1960), Nye (1985), and Rohlen (1974). The choice to consider managerial theories of culture as ideology is, of course, potentially confusing, particularly in an ethnography attempting to bring a cultural perspective to bear on the subject matter. See n. 29 to Chapter 1.

4. Such articulations are perhaps the most pervasive form in which ideology appears. They lend themselves most clearly to textual analysis, and on the assumption that the coverage is comprehensive (i.e., that all ideological formulations are translated into words), they provide a convenient analytic short cut. However, other forms are no less expressive, and a systematic study would include them too. Photographs are one important form: Goffman (1976) reveals the consistent messages conveyed by commercial art; Nye (1985) demonstrates the value of photographic analysis for ideological analysis in his study of the General Electric archives; Dougherty and Kunda (1990) examine photographs in corporate annual reports and reveal the underlying ideological themes they contain.

5. Articulating the "corporate philosophy" is a widespread practice in American

companies. Many managerial textbooks and cookbooks suggest that it is crucial for success, and some of them cite with approval Tech's version (along with others). At Tech, "the philosophy" is considered by senior managers "a living document": senior management, with the help of staff people charged with expressing their managers' ideas, has gone through numerous iterations of proposal and discussion and spent many hours debating the appropriate formulations— a process somewhat cynically referred to as "wordsmithing" by those who are skeptical of the corporate "love of wisdom." The current version of the philosophy has been in place for a number of years now, with only minor changes introduced.

6. A number of unofficial newsletters are circulated on the technet at the initiative of employees. They range from the playful to the openly subversive. Use of the technet for these purposes is condoned, or at least tolerated, by managers, who seem to operate on the assumption that even subversive play is a form of attachment and that, in any case, nothing can keep engineers from tinkering.

7. See Jackall (1988: 162–90) for a discussion of the history and use of public relations in corporations.

8. Miller's presence is strongly felt throughout the company. A handbook titled "The Sayings of Chairman Sam" has been broadly distributed in training workshops as a lighthearted but still respectful rendition of the founder's thoughts. A more straightforward version of Miller's ideas is found in one of the first sections of the "Engineering Guide," along with the corporate philosophy. Many Tech watchers attribute the culture directly to Miller's innovative thinking and to his longstanding (some would say obstinate) insistence on the preservation of some of its manifestations. Such a perspective is supported—and perhaps influenced—by managerial theorists who emphasize the role of founders and leaders in the formation of a culture, occasionally going so far as to present the company as an extension of the founder's personality (Kets de Vries and Miller, 1984; Schein, 1985). Regardless of one's stance toward such causal arguments, it is beyond doubt that this particular founder is a central symbol in whatever cultural formation has been accomplished or has developed at Tech.

9. Like *philosophy, mission* is a popular term in managerial circles. Formulating a "mission statement" is a widespread consulting technique in which layers of management are asked to formulate their goals in light of the more general ones of their superiors. The military and religious connotations of the term are obvious and by now hackneyed, yet they are indicative of the kind of "team spirit" management wishes to generate.

10. Miller is referring to Douglas McGregor's (1960) influential typology of managerial views of workers: "Theory X" refers to the view that workers are inherently lazy and require close and authoritarian supervision; "Theory Y" refers to the

view (obviously preferred by McGregor) that workers, given the chance, prefer to work out of a sense of responsibility and intrinsic motivation. This perspective, derived from the Human Relations tradition (see Chapter 1), led to much applied and educational work in industrial settings and is still taught in Organizational Behavior classes in many an MBA program. Tech, in particular, has used academic consultants of this persuasion throughout its history, and its senior management has had massive exposure to such theoretical formulations and to the people behind them.

11. See note 4 to Chapter 2.

12. The text is based on an academic study of Tech culture (Dyer, 1982), rewritten and modified to conform to the author's own experience and sense of what the appropriate terminology should be. One assumption in particular has been toned down: the original study emphasized conflict as the source of truth; here we find "multiple viewpoints" and "some conflict."

13. See Chapter 4 for an analysis of the role of internal experts in training and education events.

14. The lines between these groups are not neatly drawn. Overlap—a topic worthy of a separate study—occurs most frequently when popular writers are themselves academics (Deal and Kennedy, 1982; Kanter, 1983) or when they draw on scholarly research (Peters and Waterman, 1982). Published scholarly work of the "applied" sort resembles the popular genre, and journalists often cite the popular literature in lieu of their own brand of research and theory. Consequently, these forms of observation, analysis, and reporting do not always fall into distinct categories, but belong on a continuum. What is academic and what is popular is in the mind of the beholder as much as in the intent of the authors. Here I will use the insider's distinction between categories, as well as my own judgment based on style.

15. The body of work produced in this genre is generally distinct in style and form, and conforms to the accepted rules of scientific representation in the social sciences.

16. Academics who study organizations often categorize themselves according to the degree to which they engage in "consulting"—the application of their knowledge to practical managerial problems. For the purists, consulting can only distort the scientific stance required by the norms of academia; others view it as a justified extracurricular activity (for which one can command fees ranging from $1,500 to $4,000 a day) that exposes one to the real world and thus enriches teaching and research; still others view consulting as a legitimate research method, labeling it *clinical research* (Schein, 1985) or *action research* (Argyris and Schon, 1974). In any case, many, if not most, academic students of organizations engage in consulting in one form or another; more crucially, most managers in the course

of their careers have interacted with academics of all types and statuses and have been exposed to their ideas. Critics might point to the underlying economic interests and the continuing interaction and familiarity with management as one explanation for the generally pro-management tone of the academic literature on organizations.

17. Although it is cast as a description of the organizational culture, the author carefully limits its applicability. The data, he discloses, were collected from managers, and the description is really of their occupational culture. Moreover, most of the interpretations reflect the view of the more senior managers and not those of newcomers, who might have a totally different perspective. This leads the author to question the existence of a "single culture" and to propose that the company be viewed as a pluralistic society. Such qualifications, however, are usually lost in the transition from academic to corporate text. Ellen Cohen's rendition of this material is a case in point.

18. Like their academic counterparts, authors of these materials make their way into the corporation. The more successful charge up to $30,000 for a one-day seminar, and many also market videotaped versions of their ideas and other corporate paraphernalia.

19. The press is, of course, an independent entity and not under the control of corporate ideologists. Nevertheless, the relationship between the company and the press entails modes of influence not unlike those found in the political world. Public relations people at Tech make it their business to maintain constant ties to the press: occasionally they try to plant stories; journalists are frequent guests at product announcements and rely on insiders for their information; and so forth. More crucially, however, journalists are themselves influenced by descriptive materials and the generally accepted terminology and common sense concerning corporate life. This is evident in their frequent reliance on academic or popular material, as well as on the words of corporate spokespersons.

20. "Family" is a much used metaphor for corporate life. Rosen (1984) suggests that its use is an attempt to legitimate authority relations by equating managerial power with parental authority and portraying employees as children. This, of course, presumes a certain view of the family, itself a matter of ideological representation. A Dad who brings home the bacon has very different metaphorical implications from one who creeps into his daughter's room at night.

21. The similarities between the ideology of Tech culture and popular conceptions of Japanese management are striking. Rohlen (1974) studied a Japanese bank where employees are supposed to develop an emotional attachment and express it through pride, dedication, and enthusiastic participation. The general ideal is "that of a collectivity, constituted of emotionally satisfying personal relationships, working in the spirit of concord for the general interest." In this system,

"considerable attention is paid to the individual . . . as a human being with an inherent urge for satisfaction and accomplishment. . . . There is no need for a person to be independent of his institutional connections in order to achieve happiness. There is no contradiction, that is, between institutionalized work and personal aspiration. . . . Devotion to duty, perfected through greater self-discipline, in time leads to a reduction of the disturbance caused by conflicting demands. The result is an improved state of personal spiritual freedom and a sense of joy focused on fulfillment in one's work" (pp. 51–52). Rohlen sees in this ideology echoes of the Confucian heritage, a way of relating the organizational ideology to the larger social environment.

One would be tempted to explain similarities to Tech culture as a manifestation of the current interest in Japanese management techniques in popular managerial literature. The concept of culture in organizations is in fact closely related to an interest in Japanese management (Ouchi, 1981). In this view, Japanese organizations have found the solution to the problem of control, and Tech ideology is an American attempt to emulate Japanese management by developing a complex and all-encompassing relationship between the company and its employees, most notably in the practice of guaranteed employment in return for "loyalty."

This explanation, however, is not sufficient. The roots of Tech policies and associated practices are in the 1950s, and its current language and ideas appear to be derived largely from local traditions, from Emerson through the "company town" to the Human Relations approach to management. Current discourse is full of references to these sources, as in Sam Miller's reference to Douglas McGregor (see n. 10 above). When the groundwork for Tech's organizational ideology was laid, Japan was still reeling from its encounter with the products of Western rationality. Moreover, as Rohlen points out, Japanese managers seem equally obsessed with Western management and its perceived efficiency and rationality. This ironic reversal highlights the universal managerial quest for more control and the role of cultural arguments in this process. Others, it seems, are seen through the mediating lens of the perceived deficiencies of one's own way of life.

22. A "vocabulary of motives" (Mills, 1940) is a recurring set of words that serve in particular situations to provide definitive answers to questions concerning social or lingual conduct. Not indexes of individuals' "real," internal motivations, they are better seen as providing the source and circumscribing the limits of the actors' construction of their own motivational scheme, and are therefore a worthy (and, half a century later, still an underexploited) topic for sociological investigation.

23. Critical statements, for the most part, are presented as evidence of the company's openness and tolerance of dissent. This is akin to the way in which dissent is structured in the rituals described in Chapter 4.

Chapter 4: Presentational Rituals

1. This definition, borrowed from Lukes (1975: 291), is designed to separate the definition of *ritual* from its presumed social functions, and to extend it beyond its earlier, more limited application to settings traditionally frequented by anthropologists and to events with distinctly religious overtones (Douglas, 1966). Kertzer (1988: 9) offers an even broader definition: "symbolic behavior that is socially standardized and repetitive." From this perspective ritual is an integral feature of modern secular life (Moore and Meyerhoff, 1977). Obvious examples are the large-scale and publicized events characteristic of modern politics, sports, organized religion, legal institutions, and organizational life (Kertzer, 1988; Lukes, 1975; Meyer and Rowan, 1977; Moore and Meyerhoff, 1977; Trice and Beyer, 1984; Van Maanen and Kunda, 1989). Furthermore, as Goffman (1967) has shown, ritual phenomena lie also at the foundation of routine and seemingly inconsequential social interactions. Such a broad domain, however, sets the stage for semantic and analytic confusion. Taken to the limit, Goffman's view—that interactive behavior that takes into account cultural rules has ritual properties— suggests that ritual, like prose, is everywhere. Thus, for analytic purposes, it is necessary to distinguish types of rituals according to the nature of the social configuration within which they occur, the aims of participants, and, perhaps, the degree to which their ritual nature is openly and self-referentially acknowledged. See Moore and Meyerhoff (1977) for various taxonomies of ritual.

2. Two views of the social significance of ritual have traditionally been pitted against each other. The functionalist perspective follows on the work of Durkheim (1965), and sees rituals as collective, symbolic behaviors that serve an integrative and unifying function by reaffirming those understandings and intensifying those emotions that create group solidarity. Those oriented to the study of power and conflict processes suggest that rituals help dominant groups achieve and maintain their position by serving as a vehicle for defining (and also obscuring) social reality (see Lukes, 1975).

   A third perspective attempts to transcend both functionalist and conflict views by taking an interpretive or dramaturgic approach to the analysis of ritual (Cohen, 1974; Geertz, 1973; Turner, 1969). In this view, rituals are a dramatic form that may contain both conflictual and integrative processes; and ever-vigilant interpretation is needed to counter the careless application (with a bias toward either integration or domination) of past insights into ritual's latent functions, implicit rules, and hidden meanings.

3. The concept of "frame" as a building block in the construction of social experience was most recently elaborated by Goffman (1974). Developing notions

proposed by Bateson (1972), Berger and Luckmann (1966), Schutz (1967), and others of the phenomenological persuasion, he extends his own unique take on "the interaction order" (Goffman, 1983) to examine in minute detail the social mechanisms whereby a well-defined and bracketed version of reality is established and sustained in the course of social interaction, while others are ignored or denied. Goffman is generally concerned with how frames are jointly negotiated and defined; how they are challenged and broken; what forms of engagement with, or detachment from, their implications occur in the process; and, ultimately, what all this implies about the construction of the subjective experience of reality. In this sense, as Douglas (1966: 62–64) has noted in passing, ritual is a form of framed action. In the analysis that follows, the full implications of this view will be developed.

4. Turner's view reflects a broad consensus concerning the power of ritual to shape human experience. Langer (1967), for example, in an influential discussion, suggests that ritual leads to a state of mind she calls "transformation" wherein object and symbol become fused; similarly, Geertz (1973) views ritual as an occasion where the world as lived and the world as imagined become one. Such a view has often been associated with a conservative bias, but nothing in it suggests that such experiences are elicited only with regard to traditionally defined societies; they might (and probably do) occur in the rituals of countercultural, radical, or revolutionary groups (Kertzer, 1988). At its deepest level, then, this view of ritual is concerned not with politics narrowly defined but with the politics of the human condition.

5. For analyses of the relationship between symbolism and power, see also Bourdieu (1977), Edelman (1964), Geertz (1973), and, in a managerial context, Pfeffer (1981).

6. This perspective on ritual reflects the dominant view in the managerial community (see Chapter 1). Many of these ideas are derived from the practical, academic, and quasi-academic literatures on culture to which managers at Tech—as well as other members—are constantly exposed (see Chapter 3). Much of this work shows a strong bias toward the functionalist perspective on ritual (Van Maanen and Kunda, 1989). In studies of business organizations in particular, the focus is on those rituals and those aspects of ritual that bring about integration and value consensus and result in employee "loyalty," "commitment," and "satisfaction"—themselves ideological references to member emotions that masquerade as social scientific variables, usually of the dependent sort (see, for example, Deal and Kennedy, 1982; Trice and Beyer, 1984). The scholarly work in this tradition, however, often concludes with "implications for management" (thus mildly contradicting its own assertions), and the popular work is more openly self-contradictory in framing its view of ritual in the service of employee

solidarity and harmony as cookbook advice to managers for the furthering of their goals.

While a number of studies of organizational rituals have highlighted conflict, the counterculture, and rituals of resistance, they are the exception, and they tend to examine lower-level participants (Roy, 1959) and noncorporate settings (Goffman, 1961a; Van Maanen, 1986). In both cases the focus is on alternative rituals rather than on alternative views of the same rituals. In other words, they have conceded a vast and important domain to the functionalists and the prescribers. With few exceptions, dramaturgical or interpretive empirical studies of organizational rituals are notably lacking among students of business organizations, perhaps because currently popular methodological conventions are conducive neither to the kind of sustained fieldwork that such an approach requires nor to the textual form it invariably takes.

7. Modern secular society has been portrayed as "de-ritualized" (Moore and Meyerhoff, 1977). From this perspective, as Goody (1977) suggests, ritual often becomes little more than form devoid of meaning.

8. Turner (1974: 55) refers to this quality of ritual symbols as "multivocality." See also Cohen (1974).

9. From this point of view, establishing a valid interpretation of ritual poses a difficult problem. How is one to trust the accounts of informants? Or choose one interpretation over another? Following the logic of this interpretive dilemma to its conclusion, the best one can do is establish a plausible account that is consistent with those descriptions and native accounts one has managed to uncover.

10. The conceptual framework for the analysis is based on an interpretive perspective (n. 2 above). In particular, I rely heavily—if sometimes loosely—on two complementary theoretical positions: Turner's (1969, 1974) dramaturgical approach to ritual and Goffman's (1974) frame analysis.

11. The interpretive perspectives in general and Goffman's in particular have been criticized for overemphasizing interaction and ignoring larger structural issues—as well as, in Goffman's case, narrower psychological ones (Gouldner, 1970; Hochschild, 1983). Goffman, however, was well aware that the interaction order can and should be theoretically linked to larger (and narrower) concerns (1983). Relating the ritual framing of reality to the question of normative control in corporate settings is the contribution I wish to make.

12. The typology of rituals offered in this chapter consists of broad categories. Within each category, presentational rituals may vary considerably. In order to maintain a broad perspective and not lose the central thrust of the argument in the complexities of minute social interaction, a few examples of the most frequently occurring types within each category are presented and contrasted. Also, the implications of the frequency and timing of the events, and the degree of relative participation,

although relevant to a comprehensive understanding of the impact of ritual, are undertaken only in passing.

13. In-house training and development activities include workshops with titles like "Making Effective Presentations," "Supervisory Skills—The Tech Way," "Managing Problem Employees," "Coping with Stress," "Effective Time Management," and "Intrapreneurship." Many of these are designed and marketed by a large number of training and development groups throughout the organization, which constantly compete for clients in the internal marketplace. A broad range of training activities offered by outside consultants are also available, running from standard packaged workshops on managerial skills to more specialized sessions like "Managing Office Politics."

14. Management development takes a variety of forms. Managers may attend courses offered by business schools; they may participate in on-site programs offered by academics (one famous anthropologist conducted an extended seminar on corporate culture, using the technet as a major means of communication); they may invite consultants to participate in their work activities (often referred to as "OD," for "organizational development") and then confer with them privately. At Tech, unlike many other corporations, use of consultants is not necessarily seen as a weakness, and many managers make no bones about it.

15. Readers interested in corporate self-help and survival literature will find the business section of any bookstore overflowing with examples, including the titles the trainer cites here.

16. The frequency of participation in such events and the reasons for choosing to attend vary considerably. Almost all the people I encountered had attended at least one training session in the preceding year and planned to take more. For some the training itself was important; others viewed the sessions as a way of meeting people, socializing, and networking; others still regarded them as company-sponsored free vacations.

17. Things are never quite so simple. While the main principle guiding participation in staff or team meetings is a direct reporting relationship, the matrix design (see Chapter 2) creates the usual complexities. Some participants belong to more than one group. Others are invited as "individual contributors," or by virtue of a "dotted-line" relationship. While members like to play up this seeming chaos, a count of the numerous meetings I observed revealed that more than 90 percent of participation was determined by a simple, straightforward reporting relationship.

18. Such working relationships are often referred to in the literature on matrix structures as "lateral relations" (Galbraith, 1973). Their degree of formalization may vary: ad hoc meetings, temporary task forces, standing committees, continuing programs. The more formalized types of lateral relations often have formally des-

ignated managers with a measure of authority and accountability, as well as some
control over budgets and facilities.

19. See Van Maanen (1986) for a detailed analysis of timeouts in organizational
settings.

20. In the meetings described below, technological matters were not a central concern. A sound interpretation of more technologically oriented occasions would
require mastery of the subject matter—something I can neither claim nor expect
from most readers. Thus, the descriptions that follow are generally biased in the
direction of managers or engineers with managerial concerns and responsibilities.

21. See Bourdieu's (1977) analysis of symbolic and cultural capital as a form of
wealth and its relation to other forms of accumulation.

22. Turner (1974) saw social drama as a key concept for analyzing social process.
In his view, social dramas are conflictual situations that may—but do not necessarily—occur in conjunction with ritual occasions. The essence of social drama
is the unfolding of a "conflict between paradigms" to which key actors subscribe.
While Turner applied the concept broadly—to neighbors' disputes in African
village life (Turner, 1969), as well as to historical and political analysis (Turner,
1974)—I will extract the essence of the notion and apply it to minute and momentary episodes of what Goffman (1974) called "frame disputes" in the context
of organizational rituals.

23. Reintegration, or its appearance, is by far the dominant outcome of these mini-
dramas. Such episodes, however, can also result in schism, most notably of the
delayed and cumulative sort: participants may choose to leave the company or
redefine their relationship with it or with other participants as a result of their experience. More than one member attributed a decision to quit or transfer to being
"beat up" by superiors or peers once too often. More immediate and dramatic
schisms are the stuff of myth, but something I never observed: it is not far-fetched
to predict that security guards or police would quickly appear if reintegration
was denied and the schismatic script followed through. Occasionally mentioned
is the late-night murder of a senior executive by a "deranged" engineer, a case
whose reported details seem to be borne out by journalistic accounts. Others tell
of members "losing it" or "going nuts" in the middle of meetings. But such dramatic events are exception; and their infrequent enactment is, if anything, proof
that the potential for simple coercion that backs up symbolic power is taken for
granted, largely ignored (not to say unconscious), and very rarely actualized.

24. For a discussion of cognitive dissonance, see Cooper and Fazio (1984) and Festinger (1962).

25. Hochschild (1983) uses Stanislavski's (1965) view of acting as "self-induced real
feelings" to develop her elaborate and sophisticated theory of emotions.

26. Emotive dissonance is modeled on the more established notion of cognitive dis-

sonance. The social psychological and sociological studies of emotion, however, pale in comparison with the extensive analysis of cognitive processes in these disciplines. Although Hochschild assembles strands of evidence from diverse sources and offers an insightful analysis of the plight of flight attendants asked to display emotions as part of their airborne working routine, the workings of emotive dissonance are more hypothetical than established. See also Van Maanen and Kunda (1989) for a similar view of emotions and their management in corporate settings.

27. Turner borrowed the term from Van Gennep's highly influential and prescient *The Rites of Passage* (1960), where it was used to refer to the passage-like quality of rituals: transitional episodes that serve as the threshold between culturally defined states or stages. In Turner's rather complex scheme, liminality has both a structural and an experiential component. These, too often, he does not clearly distinguish: the former refers to identifiable passage-like states that occur as part of rituals; the latter—the contribution Turner is most often cited for—refers to the experience of those engaged in a liminal event: "unmediated relations," an experience of "I-Thou," the temporary loss or inversion of roles, and generally the experience of "communitas." The former use is more etically sound and therefore generalizable across settings and cultures; the latter is, in essence, an emic question that refers to the subjective experience of participants and thus might vary across settings. Turner himself was circumspect and sometimes vague about the possible variability in the meanings of liminal phenomena. At times he distinguished *liminal* from *liminoid* experiences (Turner, 1982): the former, he claimed, are found in primitive societies, while the latter are metaphoric applications of liminal experiences to modern societies. Elsewhere he commented on the differences between spontaneous, normative, and ideological communitas (Turner, 1969: 132), which depend on the extent to which the accomplishment of communitas is an explicit and formal part of the ritual. These notions, however, were never fully developed, and it is the legacy of communitas and role reversal that is most often associated with Turner's view of liminality (see, for example, Moore and Meyerhoff, 1977).

28. Geertz (1973) discusses common sense as a cultural system.

29. See Goffman's (1974) insightful analysis of "keying"—the intentional shift from one frame to another in the course of interaction. "Downkeying" decreases the distance from the initial activity (as in a playful fight that suddenly becomes real); "upkeying," in contrast, is a shift away from a given reality. Goffman's metaphoric allusion to music is intentional and particularly apt: in this sense, Mike's presentation in the intro workshop is a one-man philharmonic performance. See also n. 3 above.

30. Turner's terminology, with its "scientific" and "humanistic" connotations (see

n. 9 to Chapter 1), fits well into the list of terms expropriated by popular managerial writers. Turner, of course, was not unaware of the potential for such usage.
As he points out (1982), the ritual celebration of communitas, when associated
with structure and authority, leads to attempts to escape from a communitas that
is ideological—and therefore potentially self-destroying, if not false by definition—to a more spontaneous form.

31. In this sense, the dynamics of control in the course of ritual performances begin
to resemble, at least metaphorically, some of the qualities of total institutions
(Goffman, 1961a): there is no escape from observation.

32. It is worth noting that Barthes (1967) considered self-referential signs that openly
convey their own artificial status "healthy" rather than "pathological." In this
view, signs that pass themselves off as "natural" rather than contrived are a
weapon of ideology.

Chapter 5: Self and Organization

1. The self is the locus of subjective experience, and its definition in objective, scientific terms has proven to be a difficult and often self-defeating task. For the
purposes of this discussion, I see the self as consisting of cognitive and affective
components—thoughts and feelings directed at the social world and one's place
in it—and of the capacity to act spontaneously as well as to reflect on one's experience and behavior. Each of these elements has, of course, been subjected to
endless analysis in the various disciplines of social science. For a historical overview and a review of psychoanalytic approaches, see Fine (1986); for a review
of cognitive theories of the self, Kihlstrom and Cantor (1984); for a review and
integration of psychological and sociological theories of emotion, Hochschild
(1983); for a review of the symbolic interactionist perspective, Rosenberg and
Turner (1981); and for an anthropological perspective, Carrithers, Collins, and
Lukes (1985).

2. The self, most students of society would agree, is a social product that emerges
as individuals internalize—or are "socialized" into—the requirements of the
society into which they are born or in which for one reason or another they
find themselves. This insight (albeit with different emphases) is shared by major
theorists as diverse as Durkheim (1933), Freud (1961), Marx (1975), and Mead
(1934); all converge on the notion that individual selves and social institutions
evolve as the underlying tensions between individual and collective interests are
created and resolved.

There is less consensus, however, about the weight of social factors in the
shaping of private experience. At one extreme are those who postulate the exis-

tence of internally generated modes of experience—an independent "real" self whose experience of the world is at best moderated by the external culture. At the other extreme are those who see the self as social to its very core. In this view, what we take to be subjective individual experience is no more than a fleeting, epiphenomenal shadow of large and very powerful social realities. For reviews of these perspectives, see Fine (1986) and Van Maanen (1979a). In the tricky terrain in between are those who see the self as a social phenomenon that develops in a dialectical relationship with society. In their paradigmatic statement of this point of view, Berger and Luckmann (1966) depict society as a dynamic reality that is socially constructed, and the self as a social phenomenon that is inseparably tied to the evolution of social institutions and the forms of collective knowledge they embody. They suggest three significant and interrelated moments of this dialectic: externalization (the attribution of meaning to social events), objectification (the creation of stable social arrangements based on shared meanings), and internalization (the process whereby successive generations are introduced to and molded by objectified institutions). See Giddens (1979) and Strauss (1978) for similar attempts to combine theories of structure and meaning.

3. Goffman's perspective has been frequently criticized. Coser (1966), for example, suggests that he ignores the creative aspects of the self, and Fine (1986), like many others, suggests that Goffman overemphasizes outward appearances at the expense of in-depth analysis. Goffman, however, is unrelenting in his pursuit of self-presentation and the minor liberties people take with role requirements as essential constitutents of the self. In *Frame Analysis* (1974), he takes this view to its logical conclusion. "The self," he asserts, "is not an entity half concealed behind events but a changeable formula for managing oneself during them. Just as the current situation prescribes the official guise behind which we will conceal ourselves, so it will provide for where and how we will show through. The culture itself prescribes what sort of entity we must believe ourselves to be in order to have something to show through in this manner" (p. 573). The nature of this formula, and the meanings associated with it, must always be an empirical question; and generalizations, at best, become one more example of coded and publicly stated demands.

4. That these selves coagulate, as it were, into an overriding "integrated" self that transcends specific situations is a proposition that derives considerable support from commonsensical notions of the self. In this view, the self is formed through primary, secondary, or tertiary socialization (Berger and Luckmann, 1966), and the result is a core self (Schein, 1980) or a "master identity" (Hughes, 1958) around which others are constructed. Others prefer to posit the notion of situationally specific, fragmented, or loosely coupled selves as an existential con-

dition (Becker et al., 1961; Goffman, 1974; Shotter and Gergen, 1989; Van Maanen, 1979).

5. A large and diverse body of empirical studies examine various aspects of the content and process of self-definition in occupational and organizational settings (Van Maanen, 1976; Van Maanen and Barley, 1985). These studies, most generally speaking, relate specific cognitive and affective dimensions of the self to work-related behaviors and structures.

   The "work attachment" literature focuses on predefined forms of experience and their relation to structural variables. Seeman (1959), for example, uses a Marxist framework to suggest that the experience of "alienation" (operationalized as "powerlessness," "meaninglessness," and "normlessness") in industrial settings is related to the lack of control over work arrangements. Using the inverse of the same approach, countless others explore aspects of engagement. Here "satisfaction," "motivation," and other managerial attributions of experience are related to job design. See Locke (1983) for a review.

   Context-sensitive case studies of work organizations have documented the evolution of worker subcultures with norms and beliefs that often run counter to managerial interests (Burawoy, 1979; Gouldner, 1954; Homans 1950; Roethlisberger and Dixon, 1939; Roy, 1960). More recently, Hochschild (1983) drew attention to the plight of lower-level service workers engaged in what she called "emotional labor," and the resulting forms of disengagement and their consequences.

   Studies of managers and professionals in organizations have documented similar patterns of engagement and alienation (Bailyn, 1985; Becker et al., 1961; Dalton, 1959; Jackall, 1988; Kanter, 1977; Light, 1980; Merton, 1957; Mills, 1956; Rohlen, 1974; Rosen, 1984; Whyte, 1956). Here, however, engagement is more intense, and alienation, when it exists, is not a retreat from a repressive and depriving world, but confusion in a world that makes heavy and conflicting demands and does not live up to its excessive promises.

   More specific attention to the intentional shaping of the self by organizational agents is addressed in the literature on organizational socialization. This literature generally emphasizes engagement (Schein, 1968) and the attributes of organizations that facilitate and encourage it (Van Maanen and Schein, 1979). In a review of the theory and research on organizational socialization, Van Maanen (1976) points out that little is known about "inefficacious socialization" and types of deviant behavior in which some members resist or confront the socialization process.

6. In corporate settings, interviews generally elicit in the interviewee a tendency to theorize, often using the concepts, language, and style that the interviewer brings

to the field. It is easy to find in such responses support for one's own views, rather than interpret them in a broader context as one specific arena of self-presentation. See Jackall's (1988) excellent interview-based study of managerial ethics for an example of the advantages and disadvantages of this method.

7. Van Maanen and Barley (1985) distinguish between organizational and occupational culture. The former relates to the organizational boundaries and has cultural elements associated with it. The latter views occupational groups within (and across) organizations as culture-bearing collectives. The two sources of meaning for members of work organizations often clash, as indeed other subcultures might. In this chapter, the primary focus is the members' response to the organizational locus of meaning and the ideologies associated with it. A more comprehensive analysis would focus on distinct subgroupings such as engineers or secretaries as having implications for self-definition.

8. No statistics on married members are available. Such couples, however, are frequently encountered, and their presence is often an issue for their managers and peers. A company policy forbids employing a couple in the same group, but there are a number in the same engineering organizations, and more with spouses elsewhere at Tech.

9. Many Tech policies are designed with this in mind. See Chapter 2.

10. See Chapter 4 for definitions of role embracement and role distancing.

11. This attitude was frequently encountered among members. The emphasis on networks, the relative ease of communication, the limits on formal authority, and the encouragement of the internal labor market seem to have relegated the primary work group to a secondary role in forming work-related attachments. The work group is often viewed as a temporary arrangement; the primary attachment is to the company as a whole and to the possibilities it offers.

12. Other types of contrasts are also the basis for evaluation. Thus, for example, the distinctions between Wage Class 4 and other groups, between engineers and managers, between types of engineers, and between managers from different functions often elicit a cultural description, a criticism, and an implication by way of contrast that the presenter is a manifestation of the most appropriate cultural type.

13. See n. 6 above.

14. "Burnout" is both an emic and an etic concept. Those interested in the psychological aspects of work life use it as a technical term referring to a variety of work-related pathologies (see Shirom, 1982). At Tech it is commonly used by members to describe certain work-related experiences, some of which are thought to be specific to Tech. Both modes are obviously related. In this discussion I will focus on the latter, emic use.

15. These prescriptions are an ironic inverse of the conventional (and academic)

wisdom regarding organizations dedicated to the shaping of people. In schools, prisons, prisoner-of-war camps, psychiatric hospitals, military organizations, and public bureaucracies, as well as in traditional work organizations, it is the clients, inmates, and lower-status members who are often depicted as the objects of attention and influence, the people to be "processed"; it is for them that elaborate theories are developed and implemented, whole disciplines and occupations evolved (see Hasenfeld and English, 1974; Lipsky, 1980; Prottas, 1979; Van Maanen, 1976).

16. As Geertz (1983) suggests, the drama analogy has come into its own as a mode of analysis of social life. This is reflected in its extensive and systematic application in the social sciences, coupled with a shift away from its earlier depreciatory connotations. To this one might add that in normative systems such as the one found at Tech, it appears—along with the terminology of culture—as an emic concept, central to the members' own understanding of what they are up to.

17. This view of the organizational self has intriguing parallels in theories of literary criticism. The various relations of members and meanings and the stance members assume toward their production of versions of organizational reality resemble what Frye (1957) calls the "ironic mode" and Booth (1974) terms "unstable ironies." See also Shotter and Gergen (1989) for an example of recent attempts to apply techniques and concepts drawn from currently popular—and somewhat trendy—theories of literary criticism to social scientific investigations of the self. Although I have tried to avoid the jargon associated with this approach and its concern with "postmodernism," "deconstruction," and "the text," readers familiar with this brand of theorizing will recognize that it has much in common with the perspective taken in this book. In this sense, the findings point to the emergence of what might be termed an "ironic" or perhaps a "postmodern" view of organizational man to complete Schein's (1980) frequently cited taxonomy of perspectives (economic, social, and complex man).

Chapter 6: Conclusion

1. The complex relationship between academic perspectives on corporate culture and those developed by corporate ideologists is a worthy yet relatively unexplored topic for the sociology of knowledge. These ties, including the large consulting fees available to academics, the corporate support for research, and the intricate ties between corporations and business schools, where much of the research on organizations is produced, might explain the considerable overlap of perspectives that this study documents. See Chapter 3 for additional comments on this matter. For studies that deal more extensively with the influence of corporate interests on

the content of social scientific production, see Baritz (1960), Barley, Meyer, and Gash (1988), Bendix (1956), and Kunda and Barley (1988).

2. Students of organizational ritual suggest that the intentional use of the persuasive aspects of ritual is of increasing importance to management and more prevalent when normative control is a salient mode of member-organization relationships (Van Maanen and Kunda, 1989)—or, as a partial corollary, when traditional bureaucratic control structures are perceived to be ineffective (Meyer and Rowan, 1977). In both cases, the use of symbolism in its various forms—myth, ritual, ideology, and so forth—becomes a prominent mode of managerial behavior (Pfeffer, 1981).

3. Following Edwards (1979), we propose a fourfold scheme for analyzing control systems: market control of labor, technical control of the production process, bureaucratic control of the rules and procedures of the workplace, and cultural control of the workers' felt involvement. These correspond to the control of objects, behavior, beliefs, and emotions. Aspects of all four types are found in any specific situation, and their mix is forever changing. See Czarniawska-Joerges (1988) for an alternative taxonomy of forms of control.

4. A comment is necessary about the scope of my conclusions. Ethnography is, by its very nature, a limited endeavor characterized by the contrast between claims of heroic efforts and rather modest returns. Consequently, despite the temptation to engage in speculative flights of causal fancy, two kinds of frequently asked questions cannot be satisfactorily addressed with the data in this study. The first set concerns the structural, historical, and technological causes of Tech culture. Is Tech culture unique, a product of the history and managerial style of Tech's founders and managers, or is it characteristic of high-tech industries or professional bureaucracies in general? Do such organizational forms tend to arise in new growth industries, during periods of economic expansion and technological innovation, or during certain periods of an organization's life cycle? Some of these factors have been treated by students of organizational culture. The crucial role of leadership in establishing culture is a favorite subject in the applied literature (see, for example, Schein, 1985), but its empirical base is weak, and its more popular versions often seem to fluctuate between tautological statements and an attempt to cater to the fantasies of a managerial audience (Peters and Waterman, 1982). A better case has been made for the strong relationship between professional work in bureaucratic settings and normative control (Etzioni, 1961; Perrow, 1986).

The second set of questions concerns the economic consequences of the culture. Is Tech's cultural management indeed an efficient, productive, and profitable mode of organization? Was it a necessary condition for the company's success or an inhibiting factor in its development? That strong cultures require the investment of resources is self-evident, but no clear relationship has been established between such systems and profitability (despite the promises of the more extreme branch of culture consultants; see, for example, Deal and Kennedy, 1982). Tech has clearly been very profitable over the years, but internal conflicts over the policies derived from cultural principles have raged (particularly during downturns), and the policies' connection to the company's profits and losses has been debated endlessly.

Answers to these questions, while no doubt crucial to a full understanding of the issues at hand (at least for those—and they are many—for whom establishing the validity of causal arguments is the purpose of social analysis), must await further, and perhaps more systematic, investigation. In the meanwhile, the ethnographic materials in this book allow us only to explore Tech culture in its own terms and to proceed very tentatively and cautiously to more general conclusions.

5. The stratification of member groups along lines of cultural inclusion may be seen as a necessary condition for the successful implementation of normative control. In particular, the use of temporary workers allows the flexibility in employment levels required to keep commitments to central members. For an extensive development of these issues consistent with the findings here, see Pfeffer and Baron (1988) and Sabel (1982).

6. Claims to describe or to capture aspects of the "true culture" must, in light of what this book has already revealed, be taken with a grain of salt. The scientific use of the concept of culture has always been regarded as problematic: the observers' frame of reference, cultural background, value system, and interests, it is asserted, must necessarily color their observations. But the explicit use of culture by organizational ideologists and the easy availability of social scientific expertise turns an arcane and easily neglected point into a serious conceptual and methodological problem regarding the status of social scientific concepts and their relationship to everyday discourse. Is it possible to objectively describe the organizational culture in a context so highly laden with reflexive articulations and strong interests concerning the shape of reality? Who, in this setting, is the ethnographer and who is the ideologist? And is the boundary between the two so clear? Although I stand by my descriptions and my own expropriation of the concept, I do so with all these problems in mind, and I suggest that the reader do so as well.

7. That culture is laden with contradictions is not a new insight, but their particular nature is an important empirical question. Tech is characterized by a continuing attempt by ideology to colonize common sense. For an insightful theoretical discussion of the relationship between these forms of knowledge not clouded by the use of the concepts of ideology and culture, see Bourdieu (1977).

8. See Schein (1961). In a personal communication he describes how the publication of his work on brainwashing generated some corporate interest in investigating ways of influencing workers and managers.

9. The power of such total institutions of meaning is, of course, enhanced if those who choose to leave find the same pressures behind different corporate logos, or in other arenas of life.

10. See Miller (1988) for a similar argument concerning the impact of television as an ideological medium on the experience of its viewers. Miller claims that television's pervasiveness and its constant suggestion that it understands and can articulate the innermost experiences and drives of its viewers destroys any possibility of authenticity and leaves viewers jaded, hollowed out, and ready to fill themselves with the dominating logic of consumption—the medium's overarching message and justification. Turning George Orwell's *Nineteen Eighty Four* on its head, he suggests to the prototypical viewer, and to all of us, that "Big Brother is you—watching." Life at Tech appears to complement this view. Here Big Brother assumes a more concrete form; yet, like television, the ever-present organizational ideology undermines both the right to privacy and aspirations to authenticity—long, it has been persuasively and extensively argued, driving forces in our civilization (see Trilling, 1972). These two views of corporate influence suggest the existence of an overarching and pervasive ideology that originates in the logic of corporate goals, transcends particular regions of life, and traps people in a never-ending and mutually reinforcing cycle of production and consumption.

11. See Pfeffer and Baron (1988) and Mangum, Mayall, and Nelson (1985).

12. See Bellah et al. (1985).

13. See Jackall (1988) for a study of how bureaucratic forces shape the construction of moral meanings in corporate settings.

14. Although Whyte's work was considered radical at the time of its publication, it contains in fact many conservative elements. In particular, Whyte places much of the burden of change on the individual. Using a quasi-Freudian framework, Whyte calls for a sort of emotional maturity in the face of the corporation and an acceptance of its underlying structure of authority.

Appendix: Methods

1. See Marcus and Cushman (1982). Concern with the stylistic conventions and textual and narrative forms that ethnographers use to establish the authority of their reports has been on the rise in anthropological circles. See Clifford and Marcus (1986) and Van Maanen (1988) for extensive discussions, and Roth (1989) for a critique.

2. Self-application of one's conceptual tools is a typical and understandable approach to reflexive discourse: psychoanalysts analyze countertransference, sociologists "do" a sociology of their own knowledge, ethnographers reconstruct the culture of research. When properly done, such reflexive analysis is a crucial and enriching part of any research process; however, it also leaves some blind spots that could be eliminated by mixing perspectives (for example, countertransference in ethnography, or the sociology of the psychoanalytic encounter).

3. Not for lack of trying. Marcus and Fischer (1986) point out some of the experimental techniques used in an attempt to address this problem. These include providing unedited transcripts of interviews or fieldnotes, and introducing the fieldworker into the description as an actor. More extremely, some have attempted joint authorship with informants, in line with Schutz's (1967) uncomfortable (from the researcher's point of view) "third postulate of adequacy": confirmation of the validity of findings by the subjects. Less drastic and more mundane suggestions include teamwork in the field (Gouldner, 1954; Strauss et al., 1964). Alternatively, one might consider working with constant supervision of the sort often used in psychotherapeutic training (although this is not exactly consistent with the image of the heroic and individualistic fieldworker). Experimental attempts notwithstanding, there appears to be no easy solution to the problem. Ultimately, the researcher must take authority, ask the reader for a leap of faith, and perhaps do battle with critics. As Geertz (1973) points out, the ultimate test of anthropological (and perhaps other) claims lies in the crucible of continuous debate and survivability.

4. Israeli society is the product of a historical attempt to recreate—or perhaps invent—a territorially-bound Hebrew culture. The degree to which this has been successful and the form it takes is not of concern here; of interest, rather, is the observation that under such circumstances the tension between "cultural authenticity" and invented culture is a salient theme for those who are to become the manifestation of that culture. Concern with this issue in Israel has to some extent subsided as, for better or for worse, cultural forms developed their own momentum; but it riddled almost every aspect—high and low—of the cultural scene of my childhood and youth.

5. Emigration from Israel is usually referred to in Hebrew as *yerida* (meaning "descent"), in contrast to *aliya* ("ascent") for immigration. In the past, emigration was considered a social and a moral problem by most Israelis, who habitually viewed emigrants with a mixture of anger and scorn. In recent years, with the large waves of emigration from Israel to the West, the negative connotations have subsided somewhat, and *yerida* has come to be seen also as a form of economic and political protest. See Shokeid (1988a) and Cohen (1988) on Israeli emigrants and emigration.

6. For a discussion of the debates on matters methodological that characterize the field of organization studies, see Bacharach (1989) and Bryman (1989).

7. For a review of the various streams of Zionist thought, see Avineri (1981). For a critique and an alternative ideological construction, see Said (1979).

8. Here, too, of course, lie the foundations of a critique: ethnography in general and this one in particular may be (and indeed have been) viewed as little more than what psychologists would call a "projection": a reading of the experience of others distorted by one's own.

9. At the time of my fieldwork, I regarded Berger and Luckmann (1966) and Taylor (1979) as paradigmatic statements of the rationale for interpretive research methods. I still do.

10. "Clinical research" refers to the use of consultation as a basis for research, in the tradition of Lewin's (1948) action research program. Schein (1987) contrasts this process with ethnography. I myself engaged in consulting work before beginning graduate studies, and in the course of the fieldwork I supported myself by working (an average of one day a week) as a paid consultant in another company— an experience that I believe both enriched and confused the fieldwork at Tech. Although I chose to identify with ethnography, I believe there is important unexplored shared ground in the kinds of interpretive work both methods offer. In particular, it seems that the clinical mode affords broader access to managerial practices and thinking (at the risk, of course, of losing contact with other strata and, ultimately, "going native"; this danger, however, is a matter of skill and commitment, and not a logical necessity). Conversely, as Marcus and Fischer (1986) point out, ethnography is a research method most suited to clinical, interventionist, or psychotherapeutic theory, fields notoriously lacking in empirical research of any scientific persuasion.

11. Although it was clearly a condition of entry, this promise was, I felt, problematic. The commitment was loose enough, I told myself at the time, to allow me to preserve discretion and privacy and to adhere to my standards for valid and unbiased observations. Nevertheless, I generated some expectations and may even have misled some people by insinuating, if not promising, that there would be some managerial value in my findings. Also, I was making myself a potential ally of management, a position I did not want for both personal and instrumental reasons: that is, I was concerned about how I would be perceived by those whose confidences I sought.

12. My status was a concern for many members faced with deciding whether to spend time with me. My technological prowess—the primary criterion of personal worth for many at Tech—was, of course, negligible, and I often had to rely on my other, limited resources. Some of these, like my MIT connection, seemed to dwindle with time. My appearance on television (as a participant in a mildly

violent demonstration against an Israeli politician visiting Boston to gather funds, a man I considered both immoral and dangerous) gave, much to my surprise, a big boost to the research process. I became, for a brief period, something of a celebrity; this injection of cultural capital opened a few more doors, drew almost friendly recognition from people who had in the past shown no interest, and temporarily gave me, it appeared, something to offer.

13. Conversational interviews are unstructured discussions in which I started with basic facts about the person but tried to follow whatever lines of thought people were willing to develop. Generally, once they agreed to talk, the problem was when to stop them rather than how to get them going. In many cases they also asked for my opinions about the company, about actions they had taken, and so forth. Within the limits of respecting confidential information gained from others, I was usually happy to respond. During interviews I took notes that I filled out into comprehensive transcripts as soon as I could that same day.

14. Participation of this sort in organizational life elicited a strong emotional involvement that seemed to have an impact on my work. Although there are limits to a confessional, it is worth noting that I found informal and personal discussions with one of my advisors, as well as ongoing psychotherapy, very helpful in staying in the field and managing my relationships with some of its inhabitants.

15. For a discussion of the marginality of fieldworkers and their informants, see Agar (1980) and Shokeid (1988b).

16. With most people I made sure I found out their personal and career histories, the nature and organizational aspects of their current jobs, and their views on Tech culture. Beyond that, it seems, I discussed every imaginable subject.

17. Concern with the textual forms of ethnography focuses, for the most part, on the finished text and not on the process of its creation and the kinds of thinking and analysis that accompany it.

references

Agar, M. 1980. *The Professional Stranger*. New York: Academic Press.

Allaire, Y., and M. E. Firsirotu. 1984. "Theories of Organizational Culture." *Organization Studies* 5: 193–226.

Argyris, C., and D. A. Schon. 1974. *Theory in Practice*. San Francisco: Jossey-Bass.

Avineri, S. 1981. *The Making of Modern Zionism*. London: Weidenfeld and Nicholson.

Bacharach, S. B. 1989. "Organizational Theories: Some Criteria for Evaluation." *Academy of Management Review* 14: 496–515.

Bailyn, L. 1985. "Autonomy in the Industrial R&D Lab." *Human Resource Management* 24: 129–46.

Baritz, J. H. 1960. *The Servants of Power*. Middletown, Conn.: Wesleyan University Press.

Barley, S. R.; G. Meyer; and D. C. Gash. 1988. "Cultures of Culture: Academics, Practitioners and the Pragmatics of Normative Control." *Administrative Science Quarterly* 33: 24–60.

Barnard, C. I. 1950. *The Functions of the Executive*. Cambridge: Harvard University Press.

Barthes, R. 1967. *Elements of Semiology*. New York: Hill and Wang.

Bateson, G. 1972. *Steps to an Ecology of Mind*. New York: Ballantine Books.

Becker, H. S., et al. 1961. *Boys in White*. Chicago: University of Chicago Press.

Bell, D. 1973. *The Coming of Post-Industrial Society*. New York: Basic Books.

Bellah, R. N., et al. 1985. *Habits of the Heart*. Berkeley: University of California Press.

Bendix, R. 1956. *Work and Authority in Industry*. New York: Harper and Row.

Berger, P. L.; B. Berger; and H. Kellner. 1974. *The Homeless Mind*. New York: Vintage.

Berger, P. L., and T. Luckmann. 1966. *The Social Construction of Reality*. New York: Doubleday.

Beyer, M. J. 1981. "Ideologies, Values, and Decision Making in Organizations." In P. C. Nystrom (ed.), *Handbook of Organizational Design*, vol. 2. New York: Oxford University Press.

Blau, P. M., and R. Schoenherr. 1971. *The Structure of Organizations*. New York: Basic Books.

Blauner, R. 1964. *Alienation and Freedom*. Chicago: University of Chicago Press.

Boje, D.; Fedor, P. B.; and K. M. Rowland. 1982. "Myth Making: A Qualitative Step in O.D. Interventions." *Journal of Applied Behavioral Science* 18: 17–28.

Booth, W. C. 1974. *A Rhetoric of Irony*. Chicago: University of Chicago Press.

Bourdieu, P. 1977. *Outline of a Theory of Practice*. Cambridge: Cambridge University Press.

Brandes, S. D. 1976. *American Welfare Capitalism*. Chicago: University of Chicago Press.

Braverman, H. 1974. *Labor and Monopoly Capital*. New York: Monthly Review Press.

Bryman, A. 1989. *Research Methods and Organization Studies*. London: Unwin Hyman.

Burawoy, M. 1979. *Manufacturing Consent*. Chicago: University of Chicago Press.

Business Week. 1980. "Corporate Cultures: The Hard Way to Change Values That Spell Success or Failure." 27: 148–60.

Cameron, K. S., and D. A. Whetten (eds.). 1983. *Organizational Effectiveness: A Comparison of Multiple Models*. New York: Academic Press.

Carrithers, M.; S. Collins; and S. Lukes (eds.). 1985. *The Category of the Person*. Cambridge: Cambridge University Press.

Chandler, A. 1966. *Strategy and Structure*. New York: Doubleday.

———. 1977. *The Visible Hand*. Cambridge, Mass.: Harvard University Press.

Clifford, J., and G. E. Marcus. 1986. *Writing Culture*. Berkeley: University of California Press.

Cohen, A. 1974. *Two Dimensional Man*. Berkeley: University of California Press.

Cohen, Y. 1988. "War and Social Integration: The Effects of the Israeli-Arab Conflict on Jewish Emigration from Israel." *American Sociological Review* 53: 908–18.

Cooper, J., and R. H. Fazio. 1984. "A New Look at Dissonance Theory." In L. Berkowitz (ed.), *Advances in Experimental Social Psychology*, vol. 17. Orlando, Fla.: Academic Press.

Coser, L. A. 1974. *Greedy Institutions: Patterns of Undivided Commitment*. New York: Free Press.

Coser, R. L. 1966. "Role Distance, Sociological Ambivalence, and Transitional Status Systems." *American Journal of Sociology* 72: 173–87.

Czarniawska-Joerges, B. 1988. *Ideological Control in Nonideological Organizations*. New York: Praeger.

Dalton, M. 1959. *Men Who Manage*. New York: Wiley.

Davis, S. M. 1984. *Managing Corporate Culture*. Cambridge, Mass.: Ballinger.

Davis, S. M., and P. R. Lawrence. 1977. *Matrix*. Reading, Mass.: Addison-Wesley.

Deal, T. E., and A. A. Kennedy. 1982. *Corporate Cultures*. Reading, Mass.: Addison-Wesley.

De Tocqueville, A. 1961. *Democracy in America*. New York: Schocken.

Dougherty, D., and G. Kunda. 1990. "Photographic Analysis: A Method to Capture Organizational Belief Systems." In P. Gagliardi (ed.), *Symbols and Artifacts:*

Views of the Corporate Landscape. Berlin, New York: de Gruyter.

Douglas, M. 1966. *Purity and Danger: An Analysis of Concepts of Pollution and Taboo.* London: Routledge and Kegan Paul.

Dubin, R.; R. A. Hedley; and C. Taveggia. 1976. "Attachment to Work." In R. Dubin (ed.), *Handbook of Work, Organization, and Society.* Chicago: Rand McNally.

Durkheim, E. 1964. *The Division of Labor in Society.* New York: Free Press.

——— . 1965. *The Elementary Forms of the Religious Life.* New York: Free Press.

Dyer, W. G. 1982. "Culture in Organizations: A Case Study and Analysis." MIT, Sloan School of Management Working Paper, no. 1279-82.

Edelman, M. 1964. *The Symbolic Uses of Politics.* Urbana: University of Illinois Press.

Edwards, R. 1979. *Contested Terrain.* New York: Basic Books.

Emery, F. E., and Trist, E. L. 1966. "The Causal Texture of Organizational Environments." In W. A. Hill and D. Egan (eds.), *Readings in Organization Theory—A Behavioral Approach.* Boston: Allyn and Bacon.

Etzioni, A. 1961. *A Comparative Analysis of Complex Organizations.* New York: Free Press.

Festinger, L. 1962. *A Theory of Cognitive Dissonance.* Stanford, Calif.: Stanford University Press.

Fine, R. 1986. *Narcissism, the Self and Society.* New York: Columbia University Press.

Fortune. 1983. *"The Corporate Culture Vultures."* 108: 66–72.

Freud, S. 1961. *Civilization and Its Discontents.* New York: Norton.

Frye, N. 1957. *Anatomy of Criticism.* Princeton, N.J.: Princeton University Press.

Galbraith, J. R. 1973. *Designing Complex Organizations.* Reading, Mass.: Addison-Wesley.

Gecas, V. 1982. "The Self Concept." In R. H. Turner and J. F. Short (eds.), *Annual Review of Sociology*, vol. 8. Palo Alto, Calif.: Annual Reviews, Inc.

Geertz, C. 1973. *The Interpretation of Culture.* New York: Basic Books.

——— . 1983. *Local Knowledge.* New York: Basic Books.

Gergen, K. J., and K. E. Davis. 1985. *The Social Construction of the Person.* New York: Springer.

Gerth, H. H., and C. W. Mills (eds.). 1948. *From Max Weber.* London: Routledge and Kegan Paul.

Giddens, A. 1976. *New Rules of Sociological Method.* New York: Basic Books.

——— . 1979. *Central Problems in Social Theory.* Berkeley: University of California Press.

Goffman, E. 1959. *The Presentation of Self in Everyday Life.* New York: Doubleday.

——— . 1961a. *Asylums.* Garden City, N.Y.: Anchor.

————. 1961b. *Encounters*. Indianapolis: Bobbs-Merrill.

————. 1967. *Interaction Ritual*. New York: Doubleday Anchor.

————. 1974. *Frame Analysis*. New York: Harper and Row.

————. 1976. *Gender Advertisements*. New York: Harper and Row.

————. 1983. "The Interaction Order." *American Sociological Review* 48: 1–18.

Goodenough, W. H. 1970. *Description and Comparison in Cultural Anthropology*. Chicago: Aldine.

————. 1981. *Culture and Language in Society*. Menlo Park, Calif.: Benjamin/ Cummings.

Goody, J. 1977. "Against Ritual: Loosely Structured Thoughts on a Loosely Defined Topic." In S. F. Moore and B. G. Meyerhoff (eds.), *Secular Ritual*. Atlantic Highlands, N.J.: Humanities Press.

Gouldner, A. W. 1954. *Patterns of Industrial Bureaucracy*. New York: Basic Books.

————. 1957, 1958. "Cosmopolitans and Locals: Toward an Analysis of Latent Social Roles, I and II." *Administrative Science Quarterly* 2: 281–306, 444–80.

————. 1970. *The Coming Crisis of Western Sociology*. New York: Basic Books.

Hall, R. 1968. "Professionalization and Bureaucratization." *American Sociological Review* 32: 92–104.

Harris, M. 1968. *The Rise of Anthropological Theory*. New York: Crowell.

Hasenfeld, Y., and R. English (eds.). 1974. *Human Service Organizations*. Ann Arbor: University of Michigan Press.

Hochschild, A. R. 1983. *The Managed Heart*. Berkeley: University of California Press.

Homans, G. C. 1950. *The Human Group*. New York: Harcourt, Brace and World.

Hughes, E. C. 1958. *Men and Their Work*. Glencoe, Ill.: Free Press.

Illich, I. 1971. *Deschooling Society*. New York: Harper and Row.

Jackall, R. 1988. *Moral Mazes: The World of Corporate Managers*. New York: Oxford University Press.

Kanter, R. M. 1977. *Men and Women of the Corporation*. New York: Basic Books.

————. 1983. *The Change Masters*. New York: Simon and Schuster.

Kaufman, H. 1960. *The Forest Ranger*. Baltimore: Johns Hopkins University Press.

Kertzer, David. 1988. *Ritual, Politics, and Power*. New Haven: Yale University Press.

Kets de Vries, M., and D. Miller. 1984. *The Neurotic Organization*. San Francisco: Jossey-Bass.

Kidder, T. 1981. *The Soul of a New Machine*. Boston: Little, Brown.

Kihlstrom, J. F., and N. Cantor. 1984. "Mental Representations of the Self." In L. Berkowitz (ed.), *Advances in Experimental Social Psychology*, vol. 17. Orlando, Fla.: Academic Press.

Kilmann, R. H., et al. 1985. *Gaining Control of the Corporate Culture*. San Francisco: Jossey-Bass.

Kimberly, J. R., and Miles, R. H. 1980. *The Organizational Life Cycle*. San Francisco: Jossey-Bass.

Kroeber, A. L., and C. Kluckhohn. 1952. *Culture: A Critical Review of Concepts and Definitions*. New York: Vintage Books.

Kroeber, A. L., and T. Parsons. 1958. "The Concept of Culture and of Social Systems." *American Sociological Review* 23: 582–83.

Kunda, G. 1986. "Ideology as a System of Meaning: The Case of the Israeli Probation Service." *International Studies of Management and Organization* 16 (1): 54–79.

Kunda, G., and S. R. Barley. 1988. "Designing Devotion: Corporate Cultures and Ideologies of Workplace Control." Paper delivered at the 83rd Annual Meetings of the American Sociological Association, Atlanta, Georgia.

Langer, S. 1967. *Mind: An Essay on Human Feeling*, vol. 1. Baltimore: Johns Hopkins University Press.

La Porte, T. R., and J. L. Wood. 1970. "Functional Contributions of Bootlegging and Entrepreneurship in Research Organizations." *Human Organization* 29: 273–87.

Lewin, K. 1948. *Resolving Social Conflicts*. New York: Harper and Row.

Light, D. 1980. *Becoming Psychiatrists*. New York: Norton.

Lipsky, M. 1980. *Street Level Bureaucracy: Dilemmas of the Individual in Public Services*. New York: Russell Sage.

Locke, E. A. 1983. "The Nature and Causes of Job Satisfaction." In M. D. Dunnette (ed.), *Handbook of Industrial and Organizational Psychology*. New York: Wiley.

Louis, M. R. 1983. "Organizations as Culture-Bearing Milieux." In L. Pondy et al. (eds.), *Organizational Symbolism*. Greenwich, Conn.: JAI Press.

Lukes, S. 1975. "Political Ritual and Social Integration." *Sociology* 9: 289–308.

McGregor, D. 1960. *The Human Side of Enterprise*. New York: McGraw-Hill.

Mangum, G.; D. Mayall; and K. Nelson. 1985. "The Temporary Help Industry: A Response to the Dual Labor Market." *Industrial and Labor Relations Review* 38: 599–611.

Mannheim, K. 1936. *Ideology and Utopia*. New York: Harcourt, Brace and World.

Manning, P. K. 1977. *Police Work: The Social Organization of Policing*. Cambridge, Mass.: MIT Press.

March, J. G., and H. A. Simon. 1958. *Organizations*. New York: Wiley.

Marcus, G. E., and D. Cushman. 1982. "Ethnographies as Texts." *Annual Review of Anthropology* 11: 25–69.

Marcus, G. E., and M. J. Fischer. 1986. *Anthropology as Cultural Critique: An*

Experimental Moment in the Human Sciences. Chicago: University of Chicago Press.

Martin, J., and C. Siehl. 1983. "Organizational Culture and Counterculture: An Uneasy Symbiosis." *Organizational Dynamics* 12: 52–64.

Martin, J.; S. Sitkin; and M. Boehm. 1985. "Founders and the Elusiveness of Cultural Legacy." In P. Frost, L. Moore, C. Lundberg, and J. Martin (eds.), *The Meaning of Life in the Workplace*. Beverly Hills, Calif.: Sage.

Marx, K. 1975. *Capital: A Critique of Political Economy*. Vol. 1. New York: International Publishers.

Marx, K., and R. Engels. 1947. *The German Ideology*. New York: International Publishers.

Mayo, E. 1933. *The Human Problems of Industrial Civilization*. New York: Macmillan.

Mead, G. H. 1934. *Mind, Self and Society*. Chicago: University of Chicago Press.

Merton, R. K. 1957. *Social Theory and Social Structure*. Glencoe, Ill.: Free Press.

——— . 1976. *Sociological Ambivalence*. New York: Free Press.

Meyer, J. W., and B. Rowan. 1977. "Institutionalized Organizations: Formal Structure as Myth and Ceremony." *American Journal of Sociology* 83: 340–63.

Miller, M. C. 1988. *Boxed-In*. Evanston, Ill.: Northwestern University Press.

Mills, C. W. 1940. "Situated Actions and Vocabularies of Motive." *American Sociological Review* 5: 904–13.

——— . 1956. *White Collar*. New York: Oxford University Press.

Moore, S. F., and B. G. Meyerhoff. 1977. "Secular Ritual: Forms and Meaning." In S. F. Moore and B. G. Meyerhoff (eds.), *Secular Ritual*. Atlantic Highlands, N.J.: Humanities Press.

Morgan, G. 1986. *Images of Organization*. Beverly Hills, Calif.: Sage.

Nye, D. E. 1985. *Image Worlds*. Cambridge, Mass.: MIT Press.

Ott, J. S. 1989. *The Organizational Culture Perspective*. Pacific Grove, Calif.: Brooks/Cole.

Ouchi, W. G. 1981. *Theory Z*. Reading, Mass.: Addison-Wesley.

Ouchi, W. G., and A. L. Wilkins. 1985. "Organizational Culture." In R. H. Turner and J. F. Short (eds.), *Annual Review of Sociology*, vol. 11. Palo Alto, Calif.: Annual Reviews, Inc.

Pascale, R., and A. Athos. 1981. *The Art of Japanese Management*. New York: Warner.

Perrow, C. 1986. *Complex Organizations: A Critical Essay*. 3rd ed. New York: Random House.

Peters, T. J., and R. H. Waterman. 1982. *In Search of Excellence*. New York: Harper and Row.

Pettigrew, A. 1979. "On Studying Organizational Cultures." *Administrative Science Quarterly* 24: 570–81.

Pfeffer, J. 1981. *Power in Organizations*. Boston: Pitman.

Pfeffer, J., and J. N. Baron. 1988. "Taking the Workers Back Out: Recent Trends in the Structuring of Employment." In B. M. Staw and L. L. Cummings (eds.), *Research in Organizational Behavior*, vol. 10. Greenwich, Conn.: JAI Press.

Pollard, S. 1965. *The Genesis of Modern Management*. Cambridge, Mass.: Harvard University Press.

Prottas, J. 1979. *People Processing: The Street Level Bureaucrat in Public Service Bureaucracies*. Lexington, Mass.: Lexington Books.

Roethlisberger, F. J., and W. J. Dixon. 1939. *Management and the Worker*. Cambridge, Mass.: Harvard University Press.

Rohlen, T. P. 1974. *For Harmony and Strength: Japanese White Collar Organization in Anthropological Perspective*. Berkeley: University of California Press.

Rosen, M. 1984. "Power and Culture in Bureaucracy: A Study of Bureaucracy as a Control Mechanism in Monopoly Capitalism." Ph.D. dissertation, University of Pennsylvania.

Rosenberg, M., and R. H. Turner. 1981. *Social Psychology*. New York: Basic Books.

Roth, P. A. 1989. "Ethnography Without Tears." *Current Anthropology* 30: 555–61.

Roy, D. 1959. "Banana Time: Job Satisfaction and Informal Interaction." *Human Organization* 18: 158–68.

Sabel, C. F. 1982. *Work and Politics: The Division of Labor in Industry*. New York: Cambridge University Press.

Said, E. W. 1979. *The Question of Palestine*. New York: Vintage.

Sanday, P. R. 1979. "The Ethnographic Paradigm(s)." *Administrative Science Quarterly* 24: 527–38.

Schein, E. H. 1961. *Coercive Persuasion*. New York: Norton.

———. 1968. "Organizational Socialization and the Profession of Management." *Industrial Management Review* 9: 1–15.

———. 1980. *Organizational Psychology*. 3rd ed. Englewood Cliffs, N.J.: Prentice-Hall.

———. 1985. *Organizational Culture and Leadership*. San Francisco: Jossey-Bass.

———. 1987. *The Clinical Perspective in Field Work*. Beverly Hills, Calif.: Sage.

Schutz, A. 1967. *The Phenomenology of the Social World*. Chicago: Northwestern University Press.

Seeman, M. 1959. "On the Meaning of Alienation." *American Sociological Review* 24: 783–91.

Selznick, P. 1957. *Leadership in Administration*. New York: Harper and Row.

Sennett, R. 1977. *The Psychology of Society*. New York: Vintage.

Shenhav, Y. A. 1988. "Abandoning the Research Bench: Individual, Organizational and Environmental Accounts." *Work and Occupations* 15: 5–23.

Shirom, A. 1982. "What Is Organizational Stress? A Facet Analytic Conceptualization." *Journal of Occupational Behavior* 3: 21–37.

Shokeid, M. 1988a. *Children of Circumstances: Israeli Emigrants in New York*. Ithaca, N.Y.: Cornell University Press.

————. 1988b. "Anthropologists and Their Informants: Marginality Reconsidered." *Archives* 21: 31–47.

Shotter, J., and K. J. Gergen. 1989. *Texts of Identity*. London: Sage.

Shweder, R. A., and E. Bourne. 1982. "Does the Concept of the Person Vary Cross-Culturally?" In A. J. Marsella and G. White (eds.), *Cultural Concepts of Mental Health and Therapy*. Boston: Reidel.

Simon, H. A. 1976. *Administrative Behavior*. New York: Free Press.

Spradley, J. P. 1979. *The Ethnographic Interview*. New York: Holt, Rinehart and Winston.

Stanislavski, C. 1965. *An Actor Prepares*. New York: Theatre Art Books.

Strauss, A. 1978. *Negotiations*. San Francisco: Jossey-Bass.

Strauss, A., et al. 1964. *Psychiatric Ideologies and Institutions*. New York: Free Press.

Strauss, G. 1969. "Human Relations, 1968 Style." *Industrial Relations* 7: 262–76.

Street, D.; Vinter, R. D.; and C. Perrow. 1966. *Organization for Treatment*. New York: Free Press.

Sutton, F. X., et al. 1956. *The American Business Creed*. Cambridge, Mass.: Harvard University Press.

Taylor, C. 1979. "Interpretation and the Sciences of Man." In P. Rabinow and W. M. Sullivan (eds.), *Interpretive Social Science: A Reader*. Berkeley: University of California Press.

Thompson, J. B. 1984. *Studies in the Theory of Ideology*. Berkeley: University of California Press.

Trice, H. M. 1984. "Rites and Ceremonials in Organizational Culture." In S. B. Bacharach and S. M. Mitchell (eds.), *Perspectives on Organizational Sociology: Theory and Research*, vol. 4. Greenwich, Conn.: JAI Press.

Trice, H. M., and J. M. Beyer. 1984. "Studying Organizational Cultures Through Rites and Ceremonials." *Academy of Management Review* 9: 653–69.

Trilling, L. 1972. *Sincerity and Authenticity*. Cambridge, Mass.: Harvard University Press.

Turner, V. 1969. *The Ritual Process*. Chicago: Aldine.

————. 1974. *Dramas, Fields, and Metaphors*. Ithaca, N.Y.: Cornell University Press.

————. 1982. *From Ritual to Theatre: The Human Seriousness of Play*. New York: PAJ Publications.

Van Gennep, A. 1960. *The Rites of Passage*. Chicago: University of Chicago Press.

Van Maanen, J. 1976. "Breaking In: Socialization to Work." In R. Dubin (ed.), *Handbook of Work, Organization, and Society*. Chicago: Rand McNally.

————. 1979a. "The Self, the Situation, and the Rules of Interpersonal Relations." In W. Bennis et al., *Essays in Interpersonal Dynamics*. Homewood, Ill.: Dorsey Press.

————. 1979b. "The Fact of Fiction in Organizational Ethnography." *Administrative Science Quarterly* 24: 539–50.

————. 1986. "Power in the Bottle: Drinking Patterns and Social Relations in a British Police Agency." In S. Srivastiva (ed.), *Executive Power*. San Francisco: Jossey-Bass.

————. 1988. *Tales of the Field*. Chicago: University of Chicago Press.

Van Maanen, J., and S. R. Barley. 1985. "Occupational Communities: Culture and Control in Organizations." In B. M. Staw and L. L. Cummings (eds.), *Research in Organizational Behavior*, vol. 6. Greenwich, Conn.: JAI Press.

Van Maanen, J., and G. Kunda. 1989. " 'Real Feelings': Emotional Expression and Organization Culture." In L. L. Cummings and B. M. Staw (eds.), *Research in Organizational Behavior*, vol. 11. Greenwich, Conn.: JAI Press.

Van Maanen, J., and E. H. Schein. 1979. "Toward a Theory of Organizational Socialization." In B. M. Staw and L. L. Cummings (eds.), *Research in Organizational Behavior*, vol. 1. Greenwich, Conn.: JAI Press.

Weber, M. 1947. *The Theory of Social and Economic Organization*. New York: Oxford University Press.

Whyte, W. H. 1956. *The Organization Man*. New York: Simon and Schuster.

Wilensky, H. L. 1964. "The Professionalization of Everyone?" *American Journal of Sociology* 70: 137–58.

Wilensky, H. L., and C. N. Lebeaux. 1965. *Industrial Society and Social Welfare*. New York: Free Press.

Zurcher, L. A. 1977. *The Mutable Self*. Beverly Hills, Calif.: Sage.

Zussman, R. 1985. *Mechanics of the Middle Class*. Berkeley: University of California Press.

index

Academic literature. *See under* Corporate culture; Managerial literature; Tech culture

Addiction to work, 10, 39, 176, 182, 201. *See also* Burnout; Workaholism

Agents of control, employees as. *See under* Normative control

Alcoholism, 19, 45, 87, 102, 172, 202

Alienation, 13, 14, 215, 265n.5. *See also* Role distancing

Ambiguity: responses to, 173; in ritual, 154, 159; of role requirements, 77; of self display, 118, 189–92, 204, 216; structural, 37, 48, 220; of Tech culture, 7, 18, 22, 222

Ambivalence, 21, 197, 204, 215, 221. *See also* Sociological ambivalence

Anomie, 14

Anthropology: native, 69, 172; seminar in, 260n.14. *See also* Ethnography

Authenticity: ideological prescription of, 91, 225; loss of, 226, 270n.10; of organizational self, 17, 159, 177, 183, 215–16; questioning of, 159, 185, 216, 222, 225; and ritual, 106, 129, 156–57, 158, 159. *See also* Emotions; Self; Self, organizational

Autonomy, personal: employee views of, 181; Goffman on, 224; loss of, 224, 226; managerial view of, 62–63, 65, 67, 88; role distancing as, 178, 188; threats to, 17, 214–15. *See also* Role distancing; Self, organizational

Barnard, Chester, 12–13, 245n.20

Behavior, prescriptions for. *See under* Member role

Beliefs: business press on, 86; and corporate culture, 9–10, 83; employee views of, 170–81, 187–88; ideological prescription of, 58, 73–74, 90, 218, 220; questioning of, 216; ritual enactment of, 106, 154, 156, 219, 223. *See also* Brainwashing; Cognitive dissonance; Common sense; Corporate culture; Cynicism; Ideology, organizational (at Tech); Irony; Member role; Normative control; Role responses; Tech culture

Bell, Daniel, 12

Bendix, Reinhard, 11, 12, 223, 243n.15, 246n.25

Benefits. *See* Personnel policies (at Tech)

Berger, P., 241n.1, 251n.1

Bourdieu, Pierre, 155, 219, 261n.21

Brainwashing, 223, 270n.8. *See also* Indoctrination

Bureaucracy: commonsense views of, 244n.17; and control, 12–14, 220; defined, 244n.17; diseases of, 17; evolution of, 12; Marxist view of, 13; and personality, 15; sociology of, 12. *See also* Control, corporate

Burnout: causes of, 199–204, 223; displays of, 19, 202–3; experience of, 18, 24, 28, 96, 102, 127, 158, 175, 198; as failure of self-management, 198–204; handling victims of, 45, 138, 199; managerial view of, 75, 77, 126, 173, 203–4; propensity for, 39, 41, 42, 44; psychological aspects of, 266n.14; threat of, 216. *See also* Addiction to work; Failure; Stress, employee

Business press: attempts to influence, 255n.19; on corporate culture, 9; descriptions of Tech in, 22, 28, 51–52, 83–87, 218; employee use of,